ROCKY

ROCKY

THE TEARS AND TRIUMPHS OF DAVID ROCASTLE

James Leighton

**SIMON &
SCHUSTER**

London · New York · Sydney · Toronto · New Delhi

A CBS COMPANY

First published in Great Britain by Simon & Schuster UK Ltd, 2016
A CBS COMPANY

1 3 5 7 9 10 8 6 4 2

Simon & Schuster UK Ltd
1st Floor
222 Gray's Inn Road
London WC1X 8HB

www.simonandschuster.co.uk

Simon & Schuster Australia, Sydney
Simon & Schuster India, New Delhi

The author and publishers have made all reasonable efforts to contact
copyright-holders for permission, and apologise for any omissions or errors
in the form of credits given. Corrections may be made to future printings.

A CIP catalogue record for this book
is available from the British Library.

ISBN: 978-1-4711-5331-0
Ebook ISBN: 978-1-4711-5333-4

Typeset in the UK by M Rules
Printed and bound by CPI Group (UK) Ltd, Croydon, CR0 4YY

Simon & Schuster UK Ltd are committed to sourcing paper
that is made from wood grown in sustainable forests and support the Forest
Stewardship Council, the leading international forest certification organisation.
Our books displaying the FSC logo are printed on FSC certified paper.

In loving memory of Henry Bishop
1980–1989
My great friend who picked me first

'Remember who you are, what you are,
and who you represent!'

DAVID ROCASTLE

CONTENTS

PROLOGUE

David Rocastle first infiltrated my consciousness on Saturday, 26 November 1988.

As a seven-year-old, my morning had begun like thousands of others' my age. With a milky bowl of Coco Pops balanced on my lap, and wearing my beloved He-Man pyjamas, I sat cross-legged in front of the television, watching my favourite cartoon, *Banana-man*, which was swiftly followed by the side-splitting comedy of the Chuckle Brothers. At 9am I then settled into the meat of children's Saturday morning television, *Going Live!*, presented by Phillip Schofield and Sarah Greene.

While I marvelled at a feature on how the new movie *Who Framed Roger Rabbit* had been made, I was soon bored when the bands of the moment, a-ha and Bros, were being interviewed. I was also confused at why rich pop stars, such as Matt and Luke Goss, were wearing ripped jeans. Surely they could afford new ones?

With my interest in the morning's television swiftly waning, and me no doubt driving my parents to despair, my father suggested we visit Pentwyn Leisure Centre, Cardiff's latest public swimming pool, which had a wave machine. Nothing could have been more enticing to a child in the 1980s.

So, wearing my sky blue Speedos, with swimming badges sewn

on the front, I happily spent the next few hours being tossed among the waves, yet was also frustrated to be told I was too small to go on the big slide, and instead had to make do with the children's dinosaur version. Nevertheless, eating a burger and chips in the humid canteen afterwards certainly lessened the blow.

However, I had learnt that by midday on a Saturday we had to be home, or at the very least in front of a TV. After all, this was the one time of the week when my father, and thousands like him, could get their sport fix. While the likes of *Grandstand* were always of interest, providing a curious mix of snooker, rugby, rally driving and show jumping, it was *Saint and Greavsie* that my father adored.

Presented by former Liverpool star Ian St John and his sidekick, Spurs and England legend Jimmy Greaves, the double act were seen as beacons of light in 1980s football programming. In those pre-Sky days, football fans were fortunate if there was one match a week on TV, so this one hour of highlights, interviews and Greavsie wisecracks was essential viewing.

Although I was only seven, I had already been raised as a football fan, albeit a supporter of Cardiff City, who were then playing in the old third division. Such a standard was light years away from the glamour of the top flight, which dominated the likes of *Saint and Greavsie*, but it was my first taste of football, and I loved it.

The records show that the previous evening Cardiff had played Brentford at Ninian Park, where, in front of 3,405 fans, my beloved Bluebirds triumphed 1-0. I have no recollection of the game itself but, despite the club's crumbling facilities, the outbreaks of hooliganism and the long-ball football, the players on display were my heroes. Of that particular vintage, the most recognisable was Steve 'Lethal' Lynex, who had signed from West Brom via Leicester City, and had a reputation purely because he had played up front with Gary Lineker for the Foxes. While Cardiff fans soon learnt that he wasn't exactly 'lethal', just having a connection to the stardust of the first division seemed impossibly glamorous.

In any event, while I can't recall the events at Ninian Park, the highlights from that weekend's *Saint and Greavsie* are seared into my memory. As always, to make sure I was suitably entertained during this one hour of hallowed time, my father had bought me a pack of Garbage Pail Kids stickers, which also had the added bonus of a chalky stick of chewing gum. As the hard gum cracked in my mouth, and I sorted through the latest stickers to add to my collection, I occasionally glanced up at the television, which showed highlights of the previous week's action.

At the time Arsenal, Liverpool and Norwich were engaged in a three-way battle for the title, and as such much of the coverage was devoted to Liverpool's victory at Loftus Road and Norwich's draw at Goodison Park. However, as the footage moved on to cover Arsenal's match against Middlesbrough, Ian St John told the viewers that such was the strength of the Arsenal team that five of their players had represented England just a few days previously. Such a comment saw me lift my head and give the television my full attention.

Watching on, I saw footage of a young Paul Merson score the opening two goals but it was the third, and final, goal of the game that made my eyes widen. On a soggy, and uneven, Highbury pitch, and under the glare of the floodlights, I saw Arsenal's number 7 receive the ball on the right-hand side, around 40 yards from goal. Crisply controlling the ball with his left foot, he jinked to the right before snapping back to his left, breezing past the outstretched boot of his opponent. Setting off towards goal, using the outside of his right foot, he was immediately faced with another defender straight in front of him. In a flash, the Arsenal player stepped over the ball, moving to his right and then pushing off with the ball to his left. It was a trick I had never seen before, and if I had it had certainly never been executed as thrillingly as this.

Putting down my stickers, and momentarily stopping chewing my gum, I was transfixed as the Arsenal player beat another opponent with an explosive spurt, finding himself on the edge of the penalty area. Feinting one way, and then the other, he now deceived three defenders to make himself some space. After so much skill, and subtlety, the player now proceeded to strike his laces through the ball, which saw it scythe with vicious certainty through the gap, crash against the right-hand post and into the top corner.

With the crowd roaring its approval, the Arsenal player turned around, both hands in the air, beaming a wide smile, as the commentator breathlessly proclaimed that the man responsible for such heroics was called David Rocastle. I had never heard the name before but it was one I would not forget, although I would soon come to know him by another name – 'Rocky'. Unable to rewind the goal, or to find it anywhere else on TV, I could not work out how Rocastle had beaten a defender merely by stepping over a ball. Neither could my father. In the back garden, he tried to show me with a plastic football but it didn't look quite the same.

While I remained a devoted Cardiff City fan, the name of David Rocastle was one that from that moment onwards I always looked out for. In subsequent years, he proved that that moment of individual brilliance was far from a one-off, with breathtaking displays of virtuosity at Villa Park, Anfield and Old Trafford among many others. Starring for England, and still in his early twenties, it appeared that he was destined to become one of the game's biggest names.

When he moved to champions Leeds United in 1992 most football fans, including myself, wondered why Arsenal would contemplate selling one of their best players to a rival. Nevertheless, it seemed a good move for Rocastle, and would surely cement his standing in the game. However, from that moment on, his career was never quite the same. Swifly moving to Manchester City, and then Chelsea, he struggled for game time and, at the age of 29, ended up on loan at fourth division Hull City. By his 30th birthday he couldn't even find a club in Britain that was willing to take him on. Seemingly outcast, he was forced to move to Malaysia to continue his career.

Rumours were rife regarding Rocastle's perceived fall from grace. Drugs, bust-ups, poor attitude and bad diet were all floated around with no substance whatsoever. Yet there must have been some reason for the total collapse of his career.

By 2001 I was studying law at Brunel University and enjoying playing Saturday football on the muddy pitches of west London. After a match in Hayes, I remember walking off the pitch to hear someone from the touchline say, 'Did you know David Rocastle has died?' I must confess that at the time I wasn't even aware that he had been unwell, so this news came as a massive shock. How could the lightning-quick winger, with the beaming smile, be dead at just 33 years of age?

Over the previous years Rocastle had somewhat slipped from public consciousness, as well as my own. Spending his last few years playing football in Malaysia, his glory days were long behind him and he was certainly never someone who actively courted publicity.

Yet I felt a real tinge of sadness when I heard about his death. It was the first time one of my childhood heroes had died. I almost felt guilty that, after his career had fizzled out, I had not continued to follow him. It seemed almost traitorous that I had enjoyed the good times but then as things had taken a turn for the worse I had abanonded him in my mind, and moved on to the likes of Gazza, Cantona, Shearer and Henry.

While the newspaper obituaries told of a gentle soul with a thrilling talent for football, the reasons for Rocastle's career drifting away were frustratingly vague. No one, it seemed, could really put their finger on how a double title winner and England star could have seen his best years behind him by his mid-twenties. Over the years I eagerly read any interview with anyone connected to Rocastle, hoping for some insight into the reason for this, but again no one seemed to have the definitive answer – or if they did, they were unwilling to reveal it. When I became a writer, I suddenly realised that I now had an incredible opportunity to answer this very question once and for all.

So, with the aid of family, team-mates, managers, coaches, physios, friends and fans, I have not only tried to shed light on Rocastle's career, but also to pay homage to a gentleman and a brilliant footballer, who made a seven-year-old run into his back garden with his father and try to emulate his skill with a plastic football. I could never master the Rocastle stepover, not many could, but I hope that at the very least I have done him justice with this book.

CHAPTER I

THE SUMMER OF 1989

The front cover of the 19 August 1989 issue of *Melody Maker* was dominated by the band Tears for Fears, who were on the verge of releasing a much-anticipated new album. Inside the now defunct music paper, there was also high praise for the Stone Roses' epic gig at the Empress Ballroom in Blackpool, a glowing review of the forthcoming *Batman* movie, as well as withering assessments of the new offerings from the likes of Bon Jovi and Madonna. And if there is any concern at the state of music today, the number one single for that week was the monstrosity that was 'Swing the Mood' by Jive Bunny and the Mastermixers.

Amid all of this, there were also other nods to a now bygone age. Adverts for blank Memorex video and tape cassettes at Woolworths occupied the centre pages, while the Audioline 950 answering machine was apparently the 'Talk of the Future'. The supermarket Safeway made an appearance, as did Midland Bank, where you could apply for a student bank account merely by completing a form and posting it.

Yet one of the main features in this arbiter of cool was an interview with Arsenal star David Rocastle. It was rare to find a footballer in such a place in a decade when the sport was renowned for hooliganism, racism, high shorts and mullets. But Rocastle was far from your average footballer. To many he was seen as the perfect ambassador for a game that had so tragically lost its way.

Throughout the 1980s football had had to contend with a succession of disasters. In 1985 alone there was the Bradford fire, swiftly followed by the deaths of 39 fans at Heysel. Then, in April 1989, came the game's nadir, when 96 football fans lost their lives at Hillsborough during an FA Cup semi-final clash between Liverpool and Nottingham Forest.

As the game faced the summer of 1989 in the midst of depression, David Rocastle was one player who was a rare ray of light. Well mannered, with clean-cut good looks and a warm smile, Arsenal's flying winger was also a champion, having just helped his team to their first title win since 1971, which came courtesy of Michael Thomas' last-minute clincher at Anfield.

Such was Rocastle's status at this time that *Melody Maker*, a publication that usually shied away from football, had not only devoted a double-page spread to an interview with the man of the moment, but had even invited him to write a weekly column, in which he could answer readers' questions about music. Alongside an article entitled 'How are we going to get rid of Jason Donovan?', Rocastle gave advice on how to get hold of Skinny Puppy's first album, while he also told a new band that to achieve the success they craved, 'all it takes is hard work and dedication – hold your head up high until the end of the day, and above all, be yourself'. Such words could easily have been spoken in the changing room at Highbury.

Yet it is in the main interview that we get a real sense of the exalted heights the 22-year-old had reached in the summer of 1989. Writer John Wilde states that Rocastle can 'often be mistaken for genius' and is 'the only player guaranteed to dazzle on a Saturday afternoon'. While Rocastle typically bats such praise aside, focusing on the team and the job he is happy to do for it, Wilde is adamant that he is a rare talent who must be cherished in such depressing times.

Touting the Arsenal star for a big-money move abroad, as the domestic game struggled to come to grips with the scourge of hooliganism and racism, Wilde wrote: 'The modern English game does not deserve a player as potentially great as David Rocastle. Over here, if he remains, Rocastle will never be great. Eventually, they will all be gone, every last craftsman. Maybe then the English game will take a good hard look at itself and wonder where it all went wrong. In the meantime, David Rocastle looks forward to another season of stifling English football while we dream of greater days.'

It was just three months since Arsenal had thrillingly won the first division title at Anfield, but, as evidenced in *Melody Maker*, Rocastle had become a star. On the Sunday following Arsenal's title win, over 250,000 people had lined the streets to herald the champions' double-decker bus, which crawled towards a civic reception at Islington town hall. It seemed that wherever there was a pavement, ledge or lamppost, someone clad in red and white was hanging from it.

Rocastle, with his arms around his great friend and hero of the hour, Michael Thomas, had received a particularly loud roar, especially at the town hall, where he danced a jig of delight on the terrace. 'The parade, going on the open-top bus, is one of my best memories,' Rocastle later happily reminisced.

Just days after these tremendous scenes, he had starred for England, setting up a goal in a 3-0 win against Poland. The game was just the second capacity crowd at Wembley during Bobby Robson's nine-year tenure as manager. No doubt the thrilling scenes at

Anfield had encouraged many fans to cheer on the chief protagonists from both teams, with Rocastle one of the main attractions.

Inundated with requests for personal appearances and sponsorship opportunities, as well as to help with various charities and causes, Rocastle spent much of the summer in a whirlwind. One such letter saw him visit a four-year-old boy in hospital, who was suffering from leukaemia. While he did not expect the little boy to know who he was, he went along in the hope that it might provide some comfort to his family. But as Rocastle later revealed, 'He was lying in the bed covered in Arsenal scarves and he knew everything. His mum said, "Sebastian, look who it is," and he turned around and said, "Rocky!" It broke my heart.' Sitting on the little boy's bed, Rocastle was not only happy to answer any questions he had but also spent the next two hours watching a video of the title-winning game at Anfield.

Being recognised by a little boy was one thing, but Rocastle soon found it hard to leave his front door, such was his popularity. His brother Sean remembers him going shopping with their mother, and it taking him three hours to leave the supermarket as he signed everyone's slips of paper. Jerome Anderson, his agent, also recalls seeing his client outside his offices, in the pouring rain, happily chatting with fans and signing autographs until everyone was satisfied.

With his new-found fame, Rocastle was asked to help out those who had helped him along the way. When he had attended college, during his apprentice days at Arsenal, he had been taught by a lady called Kate Hoey, who had also been happy to give the aspiring Gunner lifts back home to Brockley, rather than see him take public transport in the rain. Rocastle never forgot her kindness and as such, when she needed him, he was only too ready to help.

Just days after the Islington civic reception, Hoey was due to contest the Vauxhall by-election for the Labour Party. It would be her first foray into politics, which would eventually culminate in her serving as Minister for Sport under Tony Blair. Having close links to many of the title-winning Arsenal team, Hoey reached out to match-winner Michael Thomas and star player David Rocastle, who were seen as leading figures in the black community and would therefore be valuable additions to her campaign

Rocastle was never a keen follower of politics but he was more than happy to assist Hoey, whom he counted as an old friend. There were certainly no speeches made by either Arsenal player, both of whom preferred to escape the limelight, but their mere presence, handshakes, smiles and willingness to talk about 'that' game as they handed out leaflets in Vauxhall proved invaluable. Unsurprisingly, with two stars heralding her, along with a socially conscious manifesto, Kate Hoey was elected to parliament as MP for Vauxhall, a position she retains to this day.

Having devoted much of his spare time to matters off the pitch, Rocastle was soon back to the serious business of preparing for the season ahead. Seen by many as the acceptable face of football, he would soon have to contend with an issue that continued to blight the game.

Following a pre-season tour of Sweden, after which Arsenal had beaten Liverpool in the annual Makita tournament at Wembley, the squad flew to Miami for a friendly with Argentinian champions Independiente. With the game being broadcast around the world, it was an opportunity for Arsenal, and Rocastle, to show an international audience what they were all about. But it also gave rise to some diplomatic issues.

Club captain Tony Adams revealed in his autobiography, *Addicted*, that, 'before the game I was asked to carry out the Argentinian flag and I agreed, until David O'Leary pointed out that there had been many British casualties during the Falklands War in the not-too-distant past and it would be disrespectful to them and their families to carry the flag. Back home it might also have caused a row since it was being televised live. David was right and I quickly told the organisers that I would only carry the British flag.'

While Adams had avoided a diplomatic incident before the game, the Argentinians seemed intent on causing one during it. To Rocastle's amazement, straight from kick-off he was met by a torrent of racist abuse, ranging from being called a 'nigger' to his opponents making monkey noises in his ear. With the temperature reaching over 100°F in the midday sun, some might have forgiven him for losing his cool. It seemed that the Argentineans had learnt racist taunts in English just for the occasion.

Incredibly, Rocastle managed to avoid rising to the bait, using the provocation as fuel to ram it back down their throats. Scoring two goals to help Arsenal win the game 2-1, he proceeded to shake hands with each of his opponents and give them a wink and a smile. As had so often been the case, his feet had done the talking for him. 'You had to be calm and collected,' he later said. 'They were doing it for a reason. At the end of the day, it's only words anyway.'

With yet more bigots thwarted by his ingenuity, aggressive pride and wide smile, he prepared to fly back to London to defend the first division title.

Sadly, for Rocastle's parents, and thousands of Caribbean immigrants like them, supreme skill on the football pitch wasn't enough to help them quell the tide of racism they faced . . .

CHAPTER 2

A TROUBLED START

Until her dying day, Linda Rocastle would tell the story of how a gypsy woman had predicted her first-born son would be famous. And nearly 22 years to the day before Arsenal's Anfield triumph, David Carlyle Rocastle was born on 2 May 1967, in the London Borough of Lewisham.

By this time Linda and her husband, Leslie, had been living in London for just over a decade. Like thousands of other immigrants, they had arrived in Britain in the late 1950s, enticed by the opportunity of an exciting and prosperous new life. The Second World War had robbed the country of many of its young men, and with much of its infrastructure destroyed, many politicians advocated inviting young men from Commonwealth countries to help carry out the urgent rebuilding work. But not everyone was on board.

A group of Labour MPs were so incensed by this plan that they wrote to Prime Minister Clement Attlee and told him that 'an influx of coloured people domiciled here is likely to impair harmony, strength and cohesion of our public and social life'. Rising above their protests, Attlee proceeded to pass the 1948 Nationality Act, which granted colonial subjects the same rights as those born in the UK, providing them with free movement to the country in the process.

Soon after, newspapers in Commonwealth countries splashed colourful adverts across their centre pages, promising an exotic new life in post-war Britain, where wages were high and jobs plentiful, with many excitedly claiming that the streets of London were paved with gold. Such adverts, and the relatively cheap boat fare, enticed 492 passengers to board the *Empire Windrush* in Kingston, Jamaica, and set sail for a bright new future.

Thousands more were to follow those on the *Windrush*, with the non-white population of the UK soaring from 30,000 in 1948 to 500,000 by 1962. Sadly, many did not find the paradise they had been promised. Battling the wet and cold weather, they also had to contend with a groundswell of resentment. It wasn't just the casual racist remarks, with insults such as 'wog' and 'nigger' being freely bandied about, but they also had to face the overtly hostile boarding-house notices that proclaimed, 'No Dogs. No Irish. No Blacks.' The upshot was that immigrants were often forced to live in houses that most British families would have deemed unfit for human habitation. Unsurprisingly, as unrest festered, violence soon exploded on Britain's streets.

With the likes of politician Oswald Mosley actively encouraging discrimination, the nation's Teddy Boys, freed from the chains of national service, sought to carry out his ill-feeling against the Caribbean community. As packs of white hooligans set off 'nigger hunting' through places such as Notting Hill, there was also a riot in Nottingham when a black man was caught kissing a white woman. Trying to contain a potentially volatile situation, and with over 130,000 immigrants arriving in 1961 alone, the government, in its wisdom, passed the Commonwealth Immigrants Act, which made it far more difficult for members of the Commonwealth to become British citizens.

By this stage Linda and Leslie Rocastle were already living and working in the UK. Leslie had emigrated from Grenada in the late 1950s and had initially lived with his aunt, where he had planned to continue his education. Yet he soon found the lure of earning money impossible to resist. Rather than hit the books, he began working in a series of local factories before training to become a toolmaker. Linda, meanwhile, had emigrated from Trinidad when she was 21. Training to become a nurse, she eventually found work in Greenwich Hospital, where she worked long hours for little pay.

Both Linda and Leslie were proud, hard workers. Never living off the state. Never causing any trouble. They were like thousands of other immigrants who simply wanted to make a better life for themselves.

Introduced by mutual friends at a house party, the pair found they had plenty in common. Gentle and friendly souls, they also shared a passion for music. Fans of ska, reggae and calypso, Linda and Leslie would often be found in the local clubs laughing and dancing to the sounds of Symarip, and Dave and Ansell Collins.

Within a year Linda gave birth to their first son, David, which led to Leslie proposing. After a small wedding ceremony, the new Rocastle family moved to the Honor Oak housing estate in Brockley, Lewisham, where many in the West Indian community had already gravitated due to its proximity to the hundreds of factories and docks that skirted the area. Colourful and vibrant, the sights, smells and sounds were often reminiscent of towns in the West Indies, rather than the capital of England, which helped to cultivate a relaxed and friendly atmosphere.

Moving into a third-floor flat at 10 Dale House, which was situated above a row of shops, the Rocastles initially had plenty of room. Boasting three bedrooms, a kitchen, a toilet and a bathroom, it was far from luxurious but compared to the conditions a lot of black families had to endure it was more than adequate. Indeed, the young David Rocastle even found himself lucky enough to have his own room, a rare luxury for a child in Brockley.

Over the next five years the Rocastle family swiftly grew, with Karen, Cynthia and Steve all added by 1971. Linda and Leslie worked all hours to feed and clothe their children, yet everyone recalls feeling happy and loved. The house-proud Linda frequently conjured up Caribbean-inspired dishes, such as chicken, rice and peas, while Leslie would always ensure that the record player was playing the latest reggae and calypso music. Sociable and generous, the Rocastles were always eager to host friends and family, and many recall Leslie and Linda showing off their dance moves in the living room together.

But with the family happily settled, the Rocastles were devastated in 1972, when Leslie was diagnosed with cancer. 'When he had worked in a factory he had been told to wear a mask, but Dad refused as he thought it made him look ugly,' Karen Rocastle told me. 'We think that might have been the cause of his illness, as he would have got stuff like asbestos in his lungs.' However, Karen also concedes that the fact he was a heavy smoker might have contributed to his illness. 'My mum used to say you could hear him coming before you saw him because of his cough.'

Despite his diagnosis, Leslie was told that his condition was treatable. As he was young and fit, it was thought an operation would see him make a full recovery. Sadly, it was not to be. 'My father died in front of me,' Rocastle later said. 'We were all in the house watching TV together and Mum, a nurse, was getting ready to go to work. Dad jumped up trying to open a window and suddenly lost all of his strength and collapsed.'

Tragically, other than his death, the Rocastle children don't have any other real memories of their father. 'People used to tell

me how lovely my father was,' Rocastle said, 'but it was a bit difficult because I didn't really understand what they were talking
about.'

Suddenly, Linda Rocastle was faced with raising four young
children alone, while also trying to hold down a job as a nurse. It
seemed an impossible situation.

'Just after my dad's funeral, there was a knock at the door,' Karen
remembered. 'It was someone from the social services. They told
her, "You're a young woman. Let us take your children into care."
My mum told me that was the only time she ever cursed at a
stranger. She told the woman, "F*** off, and leave me and my
children to grieve in peace."'

Thankfully, with the help of the extended Rocastle family, the
children were never taken into care. Quitting her job as a nurse,
Linda took a position on the shop floor at C&A, which offered more
sociable hours, while the children spent their days at her mother's
in nearby Murillo Road.

Also living on the street was Rocastle's future brother-in-law,
Junior Hamilton, who remembers the time fondly: 'Everyone was
always out playing football or cricket. Even the older guys would
stay out with the kids to play. There were a lot of windows that
were broken because of a stray ball. It was great because so many
West Indian families lived on the road you could smell what everyone was cooking, which was usually the same. It became a joke that
you could smell it was a Monday because that was chicken, rice and
peas night.'

But while Rocastle loved his time on Murillo Road, as the eldest
child he couldn't always enjoy the frivolities of youth. 'The earliest
memories I've got is looking after my little sisters and brothers,' he
later confessed.

At just five years old he had had to grow up fast. Helping with
the washing and cleaning, he also fed and clothed his siblings. If his

mother was ever short of anything, he would race down the three flights of stairs to the convenience store, Amy's, where the owners knew him well. And on those nights when Linda was too tired to cook, Rocastle would be happy to go to the chip shop.

'He was the best ever,' Karen told me. 'He was always calm, and he always knew what to do, even though he was only young.'

Mature beyond his years, Rocastle was the man of the house, rising above petty squabbles with the air of someone who had seen it all before. Such was Rocastle's standing in the house that, as he grew older, Linda would even look to him to make decisions about his siblings.

'Whatever Dave said went,' Karen laughed. 'If one of us would ask Mum if we could go down the youth club or something, she might say yes, but then Dave would come in and say, "Where do you think you're going?" and we'd say, "The youth club," and he'd say, "No you're not." And Dave's word stood. Mum always listened to him.'

Initially daunted by the responsibility of looking after his three siblings, Rocastle gradually realised it could work to his advantage. As he reached his teens he was the one now dominating the TV and record player, the Rocastle children would have to watch and listen to whatever he deemed fit. Usually this would be episodes of *Mork & Mindy* or *Empire Road*, while his musical taste ranged from lovers rock to soul. However, Karen recalls that he was also partial to a bit of Tom Jones, and from time to time he would even bring out a plastic guitar and try to emulate his hero's hip-thrusting moves to the cheers of his Auntie Irene!

Before long, Rocastle became known to his brother and sisters as a 'slave driver'. Steve made him cups of tea, Cynthia ironed his clothes, and Karen would be sent down to the shops to buy him sweets. 'He used to love his sweets,' Karen remembers. 'He loved Twixes and Kit Kats and used to hide them under his bed. You'd watch him eat a Twix and he'd bite off all the chocolate first, then the caramel, then he'd eat the biscuit. He enjoyed it so much.' In years to come, Arsenal and England team-mates would also recall Rocastle's sweet tooth, when he'd be hiding chocolate from his managers instead of from his mother.

Despite all of these demands, Karen never complained: 'I think we got it from my mum. It's an old-school Caribbean thing where you are expected to look after the men in your life.'

Yet while Linda relied on her eldest son, there was a short period of time when he moved out. His cousin Lennox, wanting a break from his seven sisters, went to live with their grandmother, and Rocastle decided to join him. Although Linda felt that it was important her son be allowed to have a certain amount of freedom, she had to resort to buying him a fish tank and a Chopper bicycle to lure him home.

There were times when life could be tough but Rocastle was always quick to make light of any grim situation. 'We didn't have any heating in the flat,' Karen remembered. 'So, whenever I wanted to keep my hands warm I would have to turn on the gas on the stove. Dave saw me one time warming my hands and nicknamed me "Witchy" because he said I looked like a witch with her hands over a cauldron. That name stuck for years.'

While Karen was known as Witchy, Rocastle was also given various nicknames by his mum and aunties. 'They used to call him "Coobiejay",' Karen told me, with a grin on her face, not having any idea why.

Despite the many responsibilities on his young shoulders, his childhood certainly wasn't devoid of fun. At the back of Dale House, in the so-called 'Quad', the Rocastle children could often be found playing with their friends for hours on end. Overseeing them, Linda and the other mothers would sit on the balcony and chat. In a sign of more carefree times, most families left their doors open, which saw the children rush in and out, and helped to foster a real community spirit.

The nearby Honor Oak sports ground, a large expanse of playing fields, and the adjoining cemetery gardens, known to the Rocastles as 'the crem', was frequently packed with young boys and girls playing, while just down the road was the Honor Oak Youth Club, which used to organise trips to the seaside to places such as Margate and Hastings during the summer holidays, a rare treat in the days before cheap air travel.

Across from the youth club there was the Honor Oak Adventure Playground, which had been lovingly put together over the years by a man known as Jumbo, a carpenter by trade. It was an impressive spectacle of wooden forts and ropes, and Karen Rocastle told me that it was a place her brother loved. 'He was fearless,' she laughed. 'He would jump from one place to the next without any thought of hurting himself.' Such fearlessness would, of course, become a trait he was renowned for on the football pitch in years to come.

While the Rocastles enjoyed a relatively happy childhood, they were fortunate in that they escaped the many outbreaks of racial tension that were marking the country. In 1974, the National Front achieved a remarkable 11.5 per cent of the vote in a Newham by-election, and soon after sought to march through Lewisham itself. They were only prevented from doing so after running battles with the police, which saw 56 officers hospitalised. Such was the ferocity of the attack, with police separating the National Front from local black youths determined to guard their manor, that riot shields were used for the first time in the UK outside of Northern Ireland.

'There was never really any racism in the area,' Karen told me. 'It was just a lovely place, where everyone seemed to get along and look out for one another.' However, her husband, Junior Hamilton, recalled that there was a reason why those in Brockley were sheltered from such matters. 'You rarely ventured too far from home,' he said. 'There were some places that you knew you couldn't go as a black man. Back then you'd never go to Kidbrooke or Eltham or places like that.'

Safe within the confines of his community, and looking after his siblings, Rocastle admitted that with so many responsibilities there was one thing he did miss out on. 'Because I was helping Mum with the kids I didn't get involved in football at an early age.'

Even though he didn't play organised football as a child, Karen remembers that her brother was nevertheless kicking a ball from a young age. 'Even before he could properly walk I think he was trying to kick things,' she recalled. 'My mum used to have a fruit bowl on the dining table with plastic fruits in there, and Dave would take them out and kick them along the passages of the flat.'

As his brother Steve grew, Rocastle soon had someone to play with. Using the sofas at either end of the living room as goals they would play for hours. However, their games would frequently result in broken glass or tantrums, with Rocastle hating to lose and demanding a rematch whenever he did.

With his interest in the game growing, a new addition to the Rocastle family would soon help him devote more time to it. A few years after Leslie's death, Linda met a bus driver from Barbados called Theodore Medford. It was a relationship that would endure until her dying day and would in time produce a son called Sean, who Rocastle affectionately nicknamed 'Eggy'.

The man the Rocastle children called 'Med' never actually moved into the family flat but Karen told me that he was a 'very positive role model'. Indeed, Sean said, 'David thought he was a saviour at the time. He helped Mum. He helped the whole family a lot.'

It seems that his calm, cheerful personality, without any parental demands, was exactly what the Rocastle children needed at a turbulent time in their lives. Such was the respect that Rocastle had for Medford that in later years, when he was making a video about his life, he told the producers that they weren't to call him his stepdad. He was always to be referred to as Dad, while Sean was always his brother.

With Medford helping to look after the family, and Rocastle by now a pupil at Turnham Primary School, the stage was soon set for his passion for football to be ignited.

CHAPTER 3

A BRUSH WITH DEATH

The sound and colours of the Millwall fans bled into a swirling kaleidoscope, turning their chants and insults into a blur. Caught up in the game, David Rocastle had by now learnt to block out the unrelenting wave of Neanderthal inanity that continually rolled down from the terraces. With his muddy shorts hitched high over his muscular thighs, he instead hugged the touchline, screaming at Michael Thomas to find him, exhaling clouds of cold air in the November chill as he opened his mouth.

However, if he had just taken a moment to turn five yards to his right, he would have been able to pick out the individual faces of pot-bellied skinheads behind the steel fences. Eyes popping, faces contorted with rage, they chanted loud and proud, 'You black bastard! You black bastard!' Children alongside them were encouraged to throw bananas on to the pitch, while even in the disabled section wheelchair-bound fans made monkey noises.

Motoring up and down the right wing, Rocastle found his black boots and yellow jersey peppered with phlegm, as large sections of the crowd tried to make the case that the majestic winger was the uncivilised one. There was certainly no help from the stewards or the referee. This was par for the course. Get on with it or get out.

Made of stern stuff, Rocastle instead concentrated on limiting the influence of Millwall's Jimmy Carter, who had started to dominate the game. While Arsenal were 1-0 up, courtesy of Michael Thomas' cool finish, they were continuing to show the signs of inconsistency that had already riddled their season as defending champions. A heavy loss away to Manchester United on the opening day of the season had been followed by a series of lacklustre performances, which had seen them drop as low as 17th in the league. Although there were brief reminders that the team could still be a force, such as a 5-0 win against Sheffield Wednesday and a dramatic 4-3 win against Norwich, this was still marred by a melee which led to a £20,000 fine and a warning about the team's future conduct, which in time would have serious consequences

Fully focused on gaining three much-needed points, Rocastle glanced across at Carter and lined him up. As Carter ran at fullback Lee Dixon, Rocastle set off, pounding across the mud, launching himself off the floor, aiming to take the ball and as much of Carter as possible. But the lunge was so wild that Rocastle missed Carter altogether, and instead his face collided with Dixon's knee. Neck snapping back, his head thudded against the turf.

Lying face down in the mud, the game continued around him, with the referee unaware of the severity of his injury. Not breathing, and slowly turning blue, Arsenal physio Gary Lewin frantically rushed on to the pitch to come to his aid.

As the game finally came to a stop, Lewin pulled the unconscious Rocastle up and tried to dislodge his tongue, which was blocking his airway. All the while, Rocastle lay limp, not responding. Suddenly the players became aware that this might be serious and crowded around him. Despite the players' concern, the crowd became restless at the break in play. The chant of 'Let him die! Let him die! Let him die!' suddenly rumbled off the terraces. Author and fan Nick Hornby, who was at the game, can remember the reaction vividly: 'The atmosphere was just poison. It really was terrifying. Pure evil. He was being jeered at as he was apparently dying. I can remember thinking, "What am I doing here? Where is the fun in this?"'

It seemed to take an age before a stuttering cough finally heralded Rocastle opening his eyes. With blurred vision he tried to regain his bearings, aided by the Millwall fans, who continued to give him little sympathy. Carried on a stretcher to the sidelines so that the game could restart, Lewin helped Rocastle to stand and tested all of his functions. Taking deep breaths, with the rabid fans just a metre away, Rocastle heard the full repertoire of south London's most racist taunts.

Many players might have decided that in such hostile surroundings, and after receiving such a nasty injury, being substituted was the easy, and excusable, way out. But despite still looking shaky on his feet, he bravely told Lewin that he was fine to continue. Moments later he was back on the pitch, running the gauntlet of hate, determined to help his team secure a valuable win. It was for his courage, as much as his skill, that Rocastle was such a valued member of the team.

Most managers would have been happy with the subsequent 2-1 scoreline in Arsenal's favour, but George Graham was not most managers. 'The manner of the performance is the worrying thing,' he told the press after the game. 'It would be nice to see us at our best again.' It was surely still a positive sign that, despite an indifferent start to the season, the win at Millwall saw the Gunners leapfrog their title rivals Liverpool into second place.

The team may have been top of the league by December but it

was clear that things were not running smoothly. Having lost to Oldham in the League Cup, four defeats in eight away games was also in direct contrast to the previous season, when they lost only three during the whole campaign. Scoring was also an issue, with striker Alan Smith going through a barren run that would result in just 10 league goals all season. However, he could blame the lack of service for such an average return. Not only was left-winger Brian Marwood out injured, but Rocastle seemed incapable of reproducing the scintillating form that had seen him break into the England starting line-up.

With the World Cup on the horizon, Rocastle knew more than anyone just how vital it was that he picked up soon. Numerous rumours floated around, but Rocastle had his own theory about his dip in form. 'Every time I get the ball, two or three players descend on me,' he told the Arsenal match-day programme. 'Other times, with Lee Dixon playing so well, I've just got out of the way and let him go charging forward!'

Some newspapers, such as *The Times*, speculated that Rocastle, as well as Michael Thomas, 'were showing signs of failing Arsenal through a lack of stamina'. Rocastle's endeavour in training and work rate in games could certainly never be called into question, but, as he highlighted earlier in the season, the intensity of pre-season may have taken its toll.

The incident at Millwall was also continuing to have a detrimental effect on his mental state. Having confided that it was the 'most frightening incident I've ever experienced on a football pitch', many of those I spoke to told me that in their opinion he was never quite the same afterwards. To most it wasn't noticeable, but it seemed to take a slight edge away from his game. Some suggested there was a slight hesitation where once he would have launched himself fearlessly into tackles.

However, it appears that a long-standing knee injury was the primary cause of his discomfort. After having his cartilage removed four years previously, his knee was starting to swell after matches. The joint filled with fluid, which meant his range of movement became restricted. While ice and rest would see it settle down, the amount of training and games he faced often meant that there wasn't enough recovery time to get it in optimum condition.

Nevertheless, his poor form certainly hadn't deterred his many suitors in the football world. On 7 January 1990, the *People* reported that Liverpool manager Kenny Dalglish was preparing a multimillion-pound move, as he was resigned to losing John Barnes in the summer. The *Daily Mirror*, meanwhile, believed that Dalglish was set to lose Barnes as well as Rocastle. Under the headline 'Lira Lure For Big Two', it claimed that AC Milan wanted to sign the two England stars for £12m, in a bid to replace Ruud Gullit, who had suffered a knee injury that threatened to end his career.

Another intriguing story appeared in the *Sunday Mirror*. It reported that Monaco were interested in signing Rocastle for £4m, where he would join the English contingent of Glenn Hoddle and Mark Hateley. At the time the Monaco manager was a certain Arsène Wenger, who was very much a Rocastle fan.

When asked about his thoughts on playing abroad Rocastle was clearly tempted. 'Playing abroad definitely interests me,' he said. 'Over there, I could mix skill with hard-running aggression. Over there, I'd have more opportunity to demonstrate my skills. But that's thinking far ahead.'

It is no wonder that Rocastle might have been tempted by a move to Europe. Not only was that where the game's great players plied their trade, but the financial rewards would also be substantial. While he was one of England's brightest prospects, he was also one of the worst paid. A salary of £60,000 a year was decent money, but not when you compared it to the £175,000 Peter Beardsley was said to be earning at Liverpool. If Rocastle were to move abroad, it was thought that he stood to quadruple his salary.

In order to counter the transfer speculation surrounding one of his star players, Graham made a move. Offering Rocastle a slightly improved four-year contract, his right-winger was only too happy to sign, saying as he did so, 'Now I've got some points to prove for Arsenal in the weeks ahead.'

However, soon the transfer speculation was replaced by 'scandal'. On 21 January, the *Sunday Mirror*'s headline read 'Love Child Secret Of Soccer Star', with Rocastle's picture beneath it. The article stated that the Arsenal star had not only fathered a daughter a year earlier, but that he was living apart from the mother. While the story might have been true, it was certainly not a scandal.

Rocastle had been in a committed relationship with his girl-friend, Janet Nelson, for three years, ever since they had met in a club in Angel in 1987. Like most young couples, while Rocastle lived in Barnet, Janet continued to live with her mum and dad. It was certainly not unusual. And while Janet had given birth to their daughter, Melissa, on 5 February 1989, Rocastle had been by her side and had continued to be a devoted father and boyfriend. The only 'scandal' to be found was that Rocastle had not deemed it information he had been willing to share with the press.

In any event, Rocastle tried to put the transfer rumours, and so-called scandal, behind him as his form on the football pitch failed to improve. Even a derby game against Spurs, where he usually thrived, saw him put in a subdued display, despite Adams giving them a 1-0 win. Marred by inconsistency, Arsenal also stuttered. Dumped out of the FA Cup by QPR, their league form collapsed, which saw them fall out of title contention.

With the team seemingly having nothing left to play for, and Rocastle struggling with his knee, it was decided that he would have an exploratory operation. Worried at the prospect of missing the World Cup, Rocastle was reassured that he would return before the end of the season, so would have plenty of time to prove his fitness to England manager Bobby Robson.

As Rocastle recuperated, Graham tinkered with his squad, selling the misfiring Niall Quinn to Manchester City for £750,000, while purchasing defender Colin Pates from Charlton for £500,000. When I spoke to Pates he recalled that Rocastle was the first to welcome him to the club. 'He came up to me and said, "It's nice to have another south Londoner here. We've got too many north Londoners. Now we can even it up a bit." Those first few weeks he really looked after me like you wouldn't believe. He was such a gentleman.' As would be seen throughout his career, Rocastle was often the first friendly face new signings encountered at a club. Just as he had been back home in Honor Oak, he was 'the man of the house', always ensuring everyone was comfortable and well looked after.

Finally making his comeback in April, it appeared that his operation had been a success. Running more fluidly, he was soon showing much of his old form. While Graham had to treat him carefully, due to a lack of match fitness, he proved against Millwall that his pace had not been diminished, as he strode forward on the break, before setting Merson up to score.

Yet time was running out for Rocastle to turn Bobby Robson's head. With Robson due to attend the last home game of the season, against Southampton, he was desperate to make an impression. However, when George Graham announced the starting line-up he was crushed to be told he was only a substitute, particularly as Robson had told him before the game that if he played he was as good as on the plane to Italy.

With Bobby Robson in the stand, running the rule over the six Arsenal players who could potentially figure in his squad, Rocastle sat on the bench, watching on as Southampton took the lead, courtesy of a Matthew Le Tissier strike. At this, the Highbury faithful chanted Rocastle's name, prompting Graham to finally make a double change, bringing on Rocastle for Kevin Richardson, and Perry Groves for Brian Marwood. It was hoped that both players could inject some much-needed pace into the sterile Arsenal attack, and they soon proved to be the difference. With 15 minutes remaining, Arsenal won a penalty, which was duly despatched by fullback Lee Dixon; then, just seven minutes later, Rocastle stamped his authority on the game.

As Paul Merson lobbed a high ball towards the back post, Rocastle found himself unmarked. Fishing the ball out of the air with a delicate touch he volleyed the ball past the helpless Tim Flowers. Clenching his fists, he muttered under his breath, 'Come on!' But what Rocastle wasn't to know was that Bobby Robson had already left the stadium.

CHAPTER 4

THE LOVE AFFAIR BEGINS

'You could just see what the outcome was going to be. Dave was dedicated. He was always going to make it.' So says Gary Hill, one of Rocastle's oldest friends, known to all as 'Ginger'. From the moment Hill first met Rocastle at Turnham Primary School, he remembers that he was totally obsessed by football. Whenever he wasn't looking after his family, he would be somewhere on the estate kicking a ball around, whether it be in the school playground, local park or community centre.

And while football was the be-all and end-all, Hill believes that there was another underlying reason for Rocastle's obsession. 'Growing up, he never had his dad around,' he said. 'That was tough and I think he thought football could be his way out for all of the family. He was the father in a way and he just wanted to be the breadwinner.'

Hill also recalls that Rocastle's talent was spotted early in his time at Turnham: 'Me and Dave were probably the best players in school. When we were in our second year in Turnham, Mr Pigden came up to us and asked if we could play for the school team the following morning. Most of the boys in the school team were in the fourth year, so we would be playing two years up. But there was a problem – me and Dave didn't own a pair of boots. Mr Pigden said, "You don't need them. Just be up the field at nine-thirty tomorrow morning."'

Due to the financial constraints on the family Rocastle always struggled to afford football equipment. However, because of his obvious talent, he was never short of offers from people only too happy to lend or even give him what he needed.

'When we turned up,' Hill remembered, 'there was a big box full of old-fashioned boots, ones with big toe caps, and which were ankle high. Mr Pigden said, "Pick your boots out of here." So me and Dave picked a pair out and never looked back.'

Despite wearing boots that had no doubt been out of fashion for over 20 years, Rocastle and Hill quickly became mainstays in their school team. Richard Rydzewski, the former headmaster of Turnham, certainly never forgot the very first time he set eyes on his school's star player. 'The first time I saw David was when I watched the cup final during the Easter holidays,' he said. 'I saw a young man who wanted to take part in every activity on the pitch. He was everywhere as opposed to playing in a particular position.'

Chris Bray, a PE teacher at Turnham, also remembered the young star's precocious skill. 'In the first year I came to Turnham, David was in the third year, a nine-year-old. By that time he had grown into a big boy, and a skilful boy, much admired by all the other boys in the school. He played for the A team from the word go. By the time he got to the fourth year he was still a very big, physically skilful boy, who used to hold the team together.'

Such was his prowess, and his desire to be involved in all areas of play, it was no doubt difficult for his coaches to work out what his best position was. 'We wanted him to play in goal,' Bray remembered. 'He didn't want to play in goal. He wanted to play centre forward. He was a prolific goalscorer. Many a time, one of the other teachers would come up to me after a game and say, "Who's that centre forward?" I'd say, "David Rocastle. Remember the name, because it will be important." And it was.'

Dominating the school team, Hill and Rocastle also played for Lewisham district, as well as for their all-conquering five-a-side team, Blue Stars.

'We were untouchable,' Hill told me with a grin on his face. 'No one could beat us. We were banging in goals for fun. We won every tournament we entered.'

However, there was one league where the boys' superior skill led to other teams complaining that they must be over age. As each member was called to prove their date of birth, Hill confidently revealed his age, only to be informed that he was 11 days too old. The team was subsequently disqualified. 'Dave went mad,' Hill remembered, still wincing at the memory. 'We must have played over 50 games, and were two games away from finishing the season unbeaten, and they took it away from us.'

It was at one of these tournaments that Micky Cheeseman, the manager of local junior team Vista, first saw Rocastle in action. 'I always used to check out the competitions to see if there were any useful players I could get to come and play for us,' Cheeseman told me. 'You'd see the likes of Dennis Wise playing in them, so the standard was always high. But one day I saw this young kid with tremendous skill. I went over to him afterwards and asked if he was playing for anyone on a Sunday. He said, "No." I couldn't believe my luck.'

As for how Rocastle learnt the stepovers and tricks that caught Cheeseman's eye, his friend Errol Johnson credits their packed playground in Roger Manwood Secondary School. 'There used to be this football game at school called pairs,' Johnson told me. 'Me and Dave always used to pair up and we would play against other pairs. We did that for about three years and we never lost a game. But the playground was always busy, full of hundreds of kids running around, so he didn't only have to watch the players he was playing against but also kids who were just playing. I think that helped him a lot because he had to learn how to dribble with close control, at pace, and to change direction quickly, so he didn't bump into anyone. He could dream up any kind of skill. A lot of it he didn't practise, it was just instinct. I think the stepover was instinct. He was better than anyone I've seen for doing that at pace and changing direction.'

Joining Micky Cheeseman's Vista, along with his brother Steve, who played a few years below, Rocastle soon made quite an impression. 'He was so good he could play anywhere,' Cheeseman enthused. 'And I think he actually did, even in goal. But it was as a winger, or up front, where he really caught the eye. He was just far too quick and skilful for most at that level. He scored some incredible individual goals and I swear he gave me a hernia in training one time where he beat me with that stepover of his!' Despite his clear talent, it was Rocastle's loyalty which really struck Cheeseman. Heralded throughout the area as a player to watch, he was approached by other teams to play for them. Most of these teams had more money, better equipment and, in some cases, superior players. In contrast, Cheeseman readily admits that Vista was a rough and ready outfit, with many of his players from single-parent families and little in the way of financial or emotional support. At times, Cheeseman could have as many as eight of his players crammed into his car as he struggled to get a team out. Yet Rocastle never wavered. He played for Vista all the way through his teenage years and was always quick to thank Cheeseman for everything that he did, even ensuring throughout his time as a professional that match tickets were available for him.

'He was such a loyal and lovely person,' Cheeseman told me. 'He never forgot anyone who helped him out.'

This loyalty meant that, while he was a 'lovely person', he was also fiercely protective of his younger brother. Cheeseman recalls that when he came to watch Steve play, if anyone tried to take advantage of him, Rocastle would put them in their place, either vocally or, from time to time, physically. Everyone knew that if they were going to mess with Steve, then they would soon have to answer to his older brother. Rocastle would never go looking for trouble but he certainly wasn't afraid to stand up for himself. A case in point saw Rocastle playing pool at the youth club one evening when a rumour went around that the local hardnut, 'Chester', was waiting outside for him.

'When I heard Chester was outside I was thinking, "He wants to fight Dave? My Dave?" No way!' Karen told me. 'I'd never seen my brother fight at all.'

Despite being goaded to go outside and fight, Rocastle continued to calmly play pool, telling Chester's friends, 'If he wants me, he knows where he can find me.' Soon afterwards, Chester arrived in the youth club looking for trouble. He landed a punch on her brother and Karen was shocked at what happened next. 'He didn't back down,' she said. 'He swung back and soon they were on top of the pool table raining punches on each other.' As everyone cheered them on, Karen was so shocked to see this side to her brother that it reduced her to tears. Still, she admits that she was proud he stood up for himself.

Teenage scuffles might have been familiar rites of passage, but there was something else Rocastle had to contend with on the football pitch: racism. 'It was horrible,' Cheeseman winced. 'We probably had more black players in our team than most, and we were good, so opposition players, and even their parents, used to try and wind the boys up. You used to hear some terrible things and usually we would be outnumbered, as not a lot of people came to watch us. But David never stood for it for long. He could certainly look after himself.'

However, reacting to extreme provocation sometimes earned Rocastle short shrift from referees. On one occasion, after he'd been sent off when playing for Lewisham Way Youth Club, the manager, Terry Nelson, reprimaned his young star, telling him, 'Never forget who you are. Where you come from. And who you represent.' They were to be words that he would never forget.

Renowned as one of the best young footballers in the area, there were, however, others who could also lay claim to being top of the pile. The Wallace brothers, Danny and Rod, were causing a stir, with both going on to play professionally, for Manchester United and Leeds United respectively, while Paul Elliott played for Chelsea. Steve Anthrobus was another who, while not quite a household name, nevertheless went on to play in the Premier League for Wimbledon. But it was a skinny kid with a big mouth by the name of Ian Wright who most on the Honor Oak estate predicted would go on to big things.

Wright was four years older than Rocastle, and while they both attended Turnham Primary School, the age gap would have seemed like a chasm. Nevertheless, Rocastle looked up to Wright in awe. 'One day David was really keen to go and watch a football tournament in Telegraph Hill Park, where some of the older boys were playing,' Errol Johnson told me. 'As we were watching he said to me, "Look at the player there." I remember watching this guy, who was probably around 16, tear the other team to shreds. I said, "Who's that?" And he told me, "It's Ian Wright."'

Despite the difference in age, there was always mutual respect between the pair, with both in awe of the other's talent. Wright was renowned for keeping an eye out on the younger kids on the estate, especially Rocastle, who in turn thought the world of him. Although their different age groups meant that they never played together growing up, Wright has previously recalled the one occasion when they did go head to head. 'We played in a five-a-side match against each other,' he smiled. 'He must have scored seven goals and I must have scored six. And his team beat us. Everyone in the area knew that me and Dave were the main footballers and everyone came to watch the game but on the day he got on top of me.'

Always respectful of Wright, Rocastle wasn't necessarily so conciliatory to others. 'If anyone ever told him another player was better than him, then that was like a red rag to a bull,' Johnson laughed. 'I remember the day he played against Sedgehill. They had a player called Robert Keys, who was at West Ham, and they all thought he was the best footballer in the area. David was really up for the challenge. A lot of people watched that game, as everyone wanted to see what the outcome was going to be. I remember Robert Keys opened the scoring, and he ran up to all these girls on the sideline and shouted, "Oi, did you see that?" That really wound David up. Soon after, he slammed two in the back of the net and ran the game. We won 4-1. To be fair, after the game Robert Keys came up to David and told him, "You're the best player I've seen." And he was. For me he was definitely the best player to have come out of south London.'

One of Rocastle's secret weapons for getting the better of his opponents was Johnson's scouting prowess. 'I like watching players,' Johnson told me, 'working them out and breaking down their game. I would go everywhere to watch David play, and on the bus on the way there I would tell him, "Don't go this side of him" or "This guy's slow on the turn". I would then stand and watch and he would beat his opponent all day. He was totally fearless, no matter who he was up against.'

Rocastle's fearlessness was a major part of his game. 'He was as tough as old boots,' Johnson continued, 'in that he was prepared to put tackles in as well as get up after he had been fouled.' For any player with a reputation for being one of the best in the area, there were some who took great pleasure in hacking him down, but Rocastle soon learnt never to show that he was hurt. This was a trait he carried into his professional career, as he never feigned injury, dived or stayed down, unless in need of medical attention.

Yet when Johnson stated that Rocastle was fearless, he also meant with the ball. 'David was never scared to try a trick, or to keep running at people, even if something hadn't come off before,' he told me. 'He understood the game and could adapt to any situation, but him being fearless separated him from other good footballers, and made him a great footballer.'

Synonymous today with all things Arsenal, no one can remember Rocastle actually being a Gunner as a child. Karen Rocastle thinks he might have been a Crystal Palace supporter, while Gary Hill recalls that it was West Ham. But Errol Johnson told me that he and Rocastle would go to watch Crystal Palace whenever they had the opportunity. 'We used to arrange to meet on the train and go to Selhurst Park, where we would stand on the terraces and get involved in all the chants,' he said. 'He liked a player called Jim Cannon, and as he got older he also liked Kenny Sansom.' In time, Rocastle would of course have the opportunity to line up alongside Sansom, a player described by many as the best left back in the world during his prime.

At a time when skirmishes between rival fans were commonplace, such trips were not always carefree experiences. On one occasion, a full-scale fight erupted on the train, which led to Rocastle and Hill both having to hide under their seats, aware that football fans could be quite unforgiving when it came to two black teenagers.

If Rocastle was not exactly an ardent fan of any particular team, then he was definitely a fan of certain players. West Bromwich Albion's Cyrille Regis, Laurie Cunningham and Brendon Batson were three he particularly idolised. Christened 'The Three Degrees' by their manager, Ron Atkinson, this trio of black players had caused a sensation in the late 1970s. With their dazzling skill, they were not only heralded as some of the finest footballers of their generation, but they also gave hope to black youngsters, such as Rocastle, that a career in the game was possible, as before they rose to prominence there were relatively few black players at the top level of English football.

However, while Rocastle idolised Regis and Cunningham, Hill can recall the occasion when his friend first fell in love with the team he would in time go on to represent with such pride. 'Dave wasn't a big one for TV apart from when the football was on,' he said. 'These days we get football on all the time, but back then it was really rare. The big game was always the FA Cup final, which would be on all day, from nine in the morning. We never missed that. No one would go out that day until the game was over and then we would all rush out to play over the fields to emulate our heroes. Dave loved the whole day. He would be glued to it, even watching the team coaches making their way to Wembley. He wouldn't move.'

This devotion was put to the test during the 1979 final, when Manchester United met Arsenal. On the day in question, Hill's sister was due to be married, and Rocastle had been invited to attend, such was his closeness to the Hill family. However, as coverage of the cup final got underway, he was unable to drag himself away from the television. Even as Hill got dressed for the big day and told his friend they needed to leave, he remained unmoving, telling Hill that he would catch him up. Of course, Hill didn't see him again that day, as Rocastle was carried away by the late drama.

Having breezed into a two-goal lead, courtesy of Brian Talbot and

Frank Stapleton, it seemed that Arsenal's name was on the cup, particularly as the game entered the final moments with United rarely threatening. But then the game sparked into life. Gordon McQueen pulled a goal back with just minutes to go before Sammy McIlroy grabbed the most unlikely of equalisers. With the game heading into extra time, there was still time for the most dramatic of twists, as almost straight from the kick-off Alan Sunderland scored with virtually the last kick of the game to win the cup for Arsenal.

Rocastle may not have been an Arsenal fan before but he certainly was now. Rushing straight to the park after the final whistle, Rocastle sported a faded red t-shirt in homage to his new team as he also did his best Alan Sunderland impression. Gary Hill, however, was not impressed. Not only had he missed the game, but his best friend had missed the wedding ceremony. 'He never lived that down with me,' Hill laughs. 'But what a game!'

As he was making a name for himself throughout Lewisham, it came as no surprise when the nearest professional football team, Millwall, began circling. While Millwall's supporters had gained a reputation for racial intolerance, the club was eager to cherry-pick south London's best black talent, which was now impossible to ignore. Both Ian Wright and Paul Elliott had already been for a trial at the club and been rejected. Although Rocastle and Gary Hill impressed enough to be taken on, they also didn't last long.

'My first ever club was at Millwall,' Rocastle later said. 'I went down for trials at Crofton Leisure Centre and I stayed there for a while. This was when I was almost 13. We used to train every Wednesday after school and I used to go training with them during school holidays. One day I got a letter at home. It said, "Dear David, thank you, but no thank you", and hoping that I would make it somewhere else. It was a killer. I thought that was it. Just get on with your schoolwork and see what happens.'

Hill also remembers that while the pair were disappointed,

Rocastle never showed it. 'You could see he was upset, because Millwall was the big local club and this was what he had always wanted,' he said. 'But it wasn't something he openly discussed. He would never show if he was down about something. He just always had a smile on his face, no matter what was happening in his life.'

However, in 1979, with the country mired in the so-called 'Winter of Discontent', this was no time to have your dreams taken away. With tens of thousands of public sector workers going on strike, bodies piled up in morgues, rubbish lined the streets and schools were forced to close, as the economy shrank by 0.8 per cent, leaving Britain to face its second recession in just four years. The prospects looked to be bleak, especially for a young black boy on a London council estate.

While Rocastle continued to play for Vista, it seemed that if he was ever going to rise above the council estate and provide for his family, then he would have to concentrate on his schoolwork. Thankfully, this was an area in which he also excelled, despite Errol Johnson telling me that all of their class at Roger Manwood Secondary School were renowned for 'mischief' and put on report within their first two days.

Described by all who knew him as a 'model student', Karen Rocastle remembered that, 'He loved school. He got really good marks and was very popular, which made it hard for me as the second child as I was always compared to him and he was an A-class student. My mum always used to say, "Why can't you be more like your brother?"'

Karen's recollections of her brother in his schooldays have certainly not been tainted by sentiment. His Roger Manwood Secondary School report, written by his tutor, C. Harrington, reads: 'David has a pleasant and friendly personality, gets on well with others and has been popular with his peers and staff alike. During his time at Roger Manwood he has shown himself to be lively and enthusiastic, displaying leadership within his peer group. David has shown that he can be thoughtful and conscientious. He tackles problems methodically and with persistence.'

Away from football and school, Rocastle still had plenty of other things to keep him occupied. Music, in particular, was always a passion. Karen Rocastle can remember him sitting in his room for hours, rewinding his tapes to replay his favourite song of the moment. And if there should ever be a disco in the community centre, or a house party, then Rocastle was never shy of hitting the dance floor.

As he grew older his good looks, athletic prowess, academic excellence and slick dance moves, meant he was always going to be a hit with the opposite sex. 'Girls loved him,' Johnson laughed. 'He was a good-looking lad so it was never a struggle.'

It also helped that he took pride in his appearance. Apparently obsessed with brushing his teeth, which accounted for his dazzling smile, he also ensured he always had the latest gear from Mr Byrite, which would eventually be passed down to his brothers. However, Roger Manwood was a boys' school. As such, Rocastle and his friends had to look further afield for female company. But their luck was in when their friend Junior Everett moved to Malory, a mixed school. With Junior excitedly telling his mates that there were girls at his school, Rocastle, Errol Johnson and good friend Kevin Arnold were soon making the trip across Lewisham to check them out. One girl Rocastle subsequently met was Jenny Fraser, and the two soon became firm friends.

'We used to hang out every day after school,' Fraser told me. 'He used to get a bus to my school, then we would all get on another bus together to get home. He was such a sweet guy. He never had any money but he always paid for everyone's bus fare and he was always buying me sweets. We were only 12 but I think he was trying to impress me.'

As Rocastle and his friends grew older, they would hang out with the girls around each other's houses, venture to roller-skating rinks, McDonald's or the ABC cinema in Catford, where they saw films like *Star Trek*, *Moonraker*, *The Empire Strikes Back*, *Superman* and *Raiders of the Lost Ark*. This also gave Rocastle an opportunity to satisfy his sweet tooth, with a pack of Butterkist popcorn always a must. Despite being an avid fan of the cinema, he always seemed to be squinting at the screen. It wasn't until his football career started that someone finally realised he needed glasses.

Despite all the distractions of girls, movies and music, Rocastle's dream was to become a footballer, yet as he approached his 15th birthday that dream seemed to be slipping away.

In a twist of fate, Nicky Milo, the Millwall coach who had released Rocastle and Gary Hill, suddenly called them both up to play for the county. 'We'll show him,' Hill remembers them both thinking. 'We played against Norwich in a cup game. We had to wear a blazer and tie and all that. Michael Thomas was captain of the side. That was the first time him and Dave met. Anyway, Dave and Michael played blinders and got picked up by Arsenal after the game.'

While this marked the game where Arsenal made their move for their future right-winger, he had actually been on their radar for a number of months. 'I was playing for Roger Manwood against a team called Tollington Park,' Rocastle once said. 'They were man-aged by a man called Terry Murphy, who in the end became my scout. I think we beat them 8-0 but I hadn't had a great game. There were other players who had scored hat-tricks, but Terry still recommended me to the people at Arsenal and told them to keep an eye on me. From there, most of my football was played for the district and from the district you get recognised from all over. That's where I got in contact with Michael Thomas for the first time, and from the district I was watched by Arsenal.'

In his book *The Nowhere Men*, author Michael Calvin interviewed

Terry Murphy, who recalled the first time he saw his future protégé in action. 'David was the difference between the sides,' he told Calvin. 'He was so comfortable on the ball. He had tricks; even as a youngster he would do stepovers and drag-backs.'

When Murphy asked Rocastle if he could play in a practice game for the Arsenal youth team, Rocastle told him that he would first have to check with his Sunday league manager, as they also had a game that day. Such was his loyalty and respect for Micky Cheeseman that he would have been willing to forgo the dream opportunity of a trial at Arsenal to turn out for his junior team. Thankfully, Micky Cheeseman gave his star player his blessing. 'I told him, "This is your big opportunity. You've got to make the most of it."'

Yet while Rocastle prepared for his trial at Arsenal in 1982, in 1990 he hoped he had done enough to make Bobby Robson's World Cup squad.

CHAPTER 5

ENGLAND

According to the *Daily Mirror*, the total value of the 1990 England World Cup squad was a record-breaking £47m. Ranking all 22 players in order of their perceived worth, in third place, just behind Chris Waddle and John Barnes and valued at £4m, was David Rocastle, apparently worth twice as much as Paul Gascoigne and Gary Lineker.

Having made his England Under-21 debut in September 1986, starring in a 1-1 draw with Sweden, Rocastle had earned 14 caps for Dave Sexton's side, becoming captain in the process. Playing right midfield, he had excelled in a strong team, which had also included the likes of Gascoigne, David Platt, Nigel Clough and Martin Keown.

In the group stages of the 1988 European Under-21 Championship, he had played a prominent role in England's biggest ever away win at that level, a 5-1 victory against a strong Yugoslavian team. On the night, Rocastle and Gascoigne had been electric. With Gascoigne netting twice, Rocastle had scored the goal of the night, sweeping past two defenders before arrowing a shot into the far corner. Such was the level of his performance that *The Times* reported that he had been 'outstanding'.

Considering the cast of stellar names, it is no surprise that the team reached the semi-finals of the tournament, but their progress was denied only because Rocastle, and eight other players, missed the first-leg defeat to France due to club fixtures being rearranged for the same date.

While the Under-21s were showing huge promise, England's senior team were struggling. After being humiliatingly knocked out of the group stages of Euro '88, they were in dire need of an injection of fresh talent. With Bobby Robson subsequently calling up Rocastle for a friendly against Denmark in September 1988, he said of him, 'He's a 10-year investment. I'm sure he is for Arsenal. As long as he's an investment for Arsenal, then he's got to be for England.'

Rocastle found himself joined in the squad by his Arsenal teammates Paul Davis, Michael Thomas and Tony Adams. 'There was a lot of speculation that Paul Davis and Michael Thomas would be involved, but no one thought I would be,' he said. 'It was only later in the day someone said, "Dave, you're in." No one at Arsenal knew! I couldn't believe the three of us were going to be involved in the England squad. It made it easier for me.' Seeing the three black Arsenal players together certainly caused a stir. As the press surrounded the trio for pictures, they immediately christened them 'The Three Degrees', a source of particular pride for Rocastle, who'd been such a fan of the original trio, Regis, Cunningham and Batson.

Yet some believed that there was more to Rocastle's call-up than talent alone. With the ticket sales for the visit of the Danes struggling to reach 20,000, Wembley was set to be all but deserted. The suggestion was that Rocastle had only been included to help attract more fans. The doyen of football writers, Brian Glanville, certainly questioned Rocastle's selection in his column in *The Times*. 'David Rocastle at his best is an exciting, dynamic right-flank player, but too inconsistent to demand selection yet.'

In front of a dismal turnout of just 25,000, with a pregnant Janet Nelson among them, Rocastle proved the doubters wrong. As Paul Gascoigne sat on the bench, Rocastle was involved in all that was good about England in the 1-0 victory. Displaying an innate subtlety, combined with swashbuckling aggression, the few times he got on the ball he had managed to supercharge the meagre crowd.

As such, while Glanville had not given Rocastle a glowing pre-match endorsement, he was now forced to think again: 'David Rocastle, the one "daring" selection Robson made, gave an impressive performance which confirmed his class.'

After the game, the smiling debutant shared his delight. 'The other lads made me feel part of the team straightaway,' he said. 'It is different playing for your country. It's something everyone wants to do, and having fulfilled that ambition, I'm not satisfied. I want to be part of the squad for hopefully the next 10 years at least.'

When asked if he had felt any nerves, a broad smile spread across his face. 'I had a few nerves before the game,' he confessed. 'But the lads looked after me out there, and my role was basically the same as I play for Arsenal. As the game went on, I tried to go forward more, but the way the play developed I couldn't manage it.'

Most importantly of all, the manager had been impressed by Rocastle's sizzling debut. 'With his skill factor he can go past people,' Robson enthused. 'He has pace, a jink and a little trick. He's very accomplished with most skills and can only get better.'

Such was Rocastle's impact, and the form of his fellow midfielders at Arsenal, that ex-Spurs manager David Pleat even urged Robson to go one better in the next game and pick all of Arsenal's midfield. Robson almost did just that, when he selected five

Arsenal players for the following friendly against Saudi Arabia, which included Adams, Thomas, Rocastle, Marwood and Smith, with only Paul Davis missing out from the Gunners' midfield. However, the humiliating 1-1 draw, in front of just 8,000 fans in Riyadh, meant this was an experiment he would not repeat.

Following a lacklustre start to the World Cup qualifying campaign, and with Robson only picking Rocastle and other young players of promise for friendlies, the England manager was soon involved in a furious row with the press. As journalists rounded on Robson, with some suggesting he should resign, his reply was that, 'No young player, not even Gascoigne, has yet grasped the Football League by the throat with his club. Even now, I am not in a position where I can risk everything on some of the younger players. Rocastle, Clough, Thomas, Parker and Walker are all finding their feet in the first division. They are potential England players, but are they ready to challenge the established players?'

But with pressure building on Robson to select Rocastle in competitive games, and with Rocastle gearing up to prove he could be trusted, his participation in a friendly with Greece was suddenly thrown in doubt. Preparing to travel to Athens at 9pm on the Sunday night, Rocastle awoke at 7am to find his girlfriend, Janet, going into labour. In a panic, he telephoned Arsenal physio Gary Lewin for advice, and was told to get to hospital as quickly as possible.

Pacing the corridor, Rocastle found himself in a quandary. There was no way he could leave Janet if she was in labour, while he also knew that the game against Greece was a huge opportunity for him. Thankfully, at 11am, the shrill cries of his first daughter, Melissa, settled any nerves he might have had. 'I was the first one to hold her,' Rocastle remembered happily. 'The feeling was unbelievable.' Kissing Janet and his newborn daughter goodbye, Rocastle set off for England duty with a smile on his face.

Although the uninspiring 2-1 away win may not have quietened the ever-growing band of supporters demanding Robson's head, it did allow Rocastle to prove that he may just be worthy of a regular place. Again showcasing his ability to make things happen, his exuberance and penetration from midfield had caught the eye. Now a converted fan, Brian Glanville said of his display, 'A word though in praise of David Rocastle, whose performance on the right flank was full of pace, vitality, skill and energy.'

Robson could no longer ignore Rocastle. Selecting him for his first competitive England game, a World Cup qualifier away to Albania, he hoped that he could be the spark his team had long been missing. However, as Rocastle looked forward to his competitive debut he suddenly found his knee lock in training. Frantically icing and resting the joint, he hoped he could make a quick recovery.

Right up until kick-off his participation was in doubt, and though not fully fit he nevertheless found himself named in a strong midfield alongside Bryan Robson, Neil Webb and John Barnes. Helping England cruise to a 2-0 win, Rocastle had again turned heads with his performance, despite playing injured. Every time he had touched the ball, the decibels rose in the stadium, as *The Times* match report proclaimed that he had been 'impressive'.

Keeping his place for the return game against Albania, Robson's England finally clicked into place. Yet this time all the headlines belonged to Gascoigne, who had announced his arrival on the international stage with a thrilling performance, and brilliant solo goal, in a 5-0 win.

Making his debut that day was QPR fullback Paul Parker, who had also been assigned as Rocastle's roommate. When I spoke to Parker, he recalled his excitement at seeing Rocastle at close hand for the first time: 'At the time he was like a young superstar. Everyone was talking about him and he was one of those players I never wanted to play against. He was very, very quick, and one of the first players who used to do stepovers at speed. I remember he had thighs like tree trunks, and if he needed to be he could be very aggressive. He had all the attributes every young footballer would want.'

Also getting to know Rocastle off the pitch, Parker was struck by the person he found. 'There was no arrogance with him at all,' he revealed. 'He was so laid-back, so relaxed. Sometimes I'd wish I was like that. He wasn't bothered about anything.'

Parker laughed when he recalled what he and Rocastle would get up to behind closed doors. 'I was from Essex, so I was a beer drinker, but with Dave coming from south London, he was a little cooler, so used to like a brandy,' he revealed. 'We used to have a little drink in the room while we were away with England. I'd bring beers and crisps and Dave would bring brandy and chocolate. We'd have a great time arguing over what to watch on telly, or what music to listen to.'

Parker also described how Rocastle would constantly be on the phone to Janet and newborn daughter, Melissa. 'At the time she was only a baby,' Parker smiled. 'But he used to say all these little baby things to her. I would be sat on the bed, raising my eyebrows at it all, but that's how he was with his little girl. Two or three times a day he'd call. He was soft in that way.'

Continuing his good form for club and country, just days after Arsenal had dramatically won the title at Anfield in 1989 he had set up a goal for Webb in a 3-0 win against Poland, wreaking precise devastation every time he ran at his quaking opponent. Earning yet more praise, he was fast becoming a fan favourite.

However, a 1-1 draw against Denmark in a friendly was then followed by a 0-0 draw with Sweden in a qualifier. On both occasions Rocastle had cut a frustrated figure. For the first time in his England career, the games had not fallen under his hypnotic spell. Although the results and performances were disappointing, it was the racist behaviour of the crowd in Stockholm that gave the most cause for concern. 'It was disgraceful,' *The Times* wrote, 'that, in the capital of a country so passionately dedicated to the anti-apartheid cause, a large section of the crowd behind one goal should have persistently indulged in racist chants against Barnes, Walker and then Rocastle.'

Paul Parker wasn't in the squad that night but he was not surprised to hear that such a thing occurred. 'We got it everywhere, to be perfectly honest,' he sighed. 'That's the way it was. Me and the likes of Rocky were really the first generation of black players coming into the Football League so we would be targeted. Back then no one knew any different. We had to be mentally strong. I even got it off of England's supporters when I played in the B game in Iceland. That's how bad it was.'

The black players in the England squad learnt to keep their thoughts to themselves. 'We didn't really discuss it,' Parker said. 'There was nowhere for us to go. It's not like today when there are a lot of societies and things against racism. There wasn't anything then. We knew we couldn't moan about it. We knew we couldn't go to the manager. We knew we couldn't go to the papers. We would have been called weak. I remember one time I was being abused when I was at QPR. I went to the manager, and he just said, "You're going to have to deal with it. I can't help you. I can't stop it. Deal with it or get out." That was it.'

Disregarding the racist abuse, the result against Sweden had once again seen fans and sections of the media rage against Robson. As the pressure mounted, he faced travelling to Poland in the last game of the group, needing a draw to secure qualification. Robson knew that, with his job on the line, it was vital he got his selection right. Putting his faith in Rocastle, he selected him on the right-hand side of midfield, hoping that he could put the Swedish display behind him and conjure up some magic.

The game that followed was far from a classic. In front of 30,000 intimidating Polish fans, it took an inspired display from Peter Shilton to keep England in the game. As the noisy enclave of England supporters tried to inspire their team, they saw their midfield being constantly overrun, with Rocastle in particular struggling to contain the Polish winger Jacek Ziober.

Although the 0-0 draw didn't exactly quieten the critics, it was still enough for England to qualify. Yet for the first time in his England career, Rocastle earned negative headlines for his sub-standard performance. 'I was slated,' he later said. 'My big trouble was that I felt in awe of established internationals like Bryan Robson, John Barnes and Chris Waddle. Every time I got the ball I just wanted to give it to them.'

But Rocastle had no reason to be so in awe of his team-mates. By this stage Robson had him down as one of the first names on the team sheet. Still, while he was desperate to prove a point after his poor showing, he was forced to miss the subsequent friendly with Italy through injury, which saw David Platt make an encouraging debut in his absence. Fighting for his place, Rocastle was eager to play in the following game against Yugoslavia, despite not being fully fit. Sadly, it showed, as he was again off the pace, displaying none of the virtuosity for which he was renowned.

Before Robson picked his World Cup squad, Rocastle had just three friendlies to prove his fitness. It was therefore disastrous when injury saw him miss out on wins against Brazil and Czechoslovakia, games in which rivals Gascoigne and Platt had starred. If Rocastle was to have any chance of going to the World Cup, it was vital for him to quickly find his best form for the final warm-up game.

In the last home league game of the season, against Southampton, Rocastle had of course scored for Arsenal, a statement of intent that told Robson he might just be ready. And to his delight,

Rocastle learnt that he had been included in Robson's initial 26-man squad, which would be trimmed by three before the trip to Italy. However, his ineffectual display against Denmark, and subsequent swollen knee, left Rocastle sweating. He had never been on the losing side for the national team, and had proven his worth in the qualifiers, but could he be risked, especially when Platt and Gascoigne were playing so well?

Facing a barrage of speculation, Rocastle countered, 'I've played in five of the six qualifying matches and earned some good ratings. I think Bobby Robson is aware of what I can do.'

His England roommate, Paul Parker, recalls that on the day of reckoning he and Rocastle were in their room at Bisham Abbey waiting to be told their fate. Parker was actually more nervous than Rocastle, as he had only broken into the team recently and felt that his roommate 'was a shoo-in for the World Cup'. Despite these fears, Rocastle reassured him that he would be fine and the two excitedly talked of spending the summer as roommates in Italy, with their primary concern being how they could smuggle in their supplies of alcohol and sweets.

But then came a knock on the door. Rocastle opened it to find Robson standing there with a grim look on his face. 'Can you give us a moment please, Paul?' Robson said. Parker accordingly hopped off the bed and made his way down to reception.

'I knew what he was going to do,' Parker remembered. 'I was sitting in reception in shock. My roommate, who I had just been talking about rooming with in Italy, like we were little boys going on a camping trip together, was not going to make it.'

When Parker returned to the room he found Rocastle packing his bags. It was as quick and as brutal as that. Delighted he had made the cut himself, he was still devastated that his friend's World Cup dream was over. 'He didn't say anything,' Parker remembers. 'Obviously he was hurt but he never showed anything.'

Helping Rocastle carry his bags to his car, with the press watching on, Parker told me that he became very emotional. 'I think the only thing I didn't do was burst out crying,' he said. 'All of a sudden my mate was going home and I was going to be rooming with somebody else. If Dave Rocastle had been fully fit then there's no doubt for me that he would've started in the World Cup. He was very unlucky. But David Platt came in and was a revelation in the tournament.'

While Rocastle kept his emotions in check, the next day the back page of the *Daily Mirror* quoted him as saying, 'I'm fucked off.' He had of course said nothing of the sort, and as such was rightly upset to see such a quote splashed across a national newspaper. At least Rocastle was in good company that summer. Incredibly, Bobby Robson didn't select a single Arsenal player to be in his squad, despite the team being predominantly English and title winners just a year earlier. Alan Smith was a golden boot winner and Tony Adams was a title-winning captain at just 22 years of age. Yet neither was deemed good enough.

When asked to explain his decision, Robson had some sympathy: 'Poor old Rocky. Six months ago he was a certainty but an injury, and a decline in form, made it impossible for me to pick him. I know it's no consolation but Rocastle and Adams can be leading players in four years' time.'

It would have been understandable if he had decided to go away for the summer to avoid the constant coverage of the World Cup, but first and foremost Rocastle was a football fan. He wanted to watch all of the games, particularly England.

Jerome Anderson, Rocastle's longtime agent and close friend, told me that they watched every England game together. 'He was always supportive of his team-mates, even though he wasn't there,' Anderson recalls. 'He always wanted England to do well and was just like every other England fan, getting very excited as they reached the semi-finals. But I couldn't help but feel upset for him. I knew that as a professional there were only so many opportunities you could have to play at a World Cup, and this was a great one for England. If he hadn't been injured, I think he had a chance of playing in most games and making a real impact. He knew this as well, but he never complained about it. He just wanted England to win.'

For most English football fans the summer of 1990 was a halcyon time of Gazza's tricks and tears, Lineker's goals and John Barnes rapping to the sound of New Order's 'World in Motion'. Against all odds, maligned coach Bobby Robson had inspired his team to within a penalty kick of reaching the World Cup final itself. As such, the squad had returned as national heroes, while David Rocastle could only watch on in frustration.

Faced with a summer of working on his fitness, he promised himself that come Euro '92 he would be there. But before any thought of England, he had to regain his place in the Arsenal midfield, which was by no means guaranteed with Graham looking to revamp his squad.

CHAPTER 6

BECOMING A GUNNER

It's hard to imagine now but in the early 1980s Arsenal was a club on a one-way road to nowhere. Terry Neill's 1979 FA Cup-winning success had not been built upon, and consequently a challenge for the league title seemed a long way off. Entertainment at Highbury was also at a premium. Dogged by criticism that the first team had been bereft of any flair ever since talisman Liam Brady was sold to Juventus in 1980, crowds had plummeted. As such, in the 1980/81 season, half of the attendances at Highbury were under 30,000, with one game – against Birmingham – actually attracting fewer than 20,000.

It says a lot about the style of the team at the time that to replace Brady, Neill, assisted by Don Howe, signed Welshman Peter Nicholas from Crystal Palace. Nicholas was an able player but never in the same class as Brady. What made this period even more galling for most Arsenal fans was that rivals Spurs boasted a midfield that included the finesse of Glenn Hoddle and Ossie Ardiles, while Neill missed out on opportunities to sign the likes of Ruud Gullit and Diego Maradona.

In the circumstances, the only name with any real star value to arrive at Highbury was striker Tony Woodcock, who signed from German side FC Koln. Woodcock had been a European Cup winner at Nottingham Forest, and had also represented England in the 1982 World Cup. He was by no means a stellar name like Maradona, but he at least appeased some Arsenal fans who were desperate for some stardust.

Haemorrhaging money, and failing on the pitch, the club somehow needed to conjure up a winning and attractive team. The result was a youth system that would in time produce a crop of youngsters who would go on to make their mark for club and country.

Chief scout Steve Burtenshaw discussed how he went about this in 1986, in an Arsenal programme article entitled 'Steve's Scouts Spare the Highbury Chequebook'. 'I said when I arrived back here in 1980 that it would take about five years to see the benefits of the changes we'd introduced,' Burtenshaw told Kevin Connolly, the regular interviewer for the official Arsenal program. 'We've always believed in going for quality rather than quantity, then working hard with the players we sign.'

Highlighting the three key attributes that his team of scouts looked for in a prospect, Burtenshaw said, 'Obviously you need skill, and you have to be a good athlete to withstand the competitiveness of English football. But if you haven't got the will to succeed, the other two qualities are not worth having.'

Scouring the land for players with such qualities, Burtenshaw's master plan was delivered to perfection by his team of Terry Murphy, Steve Rowley, Pat Rice, Tommy Coleman and Terry Burton. When I spoke to Burton he told me how Arsenal went about trying to attract the best youngsters in Britain. 'We had a scouting network throughout the country,' he said. 'Not really in Europe at the time but in England, Scotland, Wales and Ireland. It was in London where we really focused, though. At the time the London scene was fantastic. There was so much talent.'

This focus on London soon reaped rewards. Scouting the likes of Stewart Robson, Colin Hill and Paul Davis, each of these went on to cement their place in the first team.

However, other top London clubs had also recognised that there was a crop of talented youngsters flourishing in the city. Competition, therefore, was fierce. At the time, Arsenal's finances and lack of success on the pitch meant that the scouts had to little to rely on to attract players, other than the club's illustrious past, and an ocean of charm.

Under these circumstances, Terry Murphy was the perfect man for the job. As Martin Keown told Michael Calvin, 'Arsenal could not have had a better role model or ambassador. I can still see him coming to my school to meet the headmaster before I signed schoolboy forms. Arsenal blazer. Collar and tie. Impeccably presented. You knew here was a man with great dignity.'

Murphy made any prospective player feel as though they would be privileged to play for such a great institution. While the current team might have been struggling, Murphy would talk up the past, discussing the greats such as Herbert Chapman and Bertie Mee with great reverence, as well as heralding all of the world-class talents who had pulled on the famous red jersey, such as Brady, Charlie George and Frank McLintock. On the tour of Highbury, Murphy ensured that all the players were taken through the famous marble halls and, if there was a first-team player at the ground, he would do his utmost to get them to talk to any star-struck youngster.

David Rocastle was one of many young footballers to be given the full charm offensive. His affinity with Arsenal following the 1979 FA Cup final victory was turned into a full-blown love affair by Murphy's enthusiasm for the club.

Karen Rocastle recalls that her brother felt that Arsenal was more than a mere football club. 'He always called them "The Arsenal",' she said. 'And he really bought into the traditions of wearing the official club blazer.' To Rocastle, it was an honour to play for 'The Arsenal' and in time he would turn into a fine ambassador, and figurehead, for the club in his own right.

Following a successful trial, and being won over by Murphy, Rocastle signed schoolboy forms for Arsenal. 'This was his dream,' Errol Johnson remembers. 'He was determined to be a footballer, and once Arsenal took him the rest is history. He had so much focus and desire. He couldn't be swayed from reaching his goal. It was hard at times but he wasn't just doing it for himself, he was doing it for his family, who he wanted to support.'

Ever modest, Rocastle later told Amy Lawrence, in her book *Proud to Say That Name*, that Arsenal might have signed him due to his close friendship with one of the club's principal targets rather than for his talent. 'I heard a lot of rumours that the reason Arsenal signed me in the first place was to get Michael [Thomas], who was being chased by every single club imaginable, including Tottenham, Chelsea and Man City.' It was a joke at the time that Thomas must have been the wealthiest schoolboy in London, as prior to signing for Arsenal he had been training with three teams, all of whom were paying him subs.

Karen Rocastle can recall her older brother's dedication once he arrived at Arsenal. 'He never went out, and he started to plan what he wanted to eat so he would be at the top of his game,' she said. 'He'd say to Mum the day before what he wanted and she would make sure she got it for him. He used to get so excited the day before a match. His whole world revolved around preparing properly for a game. He was so professional, even back then.'

However, while Rocastle was thrilled to be playing for Arsenal, other top players had to be coaxed away from competing clubs. Talents such as Paul Merson, Tony Adams, Martin Keown and Michael Thomas certainly had other options, but once they had been subjected to the persuasive charm of Murphy and the rest of the scouting team there was only ever going to be one outcome.

'You like to feel Arsenal is a family,' Murphy told Michael Calvin. 'Once the boys are there you don't just say, "Right, we've got the player, that's it, forget him," and go on to someone else. I would always maintain contact with the parents and players themselves. I can go back 20 or 30 years and I'm still in contact with them. But David was special. Yes, very special.'

The caring nature of Murphy, which made his protégés want to succeed for him as well as for themselves, is illustrated by the fact that one day he noted that Rocastle's coat was worn, and his trousers a little short. Money was tight in the Rocastle household, so new clothes were often a luxury. Taking Rocastle aside, Murphy asked if he could help him out, perhaps get him a jacket as the nights were growing cold. A new jacket would no doubt have been most welcome but Rocastle was always a very proud man, and he politely declined Murphy's offer. While he might have recognised Rocastle's hardship, Murphy also respected his pride.

With Rocastle at Arsenal, and Steve Burtenshaw continuing to add the best youngsters from London and beyond, there was soon an embarrassment of riches. As if to underline this, in his autobiography Tony Adams describes the incredible day he signed schoolboy forms for the club: 'I was led into a room where there was Terry Burton, along with five boys. They were David Rocastle, Martin Hayes, Martin Keown, Michael Thomas and Gus Caesar. "That was a good day in the office," Terry has since said to me.'

When I asked Burton about this, he told me that in over 40 years in the game this was the best group of youth-team players he had come across. 'You don't realise it at the time,' he said. 'It's only in hindsight that you realise they were special days. These days if a youth player makes the first team it's big news. When you consider the amount of players we had, who played for the first team in their teens, it's quite amazing.' Indeed, six of the players from the youth team in the early 1980s would also go on to become internationals.

Manchester United's 'Class of '92' has received plenty of plaudits for the group of youngsters it produced, but Arsenal's class of the early 1980s is definitely worthy of comparison. Full of household names, such as Tony Adams, Martin Keown, Michael Thomas, David Rocastle, Niall Quinn and Paul Merson, it also contained plenty of others who went on to have good professional careers. Gus Caesar and Martin Hayes would play for the first team with mixed success, while Jon Purdie went on to Wolves and goalkeeper Nicky Hammond played in the Premier League for Swindon.

The scouting network and coaches also stand comparison with the very best. Pat Rice and Terry Burton both enjoyed long and successful spells in the game, particularly at Arsenal, where they were integral parts of the coaching teams that won many trophies, while Burtenshaw and Murphy provided them with an array of rough diamonds to shine. Terry Burton is also keen to stress that youth-team coach, Tommy Coleman, who sadly recently passed away, deserves a lot of credit, as it was he who really nurtured this group of star players.

With the 1982 youth team assembled, they met twice a week for training in an indoor hall, under the old South Stand, known as 'The JVC Centre'. Every Tuesday and Thursday night, Rocastle would make his way to Highbury after school, which would involve taking the train from Brockley to London Bridge, then two tubes, until he was finally at Arsenal. Often he wouldn't get back until late, but he never complained, instead delighting in proudly telling his siblings that Arsenal was special because it was the only tube station named after a place that doesn't actually exist.

Rocastle never missed a training session, and Burton can recall the first time he set eyes on the dedicated teenager from Lewisham: 'I remember he was a skinny, proud kid, who turned out to have these magnificent thighs and was really strong. He had a natural ability to go past people. I can still remember that trick he did, sort of dragging the ball backwards and then back around again. Tommy Coleman did a lot of work with him but none of us taught him that. We would probably fall over trying to teach him that!'

As Coleman and Burton put the boys through their paces, they were also keen to ensure that each player knew what was expected in every position on the pitch. Tony Adams and Martin Keown predominantly played as central defenders, while Michael Thomas and Rocastle were often moved around.

'Rocky actually changed positions a couple of times,' Burton recalled. 'He went from wide to centre to back out wide. I think he even had a go at fullback and striker. It was all about just trying to make him the best possible player. To make sure he understood the game, and knew his roles and responsibilities.'

When I asked Burton where he preferred Rocastle to play, he was unequivocal in his judgement. 'In wide areas,' he emphatically answered. 'But he was always good in the centre because he could read the game and was tenacious. But for me he did his best work on the wing, doing stepovers, accelerating past his fullback and whipping crosses in.'

His best position might have been out wide, but team-mate Jon Purdie recalls that Rocastle was not always happy there. 'He played on the right and I played on the left,' Purdie told me. 'But we both wanted to play more centrally, as you could get on the ball more. However, at the time there was the likes of Michael Thomas in there so it was hard for us.'

It wasn't just his obvious talent that endeared Rocastle to his coaches as well as to his team-mates. 'He was such a nice lad,' Burton said. 'He was quiet and unassuming but he always seemed to have a smile on his face. He trained hard and always listened to what the coaches had to say. It was actually quite amazing to have such a quiet, nice boy, and then see the difference on the football pitch.'

This is also how Jon Purdie remembered his former team-mate. 'He would just concentrate on his own game,' he told me. 'He certainly wasn't a shouter like Tony Adams, who would go around getting everyone going. But he was still so determined. With Rocky, actions spoke louder than words. He wouldn't hesitate to fly into a tackle, which would get the team going.'

Again, Rocastle's quiet nature certainly didn't mean that he lacked confidence in his ability. 'I remember I was having a talk to them in the dressing room,' Pat Rice recalled in the video *The Rocky Road to Success*. 'And I said, "Hold up your hand any of you who think you're going to make it in the first team here." Out of all of them David was the only one who put his hand up, and I thought, "That will do for me; he's got the determination to succeed."'

Some of the coaches were, however, still perturbed by the fact that when he dribbled with the ball he always seemed to have his head down. Finally, Tommy Coleman realised what the issue might be. Taking his young star to the halfway line, he asked, 'Can you see the goal?' Rocastle squinted, waited a moment, before finally confirming that he could not. Soon afterwards the short-sighted winger was provided with his first pair of glasses, as well as contact lenses.

On 7 August 1982, Rocastle made his youth-team debut away to Colchester. Going down 3-1, it was an inauspicious start for a team that included so many future stars, but it was Rocastle who had the consolation of scoring the Arsenal goal. While champagne would soon mark such memorable moments, Rocastle had to make do with a less extravagant reward. 'At the youth-team games a lot of the kids left home about six in the morning to get a bus,' Burton told me. 'After a day of travelling, and then a game, we used to have fish and chips afterwards. Everyone loved it. Times have definitely changed.'

Indeed, you can hardly imagine the current Arsenal manager, Arsène Wenger, sanctioning such a post-match meal, but it certainly didn't do the likes of Rocastle or Tony Adams any harm.

Combining football with school, as well as looking after his family, Rocastle played 15 matches during the 1982/83 season, starting 10 of them and scoring five goals in the process. It was certainly a respectable return on a personal level, but the star-studded team often failed to deliver during their first season together, losing five games, including a 5-0 home defeat to Norwich. Matters weren't helped when Rocastle turned out for Micky Cheeseman's cricket team and got hit in the face with a ball. Cheeseman told me that Steve Burtenshaw called him soon afterwards to thank him for his work with Rocastle, but also to suggest that he no longer play cricket. Cheeseman agreed that perhaps such a pursuit was no longer appropriate for a teenager trying to make the grade at Arsenal.

In the summer of 1983, Rocastle left school with a handful of GCEs along with the well wishes of his teachers. In his final school report, his headmaster, Brinley Morgan, wrote, 'David is a fine example of how a sportsman should be. His attitude is exemplary. He has represented the school in most sports but he is a particularly talented football player who has involved himself wholeheartedly in his community.'

With his school days coming to an end Rocastle prayed he had done enough to secure an apprenticeship at Arsenal. It had been a solid first season but competition for a coveted apprenticeship was fierce. It was by no means guaranteed and, for a few months, his future career very much hung in the balance. In moments of doubt, he told his friend Jenny Fraser that he would like to try his hand as a plumber if he didn't make the cut, while his family believe that he probably would have ended up working in a leisure centre. He would no doubt have succeeded in whatever career he chose to pursue, but football was his dream. And now it was decision time.

With the Arsenal coaches having not yet made their decision, the youth team travelled to Haarlem, Holland, in May 1983, to participate in an under-21 tournament. All the players were aware of just what was at stake. Anyone who had a bad tournament could very well see their hopes of an apprenticeship vanish. Thankfully, in the games against Sunderland, Brugge, Haarlem, Feyenoord and Ajax, Rocastle flourished on the wide right. Playing against older players didn't seem to daunt him at all. Ferociously competitive, he was more than physically capable, while his balanced grace and effortless control, all at speed, caught the attention.

Terry Burton fondly remembered the trip where Rocastle came to the fore. 'These tournaments were a big part of the players' education, when they started to play against top European teams in a different environment,' he said. 'It was a real test for the boys, and I remember the likes of Rocky and Tony [Adams] showed us, "I've got a hold of this now. I understand the game. Look at me." Their performances stood out.'

As such, when Rocastle returned to the UK he received the news that he had been dreaming of – 'The Arsenal' wanted to sign him as an apprentice. The dream was another step closer. And Arsenal could hardly wait to unleash its burgeoning stable of youth players on the first division.

Following another mediocre season, with the first team finishing in a lowly 10th position, manager Terry Neill had the following to say in his programme notes: 'This was not good enough ... something has got to be done about next season, and I have got to spend the summer working out what that something will be. I assure you that changes will be made.'

Changes certainly would be made, as the club was soon transformed on and off the pitch.

CHAPTER 7

THE BATTLE OF
OLD TRAFFORD

Saturday, 20 October 1990 was the day when many thought Arsenal had blown any chance of winning the title. Matches with Manchester United had been feisty affairs in recent years, marked by a number of unsavoury incidents that had only served to stoke the fire. And this was the day when all the underlying tension finally exploded at Old Trafford.

Going into the game, Arsenal had been in scintillating form. With George Graham having revamped his squad during the summer, goalkeeper David Seaman had arrived from QPR to replace the departing John Lukic; defender Andy Linighan supplemented the already strong defence, while Swedish left-winger Anders Limpar had been a sensation.

Still unbeaten in the league, and close on the heels of leaders Liverpool, the Rocastle–Limpar combination had lit up the early months of the season. However, Rocastle still wasn't fully fit.

Following a summer jet-ski accident in Australia, in which he had collided with team-mate Gus Caesar, he had been knocked out cold and damaged his ankle in the process. Having put on some weight during his recovery period, he admitted that in the early games he had to pace himself.

Nevertheless, Rocastle knuckled down to lung-busting runs in order to shift the excess weight, and Graham was pleased with his commitment. 'He's been getting extra weight off,' he said. 'And we're seeing the benefits. He's looking much more like his true self. We're not asking him to do anything different – just do the things he's good at.'

It was a frightening prospect that Rocastle was still not at full tilt as he lined up at Old Trafford. Doing the 'things he's good at', he had frequently exhibited his bewildering repertoire of feints and swerves to leave defenders on their backsides while also resolutely protecting his fullback, Lee Dixon. As such, following the 1-0 win courtesy of Limpar's cheeky cross-shot, the back pages should have been heralding yet another Arsenal victory. However, this was all but forgotten thanks to an incident that has since been dubbed 'The Battle of Old Trafford'.

When Anders Limpar darted down the left wing in the second half, only to be dispossessed by Denis Irwin, it seemed an innocuous event. But as the ball broke loose and Irwin went to retrieve it, he was met by a shuddering challenge from Nigel Winterburn. Reacting furiously, Brian McClair kicked Winterburn twice while he was on the floor, as Irwin also staggered to his feet to lash out. Within seconds players from both teams were steaming in.

First on the scene was David Rocastle. Eyes popping, veins throbbing in his neck, he grabbed Irwin by the throat, as the Manchester United goalkeeper, Les Sealey, desperately tried to restrain him.

In later years, Rocastle told Amy Lawrence why he was so

enraged: 'Something happened, I don't even know what it was, but all I saw was a few of my team-mates in trouble, and if you see your team-mates in trouble, you go in, within the laws of the game, to try and help them out. It was nothing malicious towards Manchester United players but it was our team-mate, our little blood brother, in trouble. They were kicking Nigel on the floor like a nightclub brawl. That's what got us upset. If it was just a bad tackle, you wouldn't go in like that, no chance. But when I saw them kicking Nigel I ran over, thinking, "You can't have this!" It just epitomised Arsenal's team spirit. We went in there and we stuck up for each other. At Arsenal we never, ever started any brawls – we just finished them.'

The whole incident was over in less than a minute, but the damage had been done. While referee Keith Hackett booked Winterburn and Limpar, and let Irwin and McClair off with a stern talking-to, Arsenal would soon find that the worst punishment was yet to come.

With the incident against Norwich from the previous season still hanging over their heads, and the media fanning the flames, the club quickly recognised that it had to be seen to act before the FA imposed its own sanctions. Accordingly, the Highbury board fined the Arsenal players involved two weeks' wages, which amounted to £5,000 for Rocastle, while George Graham was also fined the then huge sum of £10,000.

'I felt a bit aggrieved,' Rocastle told Amy Lawrence. 'I didn't think I'd done a lot to be fined. I was going in for a team-mate in need and I didn't even do anything.'

Gordon Taylor of the PFA certainly didn't agree with this stance, as television footage clearly showed that Rocastle had grabbed Irwin by the throat. 'Players have a right of appeal to us,' he said, 'but if any take it up I would suggest they bite the bullet.'

Consequently, the club's fine stood, but as all good managers do in such circumstances, Graham tried to ensure that the incident worked in his favour. 'They're enjoying getting at us,' he said of the press, as he assembled his players at London Colney. 'Normally nothing comes out of Highbury and they're enjoying it. Again, lads, there's one way to handle it, and that's to keep winning matches. They're looking at us, and the stick we've been getting, and it seems fashionable to jump on the bandwagon and get into Arsenal. We're not second bottom. We're second from top. It's the best start we've had for over 40 years. So keep thinking football all the time. You should all be proud of yourselves.'

And the players were, especially Rocastle, who felt it was his duty to fight for his team-mates. As Rocastle showed with his schoolboy fight against Chester, he never deliberately provoked trouble or went looking for it, but if it should come his way he would not back down.

Instilling a siege mentality in his players, Graham tried to ignore the rumours that the FA would be dishing out a harsh penalty, and instead concentrated on winning matches. However, when Arsenal took on Sunderland in the following game, it appeared that the events at Old Trafford were still bubbling under Rocastle's skin. In the 34th minute, a Gary Bennett tackle on Anders Limpar had left the Swedish winger writhing in agony. Such theatrics were met by a swarm of Sunderland players, who claimed that Limpar was merely play-acting. As ever, Rocastle jumped to his team-mate's defence, which earned him a talking-to by the referee, Vic Callow.

With another three points sealed thanks to a Lee Dixon penalty, and the team's best start to a season for 43 years continuing una-bated, it appeared to the football world at large that full service had been resumed. But the incident with Rocastle had concerned Graham.

Facing an immediate return to Manchester, as the Gunners played Manchester City in the League Cup, Graham took decisive action. Dropping Rocastle from the squad, he told the press that his omission was for 'tactical reasons' despite the fact that the team lined up in the same shape, with the only change being Perry Groves on the right wing.

Although Rocastle had been in good form, *The Times* agreed with Graham's decision: 'Rocastle was at least spared an occasion during which Arsenal's behaviour, after all the attendant publicity, was inevitably under examination.'

Despite his right-winger's absence, Graham's 'tactics' worked to perfection. *The Times* said of the 2-1 win: 'Arsenal, who departed Manchester in disgrace 10 days ago, last night left the city with honour.'

The following game, against Coventry, again saw Rocastle omitted. Once more it didn't matter, as Arsenal's new star man, Anders Limpar, scored the two goals to take his team to within touching distance of Liverpool. It seemed that some of the press now thought that the team could do without Rocastle altogether. 'Rocastle was not even in Arsenal's 13,' wrote Deryk Brown of the *Sunday Times*. 'When you saw the amount of ground the excellent Dixon can command down the right it is possible to see why.'

Worse was to come at Selhurst Park. Rocastle had been looking forward to the prospect of lining up against his old friend Ian Wright, who was now setting the first division alight with a glut of goals. But not only did he miss out, he also found his manager had a few choice words for him. Despite Graham previously claiming that Rocastle had been dropped for 'tactical reasons', he now told the press that he had informed his right-winger to 'lose weight and go back to basics'.

Given Rocastle's scintillating form before the brawl at Old Trafford, this appeared to be a very harsh judgement. Rocastle might have had an issue with his weight, something he struggled with throughout his career, but he was always said to have trained like a true professional. Not one of his team-mates, from any stage of his career, told me that he didn't work hard in training. In fact, it was the opposite. Some claimed he worked too hard, and trained even when injured.

Rocastle no doubt bristled at his manager's comments, particularly as he was exactly the same weight, 12 stone 11 pounds, he had been at the start of the season. He could have been forgiven for wondering if it had all been worth it. After all, he was the only player from the incident at Old Trafford to have been hit with a fine, been dropped from the squad, as well as publicly humiliated. Despite this he refused to sulk, and still gave his all when playing for the reserves. 'Professional pride always makes you try your hardest,' he told *Highbury Focus*. 'But it's difficult in front of a few people, especially when the opposition is so variable.'

The subsequent 0-0 draw at Selhurst Park might have kept Arsenal's unbeaten record intact, but Graham saw it as two points dropped. And worse was still to come, as the FA finally delivered its verdict on the events at Old Trafford. Each club was to be fined the sum of £50,000, but the biggest shock of all was the points deduction, with Manchester United docked one point and Arsenal two.

After cutting Liverpool's lead at the top to just four points, the dropped points at Palace and the two-point penalty suddenly saw Arsenal eight points adrift. Understandably, some of the Arsenal camp felt that the FA had handed the title to Liverpool and openly voiced their displeasure. 'It is very sad,' David O'Leary told the press. 'The champagne will be out at Liverpool tonight because this makes our task very much harder. Without being disparaging to all the others in the first division, we were the team that could have provided Liverpool with a genuine challenge. They have as good as handed the title to Anfield at Lancaster Gate today.'

To many it appeared that Arsenal's title challenge had ground to a halt. Yet with the FA's judgement finally in, Graham felt that now was the time to bring his hot-headed right-winger back into the fold. Returning him to the squad for the visit of Southampton, Graham said, 'Anders Limpar is doing a great job for us on the left, and we would be some force with a top-form David Rocastle on the right. If he proves he can be as good as two years ago then we will give Liverpool a race.'

Consigned to the bench, Rocastle watched a resounding 4-0 win revive Arsenal's title hopes, which was followed by a dramatic 3-1 win against QPR at Loftus Road. Looking a formidable prospect in the league, attention soon turned back to the League Cup, which promised the tantalising prospect of Manchester United visiting Highbury, so soon after the events at Old Trafford.

Unsurprisingly, the game was billed as a grudge match, and while Rocastle would have been disappointed to miss out yet again, it was one occasion he was happy to do so. In a shocking turn of events, Alex Ferguson's stuttering side suddenly came of age. Exhibiting an awe-inspiring display of attacking intent, United blew the unbeaten Gunners away, 6-2.

Normally so faultless at the back, Bould and Adams had never looked so fragile, with teenager Lee Sharpe grabbing a hat-trick and Lewisham boy Danny Wallace setting up four and scoring one. Suddenly alarm bells were ringing, and at the worst possible time, as Liverpool, boasting the best attack in the country, were next to visit Highbury.

Following the devastating United display, Rocastle must have thought he had a chance of starting the Liverpool game, especially with the news that his replacement, Perry Groves, was set to be dropped. But against a team renowned for its attack Graham felt that he needed to shore up his shellshocked defence. Therefore, he reverted to a 5-3-2 formation, with O'Leary deployed as sweeper and the fullbacks, Winterburn and Dixon, expected to get up and down the flanks.

Unbeaten in the league, and having witnessed Arsenal's slipshod defending against United, it was thought that Liverpool manager Kenny Dalglish would go for the jugular. Yet, still wary of Arsenal's attacking threat, Dalglish surprisingly dropped Houghton, Beardsley and McMahon, and brought in the defensive trio of Nicol, Molby and Venison.

As both teams lined up in defensive formations, a shrewd observer of the game might have predicted a 0-0 draw, a result Graham would no doubt have been delighted with. But with Davis and Thomas strangling the Liverpool midfield, they set up the platform for the attacking players, Limpar, Merson and Smith, to bombard the Liverpool defence. The resulting 3-0 victory must have been beyond Graham's wildest expectations. Suddenly Arsenal were back in the title race.

However, while subsequent draws against Luton and Wimbledon represented setbacks to Arsenal's title-chasing hopes, the club was about to be hit by even bigger troubles. Once again, Highbury was set to be rocked by scandal, as a situation that had been bubbling beneath the surface for years finally became front-page news.

CHAPTER 8

THE APPRENTICE

As David Rocastle prepared for his life to change as an Arsenal apprentice, the country was also about to undergo its own significant transformation. The 1983 general election had seen Margaret Thatcher's capitalist manifesto, along with post-Falklands euphoria, overcome Michael Foot's socialist dreams, famously referred to as 'the longest suicide note in history'. With Thatcher leading the way the country was poised to embrace the fast-money culture for which the 1980s would later become renowned. *Wall Street*'s Gordon Gekko perhaps summed up the overwhelming ethos of the decade with his infamous phrase, 'Greed is Good', as city traders, mock Tudor houses, Porsches, Filofaxes and large mobile phones became clichés of the time. And Arsenal decided to go along for the ride.

After years of frugality and being unable to compete for the top stars in the transfer market, the dismal end to the 1982/83 season had seen a dramatic change in philosophy. Throwing aside all caution, Arsenal broke the bank and signed a glitzy superstar, hoping to revolutionise the team as well as excite the terraces. The man in question was 21-year-old Scotsman Charlie Nicholas. Nicknamed 'Champagne Charlie', Nicholas' £800,000 arrival from Celtic didn't only signal that the club had embraced Thatcherism, it also heralded a shift in culture on the terraces as well as in the dressing room.

A renowned fashionista, Nicholas modelled his blow-dried mullet, hoop earring, tight leather trousers and vest tops on the pop stars of the era, particularly U2's Bono, of whom he was an admirer. Many Arsenal fans instantly took to apeing their hero, and soon the bovver boy dress code of the 1970s was swept away by a tidal wave of designer labels. Ellesse, Fila, Tacchini, Pringle, Lyle & Scott and Gabicci became the designer wear of choice on the North Bank, with Man at War in Shepherd's Bush doing a roaring trade, as did Sharp Sports, just off Kensington High Street, which stocked the much sought-after blue velour Fila tracksuit top and Diadora Borg Elites. Not only did wearing the right designer label ensure kudos on the terraces it also helped its wearer evade the police, who were on the lookout for football hooligans clad in their team's colours.

Pictured with a string of page three models and known to enjoy the delights of the lap-dancing club Stringfellows, 'Champagne Charlie's' playboy image enticed many of his team-mates to join him. With the likes of Kenny Sansom, Graham Rix and Tony Woodcock already criticised for their love of the nightlife, Nicholas' arrival was said to have moved things up another notch. Within a year Rix, Nicholas and Woodcock all lost their driving licences, while at the end of Nicholas' first season Woodcock stated in his autobiography, 'We have decided to cut down on our nightclubbing. We had a get-together today and decided we were a little bit out of order last year.' Indeed, Gus Caesar recalled that at this time, 'We'd come in and you could tell when everyone had been out. The dressing room smelled like a brewery.'

Nevertheless, apprentices such as Rocastle were in awe of players like Nicholas and other household names at the club. 'At first it was quite awesome, because you're seeing players you've only ever seen on the back of cigarette packets,' Rocastle enthused. 'And then there I was sitting next to Pat Jennings at the dinner table. Arsenal had a lot of internationals at that time and the lads were a bit frightened but they tried to make us relaxed and say, "Why don't you come sit with us?" I was in awe of them, thinking, "What shall I do or say?"'

Nicholas may have earned an eye-watering £2,000 a week but Rocastle, and the other apprentices, were happy to bring home the princely sum of £104 a month. To Rocastle, this was a fortune. It was the first real money he had ever earned, and while some of it went to his mother he also treated himself to new trainers, records and some new clothes. Linda Rocastle was also delighted. With her son living at home rather than going into digs, this meant that the club also paid her £100 a month. It seemed that Rocastle's burgeoning football career was already paying off.

However, before Rocastle could even focus on football there were apprentice duties to be fulfilled. In the early morning gloom, with frost on the inside and outside of his bedroom windows, Rocastle would rise at 6am and ensure that his brothers and sisters had everything they needed before he set off in the cold to catch the bus to Highbury, where he had to report by 9am sharp.

On arrival at Highbury, the apprentices would be expected to pack all of the kit for training and then travel with it to London Colney, where they would also be required to lay it out for the first team, as well as pump up footballs for the session ahead. Only after all of this was done would Pat Rice put them through their paces.

'Pat was very disciplined but fair,' fellow apprentice Jon Purdie recalls. 'He got us all really fit. After we had done all the kits at Highbury, he would take us to this little gym area and we all would have to do something like 200 sit-ups before we would go off to training at London Colney. I remember he would always do it with us as well, so none of us could moan.'

Purdie also remembers that while Rice was fanatical about the team being well drilled on the field, a large part of what he had to say related to standards: 'He would always say to us, "Remember, you're at Arsenal now." We could never be late, always had to look smart, have our shirts tucked in and things like that. We learnt all about respect and having pride. It's something I've never forgotten.'

After training at London Colney the apprentices would finally return to Highbury mid-afternoon, where they had to unload all of the dirty kit. But this still didn't signal the end of the day. Dressing rooms, baths and toilets still needed to be scrubbed, and only after Terry Neill had given their work his seal of approval would they be allowed to leave. Despite such unglamorous work, Rocastle loved it.

Spending so much of their time with each other, helped to forge a strong camaraderie within the group from an early age.

'I knew Michael Thomas from the age of 11,' Rocastle later told Amy Lawrence. 'He was an outstanding footballer for his age compared to the rest of us, he had everything. I remember Tony Adams when he was a 12-year-old – he looked like a mod, with the old short jacket and short tonic trousers on . . . We fought for each other like blood brothers.'

With the day at an end, the apprentices who lived in digs would usually join up with first-teamers, such as Graham Rix, Tony Woodcock and Kenny Sansom, at the White Hart pub in Southgate for a few drinks, or would find a pool hall or bookies to while away the hours. 'The likes of Charlie Nicholas and Graham Rix were brilliant with us,' goalkeeper Kenny Veysey told me. 'They would invite us all out, even though we were just young lads. They were never shy at buying everyone drinks as well. Sometimes we'd even end up in the West End with them, going to Stringfellows. We didn't have a lot of money so it was unbelievable for us.'

Yet Veysey recalled that Rocastle was never really interested in such pursuits. 'He wasn't really one for going to the pub. But I remember he loved his clothes. Quite a few times after training myself, Michael [Thomas] and Rocky would go to Dunston Street [in Hackney] on the bus. Rocky knew of all these little factories in the backstreets that sold designer clothes. It wasn't like he was on a lot of money back then but he looked a million dollars.'

Always immaculate, Rocastle also dispensed friendly fashion advice to the young Irishman who had recently joined the team, informing Niall Quinn to 'lose' his duffel coat

With Rocastle looking out for him, Quinn never had to search too far for help, even when it came to socialising with the opposite sex. 'Dave was seeing an Irish girl called Ruth,' Quinn recalls. 'She had a friend, Esther. So we all went out one night in Lewisham and ended up at a dance club. I remember Dave moving about the dance floor with the same elegance he had on the football pitch and me trying to move about the dance floor with a little bit more elegance than I have on the pitch.'

While he might not have been a regular at the White Hart, fellow apprentice Gus Caesar recalls that Rocastle, his brother Steve, close friend Kevin Arnold and Michael Thomas would regularly hit the clubs of south London together. 'He always remained close to his friends who he grew up with,' Caesar told me. 'I used to tag along and we'd end up in a club or more often than not a house party.'

Although he was never a big drinker, he was certainly someone who liked to enjoy himself. Karen Rocastle recalls her brother's 18th birthday celebrations in their flat: 'So many people turned up that they couldn't all get in, so they were all waiting on the balcony. The front room was packed. And the music was loud. In the end my mum was so sick of it she called Theodore round and he had to turn off the electricity and tell everyone to go home!'

On his walk home from training Rocastle would often bump into his old rival Ian Wright. Since their schoolboy days, when they had both been heralded as the top footballers in south London, their careers had taken vastly contrasting paths. After not making the grade at Millwall, Wright had fallen in with the wrong crowd, which had culminated in a short spell in jail for non-payment of fines for driving without tax, insurance or an MOT. His hopes and dreams of a career in football now seemed to be consigned to the scrapheap.

'He was 17, and coming home from Arsenal every day,' Wright once said. 'I was 20 and working on building sites and in chemical plants. Rocky always told me not to waste my talents, to keep going, to get myself in the professional game.' Thankfully, Wright heeded his friend's words of advice. Soon after playing non-league football for Greenwich Borough, he had a successful trial at Crystal Palace and went on to become one of the great goalscorers in the modern game. Always a supporter of Wright, Rocastle could often be seen in the crowd on nights he didn't have a game himself, cheering him on.

As well as learning his trade as a footballer, fulfilling his apprentice duties, mixing with his heroes and looking after his family, Rocastle was also required to attend college once a week at King's Cross. The course was run by a pre-politics Kate Hoey, and she was only too happy to give her star pupil a lift home after class. 'I often used to give David a lift home after training,' Hoey told Jason Cowley in *The Last Game*. 'He lived with his mum and his sisters and I think he always felt he had to look after them all. I think that feeling always meant he was very responsible and he worked hard to succeed.'

With all these things to consider, it is a wonder Rocastle had any time to concentrate on actually playing football. But, true to form, in his two years as an apprentice he excelled. Scanning the fixture lists for 1983 to 1985 reveals some remarkable results, which really underlines the prowess of the team. A 10-1 away win at Spurs stands out, as does the 9-2 win in the home fixture. And these were by no means isolated, freak results. The likes of Swindon Town were also defeated 10-0, while there is an array of 5-0 victories.

The team also impressed in international tournaments. In the Borussia Dortmund Youth Tournament they put in strong displays against Bochum, Frankfurt and Schalke before succumbing to Real Madrid, while in Lille they drew with a powerful AC Milan side and defeated Benfica and PSV Eindhoven. 'We thought we were unbeatable,' Gus Caesar told me. 'Every game we played we thought we would win. We knew we were good.'

Although their foreign exploits turned heads, it was in the Southern Junior Floodlit Cup that the team finally lifted silverware. Having reached the final in 1984, they defeated Norwich City over two legs, with Rocastle scoring the decisive goal back at Highbury.

However, the real prize for any youth team to cement their legacy was the FA Youth Cup. Manchester United's Class of '92 is of course remembered for winning the trophy, and in doing so served notice that there was a well of talent waiting to erupt at Old Trafford. That the Arsenal class of 1983/84 failed to match their achievement has meant that the club's youth system of the 1980s has failed to gain the credit it deserves.

After sailing through the early rounds, beating teams like Carshalton, Bristol Rovers, Cambridge United and Aston Villa, they met Stoke in the semi-finals. The first leg at the Victoria Ground had been promising enough, with a hard-fought 3-2 victory seeing the boys travel back to London in high spirits. However, what came next was a total disaster. Inexplicably imploding at Highbury, they lost the second leg 3-0. As Keown remarked afterwards, 'There was a major inquest. They made out it was going to be the end of our careers.'

'It was a quiet bloody dressing room afterwards,' Gus Caesar remembered. 'There wasn't much said. We knew we had blown it.'

Despite this bitter blow, Rocastle's success during the season had been swift. By November 1983 he had been called up for the reserve team to play Watford away. It was no doubt a daunting prospect for a raw 16-year-old to suddenly be thrown into the deep end with hardened professionals, but Rocastle was instrumental in a 3-0 win, marked by a debut goal.

Over the course of his first season, the young midfielder had played an incredible 66 games, six of which were for the reserves, scoring three goals along the way. When you consider that today clubs are mindful not to burn out their players, it is a remarkable workload, yet one which was the norm for the time. It certainly didn't seem to have any negative effect on Rocastle. Always a galvanising influence in the dressing room, his hypnotic exhibition of deft footwork saw his coaches enthralled by his potential.

As word of his raw talent spread with breathless optimism through the marble halls of Highbury, director David Dein was keen to inspect the young starlet. A 36-year-old businessman, Dein had purchased a 16.6 per cent share of the club for the sum of £292,000 in 1983. An avid Arsenal fan, Dein was called 'crazy' by chairman Peter Hill-Wood for investing so much money in a club that was over £1 million in debt and couldn't even afford to give the first-team players a customary turkey at Christmas. But in Dein's eyes, the investment was worth every penny.

Between 1983 and 2007, he would not only redevelop Highbury and set in motion the move to the Emirates Stadium, but he would also attract some of the world's greatest players to the club, as well as the little-known Arsène Wenger. In addition, he would be hailed as one of the main protagonists behind the creation of the Premier League, more of which later. Proving his investment had been a good one, when he finally sold his stake in the club in 2007 it was worth £75 million.

Taking in a reserve game, Dein found that the hype surrounding Rocastle had been warranted. 'I ran home immediately to my wife in excitement,' he remembered, 'and said, "I've seen the nearest thing to a Brazilian footballer you'll ever see in our academy, and he's from Lewisham!"'

By Christmas 1984 a decision was made on Rocastle's future. And after becoming a regular fixture in Terry Burton's Football Combination side, there was only ever going to be one result – the offer of a two-year professional contract. It was the best Christmas present he could have asked for.

Sadly, Terry Neill had not lasted long enough to enjoy the fruits of the youth team. By December 1983, he had been sacked after losing to West Bromwich Albion, where there had been major fan demonstrations against him afterwards. This had all been building since a lacklustre start to the season had culminated in an embarrassing League Cup defeat to Walsall. The superstar arrival of Charlie Nicholas had not had the desired impact and the team was also torn apart by cliques, with half the squad out on the town regularly and the other half deemed to be 'boring' for not joining in the revelry.

While some fans hoped this might be the occasion to introduce innovative ideas, perhaps in the form of the up-and-coming Terry Venables, they instead had to contend with Neill's assistant, Don Howe, taking charge.

Howe's appointment may have stabilised the club somewhat, but English football was soon mired in disgrace. In 1985, the game was hit in quick succession by the Bradford fire disaster, in which 56 people lost their lives at Valley Parade, and then Heysel, where Liverpool fans charged at Juventus fans during the European Cup final, causing a wall to collapse and resulting in 39 fatalities. The aftermath would see English clubs banned from European competition for five years, thus encouraging more of the game's brightest stars to ply their trade abroad.

In a season where there had even been crowd disturbances during a Chelsea v Arsenal testimonial game, it seemed that English football had reached rock bottom. We were not to know then that there was still another chilling disaster to come.

CHAPTER 9

THE TUESDAY CLUB

Booze. Drugs. Women. These may be the staple diet of any self-respecting rock'n'roll hellraiser, but they are hardly prerequisites for top-class athletes. Despite this, over the years some of those at Arsenal had fully embraced such a culture. On his arrival, George Graham had seemingly weeded out those most partial to such pursuits, but the younger players had happily stepped into their places, with the hardcore becoming known as the 'Tuesday Club'.

When I caught up with Perry Groves, he explained how the so-called Tuesday Club came to be: 'We didn't usually have a match on Wednesdays, which meant that we could all go out together on a Tuesday and have a few drinks. What would happen is, on Tuesdays we didn't used to train at London Colney, we would train at Highbury. We would all park our cars at the nearby JVC Centre and leave them there so we could pick them up the next day. Then we'd start training at 10am at Highbury, which usually involved running around the track or up and down the terraces. Then we'd all get changed into our "pulling gear" and go to the pub for the day.'

The usual routine would see the hardcore regulars of Groves, Merson, Adams and Bould head to the Alwyne Castle pub, just down the road from the ground, where after a few pints they would put the world to rights. Suitably refreshed, they would then venture to a bar in King's Cross or head down Holloway Road on a pub crawl.

By 5pm Groves told me that 'the three amigos' – Alan Smith, Brian Marwood [when he was still at the club] and Lee Dixon – would join in, but only after they had done their shopping and been home to see their wives.

As dusk fell it would be time to head to the Punch & Judy pub in Covent Garden, or TGI Friday's in Piccadilly Circus. Yet as Groves revealed, 'There was never any time to eat anything; a lot of us were more interested in drinking and going on the pull. There were always a few birds hanging around us.'

It would usually be in the West End that the so-called 'Four Tops' – Rocastle, Michael Thomas, Paul Davis and Gus Caesar – would join up with the team. 'They loved their cocktails,' Groves laughed. 'They'd all sink a few of those and then David Seaman might pop along for a few before he went night fishing.'

On an average Tuesday night you could expect to see the vast majority of the Arsenal squad out in the West End. 'It was great for team spirit,' Groves happily reminisced. 'We all got on. We might not spend the whole day or night together, or even end up at the same club, but we were a really tight group. I'm not saying we were all best buddies but I genuinely can't remember a fight in training or any serious disagreements.'

Although this might sound an incredible way for top-flight foot-ballers to behave, in the 1980s this was par for the course. 'It was the same everywhere,' Brian Marwood told me. 'It wouldn't happen in today's world but I'm sure other clubs were all doing the same thing.'

While Rocastle enjoyed a few cocktails, he was never one of the

Tuesday Club hardcore. 'Rocky was the nicest bloke,' Groves said. 'For someone who was so intense on the pitch, off the pitch he was always very calm and tranquil. He wasn't really into pints like most of us. He'd order a light cocktail or a rum and coke. He was probably a bit more sophisticated.'

For the first few years of Graham's reign, the Tuesday Club had been tolerated. As long as the players continued to do the business on the pitch, and kept themselves out of trouble off it, then Graham was happy to turn a blind eye. However, although in time the likes of Paul Merson would go to rehab to be treated for alcohol, drug and gambling addictions, the first real sign that all was not well occurred in December 1990, just a few weeks after the FA had deducted the club two points following the brawl at Old Trafford.

Earlier that summer, Tony Adams had made the headlines after crashing his car into a wall following an afternoon of drinking. He subsequently spent several hours in a police cell before heading straight to Heathrow, where he caught up with the Arsenal squad for a trip to Singapore. However, Graham didn't read his captain the riot act, and with Adams due to face trial later that year it appeared that the event would soon be forgotten about. After all, no one had been hurt, and the only damage had been to a garden wall.

When Adams finally stood trial at Southend Crown Court on Wednesday, 19 December 1990, he was so confident of facing just a stern rebuke that he had told all of his team-mates he would see them later that night for their Christmas party. But the judgment that followed sent shockwaves through the game. Sentenced to four months in jail, a pale Adams was led in disbelief down from the dock to begin his stint at Chelmsford Prison.

Rocastle was on the team coach, returning from a reserve game at Fulham, when he heard Adams had been jailed. 'We thought he might get community service but, because of the time of year, they obviously wanted to make an example of him,' Rocastle told Amy

Lawrence. 'It was our Christmas party that night. We were supposed to be meeting up in Islington to go on our boys' night out and everyone was in a sombre mood. All we could think about was Tony.'

Already handicapped by a two-point deduction, the loss of the team's captain seemed to strike a terminal blow to Arsenal's title aspirations. As always, Graham regrouped his shellshocked players and had them ready to go again for the trip to Aston Villa just a few days later. Rocastle found he was among the substitutes once more, but with Arsenal struggling to break down a stubborn Villa defence Graham had no option but to turn to his number 7. 'We were losing shape up front and I thought I would give Rocastle a chance to blossom again,' he later told the media.

Neither Rocastle nor anyone else could make a telling contribution, and the match ended in a 0-0 draw. Despite surpassing their previous best start to a season since 1947, and thereby setting a new club record, Arsenal were still six points behind Liverpool, who also had a game in hand.

Of further concern was that Arsenal had drawn three games in a row, and had scored a solitary goal in the process. If they were to have any chance of catching Liverpool they needed to start turning the draws into wins, and fast.

Better news was, however, just around the corner for Rocastle. With Graham deciding to shake up his faltering attack, he reintroduced him to the starting line-up for the visit of Derby County on Boxing Day. While the poor weather and dearth of public transport saw the lowest crowd of the season at Highbury, those who turned out at least witnessed their team emphatically return to winning ways, with a confident 3-0 victory.

But the game turned into yet another disaster for Rocastle. Having waited over two months to get a start, he broke his toe in the first minute of the game. Typically, despite clearly being in pain, he shrugged it off, and bravely carried on until the 59th minute, by which stage Arsenal were 2-0 up, courtesy of goals from Smith and Merson.

Rocastle later told *Highbury Focus*: 'I remember feeling the hurt in my foot and looking up at the clock – and just 50 seconds had gone. Usually I can run off knocks. But not this one. I was pleased that I got some good write-ups, but what I remember most was the pain in my foot. I couldn't stay on any longer otherwise I'd have been a liability to the team.'

In this topsy-turvy season nothing was going Rocastle's way. He now looked set to spend at least six weeks recovering, and then faced the prospect of trying to win back his place in the team all over again.

As physio Gary Lewin treated Arsenal's injured star, Rocastle felt optimistic that he could soon start again refreshed. 'It'll be like having a new player when I come back,' he said with his usual positivity. 'It will feel like I'm making a fresh start again. The broken toe has stopped me kicking a ball but I've been able to join in the fitness training and I've done plenty of perimeter runs and cross-country work.'

In the absence of Rocastle and Adams, the team's unbeaten run continued. Victories against Sunderland and Leeds in the FA Cup saw them sail into the fifth round, while they finally overhauled Liverpool at the top with a draw at White Hart Lane and a win against Everton.

By mid-February reinforcements were also set to arrive. Not only had Adams been released from jail, but Rocastle had returned to full training. Frustratingly, having hoped to play a few reserve matches before returning to the first-team squad, bad weather hit the country which meant that Rocastle's comeback games against London University and then Luton were called off. It was typical of the luck he had endured all season.

With the weather finally improving, he eventually made his

comeback in a reserve game against Fulham. Incredibly, this gave him the opportunity to come face to face with his younger brother Steve, who was an apprentice at the club. Lining up at Highbury, Rocastle found himself on the right wing, while Steve played at left back. From playing against each other in their living room, they were now performing on one of the grandest stages of all, even if the ground was empty on the day.

While Rocastle tried to coach his brother through the game, telling him to push up whenever there was an opportunity, the one time Steve listened to him the ball found its way to Rocastle, who was now in acres of space. Slipping the ball past the goalkeeper to score, he trotted back to the the halfway line and had the cheek to give his furious sibling a smile. Steve had obviously forgotten just how competitive his brother could be. Proving that the rest may have actually done him some good, it appeared that the zip had returned to Rocastle's legs as he inspired the reserves to a 3-0 win. 'It was a good team performance,' he said after the game. 'It helped me settle in quickly again and I was very pleased with the goal. Fitness-wise I felt fine. Now it's a case of getting into the swing of things again. It's not going to be easy to get back in, because the team have done so well while I've been out. But there are a lot of matches between now and the end of the season. I want to prove I'm match fit again, then take it from there. It hasn't been a great season for me so far but I want to end it on a happy note.'

On the day Rocastle had put in a dazzling display for the reserves, the first team had lost its first league game of the season, away to Chelsea. With the business end of the season fast approaching they could ill afford any more slip-ups.

Following the reverse against Chelsea, the Gunners played host to Crystal Palace. Finally recalled to the bench, Rocastle watched on, no doubt impressed by the defensive frugality and attacking verve displayed by his team-mates. On the day, the likes of Merson and Smith were unplayable, as was young Kevin Campbell, whose introduction to the line-up provided added impetus, not to mention goals.

A revelation in the youth and reserve teams, Campbell told me just how vital Rocastle had been in his rise to the first team. 'He just made me feel so comfortable,' he remembered. 'I was just a kid but he would make a fuss of me, giving me high-fives, little things like that. Not everyone would acknowledge the younger players but he always made a fuss of everyone. Sometimes he'd even give me a lift back to Brixton. I couldn't believe it. I'd be sitting next to David Rocastle and he'd be singing along to "Mr Loverman" by Shabba Ranks. He was great.'

On 22 February 1991, with Arsenal and Liverpool engaged in another tight title race, shocking news emerged from Anfield. Not only had Liverpool lost 3-1 to Luton, but the day before manager Kenny Dalglish had dramatically announced his resignation. It seemed that the strain of managing the club following the events of Hillsborough had finally caught up with him. While it was a tragedy for a talented manager like Dalglish to walk away from the game, it certainly gave Arsenal hope that against all odds the championship might yet be achievable.

Following on from this news, Rocastle and Adams were both named in the starting line-up for the fifth-round cup clash at Shrewsbury. If it had been expected that the two might benefit from a gentle stroll before any league action then what followed was anything but.

In the cold, damp murk, Arsenal struggled to get into their stride on a boggy playing surface that certainly hindered Rocastle's natural game. Still, even though Arsenal suffered from a dearth of penetration, they came away with a 1-0 win, courtesy of Michael Thomas' cool finish.

Level on points at the top, there was everything to play for when

Arsenal travelled to Anfield on 3 March 1991. Despite being away from home, Arsenal had every right to feel the more confident of the two sides. Not only had they comfortably triumphed in the reverse fixture at Highbury, but they had put their travails behind them while Liverpool were very much in the middle of their own. Since their loss at Highbury, they had won only four of their next 10 league fixtures, a statistic that pointed to a team very much on a downwards slide.

On the day, Adams returned to the heart of the defence for his first league start since his release. Rocastle, however, had to wait patiently for his chance from the bench, which eventually came early in the second half, with the game still goalless. And just minutes after his introduction, Arsenal were ahead as a brilliant one-two between Merson and Smith saw Merson calmly slot the ball past Bruce Grobbelaar. With Bould, Adams and O'Leary again standing firm, another memorable result was recorded at the home of the champions.

Suddenly title favourites and continuing to progress in the cup, with a 1-0 win over Cambridge, Rocastle's knee issue flared up once more. This further setback meant he was forced to sit out the next few matches before he again returned, and started, at Norwich.

Despite Arsenal's disappointing display in the 0-0 draw, Rocastle earned praise from the media, as he was said to have 'combined well with Paul Davis'. However, Liverpool's 7-1 victory against Derby had swung the title race back in their favour, psychologically and mathematically.

Retaining his place in the team, Rocastle lined up for the 2-0 away win at Derby, but it was clear he was still in pain. Sitting out the subsequent 5-0 blitz against Aston Villa, described by some fans as the best performance of the season, it was eventually decided that he would require another operation. It was yet another bitter blow, as while the operation was relatively minor, he would still be expected to miss the remainder of the season. What's more, he would also miss out on a historic FA Cup semi-final against Spurs.

In Rocastle's absence, Arsenal shockingly lost to the Gazza-inspired Spurs, and so went any chance of the double. After a faltering display against Manchester City, in which they surrendered a two-goal lead, it also looked as if they would lose their grip on the league, as Liverpool hammered Leeds, Norwich and Palace in quick succession. With former Kop favourite Graeme Souness installed as the Merseysiders' new manager, it seemed to have given them new-found impetus right at the death.

As the bank holiday weekend approached, six vital points were up for grabs. Whoever blinked first looked destined to concede the title. Therefore Arsenal's subsequent draw away to Sunderland appeared disastrous. But then news filtered through that Liverpool had lost at Chelsea. With Liverpool due to play Nottingham Forest on 6 May, before Arsenal kicked off at Highbury against Manchester United, anything less than a victory would bring the title back to north London. And that's exactly how it turned out.

Without having to kick a ball Arsenal were champions, following Liverpool's 2-1 defeat. As an added bonus, this meant that their old foes Manchester United were forced to welcome the new champions on to the pitch with a guard of honour.

The game itself was a relative stroll. Laying down their sword to superior opposition in the May sunshine, United lost the game 3-1. Author Nick Hornby brilliantly summed up the atmosphere among the crowd in his seminal book *Fever Pitch*: '"You can stick your fucking two points up your arse," the crowd sang gleefully, over and over again, throughout the Manchester United game, and it began to seem like the quintessential Arsenal song: take our points, imprison our captain, hate our football, sod the lot of you.'

It seems that history has not treated this Arsenal vintage kindly, with many tending to side with the misconceived view that the league was won with a series of dour 1-0 victories. Nothing could be further from the truth. 'Everyone called us a long-ball team,' Rocastle told Amy Lawrence, 'but we played horses for courses. If we played a physical team who tried to outbattle us we'd knock the ball up to Alan Smith, who was probably one of the best players at holding the ball up, and take it from there. When we played teams who wanted to play an intricate passing game we had players of the calibre of Paul Davis, Anders Limpar. You couldn't call those players long-ball merchants.'

David Seaman's 24 clean sheets, with just 18 goals conceded, was a club record, while Alan Smith's 27 goals saw him win the golden boot. And in midfield Merson and Limpar were at times imperious. Again, many football fans might have forgotten just how brilliant the super Swede was in his debut season. His displays of skill and pace, coupled with some truly incredible goals, were breathtaking at times.

But the season had been a disappointment for Rocastle. 'I've seen both sides of it, really,' he admitted. 'When we won the title two years ago I was ever-present, I played in every game, so now I've had the other side when I haven't played too much. People keep asking, "Do you qualify for a championship medal?" It was driving me mad because people forget the first two months of the season where I played a lot.'

As for looking forward to the following season, he struck a cautionary note: 'I'm not going to say anything about next season because after last season I said I'm looking forward to this season, and it's gone how it has, so I'm just going to say I'll report back on 8 July.'

But when he did report back, Rocastle would find things had changed again, as he faced making a major adjustment to his game.

CHAPTER 10

DEBUTANT

A broken-down door. Armed officers swarm in. Shouting. Mayhem. Cherry Groce screams. 'Where is your son?' an officer shouts at her. More screaming, this time from her three young children. The officers tear through the house, 'Michael Groce! We are the police. Come out with your arms up!' No answer. A melee breaks out. BANG! A gunshot. Cherry Groce falls to the floor, blood seeping through her nightdress. So start the Brixton riots of 1985.

Since 1948, when immigrants had arrived on the *Empire Windrush*, there had been numerous racially motivated clashes throughout the country. Matters looked to have reached a climax in 1981, when in response to a steep rise in street robbery the Metropolitan Police commenced Operation Swamp. Plainclothes police officers subsequently stopped and searched large numbers of black youths on Brixton's streets, usually without any justification, which led to widespread resentment, particularly as the police were protected by the so-called sus laws, which allowed them to stop and search individuals they suspected of frequenting, or loitering in, a public place with the intent to commit an arrestable offence. Eventually the situation exploded into street warfare. Over 300 people were injured in the ensuing riots, including more than 200 police officers.

As a direct result, the sus laws were repealed in August 1981, but Lord Scarman's report on the events in Brixton only served to aggravate matters, as he concluded that 'institutional racism' did not exist in the Metropolitan Police force.

However, as many in the black community continued to criticise the police for their hostile attitude towards them, black youth unemployment rose as high as 55 per cent. It was a volatile mix, and one that would erupt into violence following the 1985 shooting of Cherry Groce. As the police lost control of the streets, dozens of cars were set alight and shops looted, which eventually led to over 50 people being injured and over 200 arrests. As further riots broke out in Toxteth and Peckham, there was worse to come.

Just 10 days later, a police search at the Broadwater Farm home of Cynthia Jarrett, an African-Caribbean woman, led to her suffering a fatal heart attack. With relations already on a knife edge, the streets again turned to violence. This frenzy of anger culminated in the murder of PC Keith Blakelock, who when trying to flee enraged rioters tripped and fell. Swiftly surrounded by a mob, he was brutally murdered, becoming the first police officer to be killed in a riot since 1833.

The shock of such an event finally brought the disturbances to an immediate halt. As police cracked down on the estates, PC Blakelock's murder was also said to have led to a change in tactics when dealing with the black community.

Football was sadly not immune to the issues of racial conflict that blighted the country, as the race divide also simmered in the Football League. In 1985, just 8 per cent of footballers in the first division were black, and no more than three black players had ever appeared on a pitch at any one time. Even by 1989, there were only 145 professional black players out of 2,000 playing in the Football League, with 24 clubs having no black players in their squads whatsoever.

This was still seen as a marked improvement on the footballing culture of the 1970s. Journalist Rob Hughes wrote in *The Times* that in that era he had been told by 12 first division managers that they would not sign a black player because 'they lacked bottle, were no good in the mud and had no stamina', though it should also be said that a similar attitude also prevailed when it came to foreign players. This attitude is all the more remarkable when you consider the multitude of world-class black players in the 1960s and 1970s, such as Pelé and Eusébio.

In 1975, the then England manager Don Revie named 84 players who were under review for the national team. Not one of them was black. This isn't to say that Revie was prejudiced, as he was one of the few club managers in the 1960s to buy a black footballer, when he signed the South African winger Albert Johanneson for Leeds United. Rather, it shows that there were so few black players in the Football League for Revie to pick from.

When you take into account the environment at many football matches in the 1970s and '80s, it is a wonder why any black player or fan would choose to associate themselves with the game. As the National Front emerged, it was not uncommon to see their racist propaganda sold inside and outside football grounds. In 1980, the *Islington Gazette* even reported that racist literature had been sold by some so-called fans outside Highbury, prompting the club to issue a threat to ban anyone involved.

Matters were just as bad inside stadiums, as all too frequently footballers found themselves playing in cauldrons of hostility. 'I didn't want to come out on the pitch,' Chelsea's first black footballer, Paul Canoville, said in his heart-rending autobiography *Black and Blue*. 'I would warm up inside the changing room and go out just before. I hated being a sub. When I warmed up, it was, "Sit down, you nigger."' Canoville also revealed how he was even booed and abused by his own fans, as well as some of his team-mates. Amazingly, he was also the only Chelsea player without a kit sponsor.

While black footballers were few and far between, there were some who had come through the system and had prospered. As West Bromwich Albion's 'Three Degrees', Regis, Batson and Cunningham slowly changed the mindset of British football, more black players made their mark. In 1979, Viv Anderson became England's first black footballer, while two years later Justin Fashanu became the first £1m black footballer in Britain. Garth Crooks, Dave and Gary Bennett and Roger Palmer also graced the first division, while there was an emergence of black players at Arsenal, with Paul Davis, Ralph Meade and Chris Whyte breaking into the team.

One of the reasons that Arsenal managed to attract such a crop of black players was due in part to the fact that Highbury remained relatively immune from racist abuse. Many credit one of the big faces on the terraces, Dainton Connell, known as 'The Bear', for this. Stamping out any racist chanting he also went out of his way to look after the black players in the team, as well as their families. The Rocastle family certainly credit him with looking out for them.

Despite this, widespread hostility to black footballers still remained, and the October 1985 events in Brixton and Broadwater Farm thrust Britain's fragile race issues back into the spotlight. Amid all of this tension, 18-year-old David Rocastle was about to get his chance.

Having reported back to pre-season training in the summer of 1985, Rocastle had looked forward to his first season as a professional footballer, along with the likes of Adams, Keown, Hayes, Thomas and Caesar, who had also made the grade. While Don Howe received widespread criticism for not adding to his squad, he knew he had a rare crop of youngsters almost ready to flourish, with Rocastle particularly impressing. 'David stood out more than anybody,' Viv Anderson told me, giving his impression of the young players at that time. 'There was a lot of talent about but he really looked something else.'

While no new players had arrived, the one addition that Howe did make was to appoint former England youth manager, John Cartwright, as first-team coach. Terry Burton, who had assisted Howe the previous season, was subsequently sent back to the reserves, while Tommy Coleman was told he could leave, despite the fact he had done an admirable job with the youth team.

Cartwright was brought in to shake things up but the senior players were not impressed. 'He wanted the ball played forward as quickly as possible,' David O'Leary complained. 'It would be channel balls and no compromise. I couldn't see the sense of that for one simple reason. Our front two were Tony Woodcock and Charlie Nicholas. They were players who needed it played to feet – not into the channels.'

Preferring the ball at his feet, and appreciating the more technical side of the game, such tactics would have been anathema to a purist such as David Rocastle. Surprisingly, O'Leary recalls that, 'Paul Davis and David Rocastle were players who thought very highly of John Cartwright. They respected the help and advice he gave them in helping them to be better players.'

Indeed, it is no wonder that Rocastle was so eager to impress. Cartwright's style of play required mobile wingers, who could get up and down the pitch, something the current incumbents, Graham Rix and Ian Allinson, were not renowned for.

Although Rocastle might have eagerly anticipated the new

season, many did not share this same view. With the game bogged down in long-ball tactics, hooliganism and racism, it is little wonder that the BBC and ITV refused to meet the Football League's demands for a new TV contract, particularly as talks came just months after the Bradford fire disaster and Heysel.

Amazingly, when you think of how we are now swamped with live football matches on television, the Football League wasn't too concerned at the prospect of a TV blackout. Sir Philip Carter, a member of the league's television committee, recalled: 'There was an underlying concern with all the chairmen that TV would reduce gates and affect football negatively. There was very little money in it. They were saying American football and motor racing had more exposure than football.'

When Arsenal kicked off the 1985/86 season, away to Liverpool, not a single TV camera was in attendance. However, David Rocastle was. Stunned to be included in the travelling squad, he may have been the spare man, consigned to the stands, but he was nevertheless ecstatic, even if he could only watch on as Liverpool predictably triumphed 2-0.

'I loved the atmosphere,' Rocastle told the Arsenal match programme shortly afterwards. 'And I'd love the chance to gain some first-team experience. But my first priority is to play well enough to establish myself as a reserve-team regular.' To achieve this he pinpointed the areas of the game he still needed to focus on: 'I want to practise and improve, particularly with my left foot. I still feel more comfortable on my right.'

Just 21,000 fans attended Arsenal's first home game, and win of the season, against Southampton, a sign that supporters were not enthused by the lack of transfer activity or the style of football. On this occasion Rocastle would not be one of them, instead playing against Fulham in the reserves, where he scored and starred in a 6-0 win.

After losing to Manchester United, the first team went on a run of six unbeaten matches, which continued to consign Rocastle to the second string, where he delivered a series of outstanding displays. Perhaps his finest performance came in a resounding 12-0 win against Charlton Athletic, where at times his speed, skill and physicality had seen him stand head and shoulders above everyone else on the pitch.

Despite the first team's run of form, it was now becoming impossible to ignore the youngster, and he was the spare man again for the home game against Sheffield Wednesday. This time there was the possibility that he might just make the bench, owing to the fact that Stewart Robson was struggling with an injury. Sadly for Rocastle, Robson passed a late fitness test, and he was once more forced to watch the 1-0 win from the stands.

However, while Robson recovered sufficiently to feature against Chelsea at Stamford Bridge, the team put in a dire display, going down 2-1. This was then followed by a 0-0 draw away to Hereford in the League Cup. Not only had the team's poor performances disappointed Howe, but Robson had again picked up an injury. With Cartwright championing the inclusion of Rocastle in the team, it now appeared the perfect opportunity to give him his chance.

On Friday, 27 September 1985, Don Howe summoned a nervous Rocastle into his office. Sitting him down, he delivered the news the anxious youngster had been waiting for his entire life: 'You're playing against Newcastle at Highbury tomorrow.'

Rushing home, Rocastle burst through the door of his family flat and breathlessly told his mother and siblings that he was in the team. Linda Rocastle was never one to get carried away with her son's success, but the array of pictures she already had on the wall dedicated to her oldest child was clear evidence of her pride. As word spread through the area that one of their own would be playing for Arsenal the following day, the Rocastle flat was soon inundated with well-wishers, photographers and reporters.

Rocastle later reflected on the experience when talking on *The Rocky Road to Success*: 'The manager told me on the Friday I'd be playing on the Saturday. It just didn't sink in. Because it was just overnight, I didn't have too much time to get nervous. I can remember getting up bright and early Saturday morning because I was going to make my debut. People came to take pictures of me. My mum didn't know what was going on. All these people were saying, "You're making your debut for Arsenal, how does it feel?" I didn't know what to say at the time.'

He later expanded on this, telling Amy Lawrence: 'The press came around and I had my big Afro and white trousers and a white jumper and they said I looked like Tubbs out of *Miami Vice* – I got some stick from the lads about that. Unbelievable, though, my picture was on the back page of the paper saying, "Young south London boy set to make his debut for Arsenal tomorrow."'

Despite so much excitement, Rocastle remained relatively calm, almost treating it as if it were just another day. Such was his demeanour that his sisters didn't appreciate the magnitude of the occasion, and therefore went shopping instead of watching him play.

Not having a driver's licence, and without transport, Rocastle's former Vista manager, Micky Cheeseman, offered to give him a lift to Highbury. 'I took him, his brother and a friend of mine,' Cheeseman told me. 'We picked him up, took him to the game and dropped him outside the marble halls. It was funny as just as I dropped him off the exhaust fell off my car!'

Entering the cramped, white-tiled Highbury dressing room, where his red-and-white polyester number 7 shirt was already hanging on a peg, Rocastle got changed as Don Howe addressed the team. Despite Howe giving Rocastle words of encouragement, urging him to run with the ball at every opportunity from centre midfield, where he was lining up, Rocastle still felt some nerves creep in.

'I can remember the clock from two to three o'clock just wouldn't go,' he said. 'It seemed to constantly be on two o'clock. I kept thinking, "What's going on here?" In the end, what seemed like three hours later, kick-off came.'

Standing in the tunnel, Rocastle accepted pats on the back from team-mates like Kenny Sansom and Viv Anderson, as he followed team captain Graham Rix out on to the pitch to the roar of the Highbury crowd.

Encouraged by the support of the home fans, and with the referee blowing his whistle to signal the start of the game, David Rocastle's first division career was up and running. However, while the game would be remembered as Rocastle's debut, it is notable for little else, such was the lack of entertainment in the drab 0-0 draw. Despite this, the debutant was ecstatic. 'I quite enjoyed the game,' he said afterwards. 'It might not have been the best of games for people to watch but from my point of view it was one of the best games I've ever had.'

This certainly seems to be an accurate assessment of how most people viewed the day. While newspaper headlines proclaimed 'Rocky Controls The Show' and praised the young midfielder's 'enthusiasm' and 'endeavour', there was little else to discuss. As former Arsenal star Steve Williams told Jon Spurling in his book *Highbury*, 'He made his debut in a bloody awful goalless draw with Newcastle at Highbury in 1985 – we used to have a lot of them back then – and the game was famous because a radio reporter had absolutely nothing to say in his match report, because absolutely nothing had happened. But in my opinion, Rocky deserved a mention, because, basically, you could see the boy could play.'

Viv Anderson was equally complimentary. 'He just had a massive enthusiasm for the game, which lifted us, and the crowd,' he remembered. 'He glided past a few people and made things happen. He was only young, so still a bit raw, but you could just see he had it.'

In the stands, author Nick Hornby had also been impressed. 'Up until then the football had been really poor,' he told me. 'Then suddenly we had this kid, with quick feet, who wanted to attack, and got us all on our feet. It was unusual at the time. He immediately stood out. There were some fantastic young players coming through, but to most fans he was the beacon of light.'

Lavishing praise on his debutant, Don Howe made it clear that he was not yet the finished article: 'David passed when he should have shot, and shot when he should have passed, but he's going to be a great player. Although he has a good ability on the ball, he's got good vision and is a terrific defender. He gets his foot in.'

David Rocastle had arrived. He could now call himself a first division footballer. The future apparently sparkled with promise, although a significant setback was on the horizon.

CHAPTER II

ROCKY 2

'I've had two nightmare seasons after four good ones,' Rocastle candidly told Kevin Connolly on the eve of the 1991/92 season. 'It feels like taking money under false pretences sitting on the bench. I want to be in the thick of it, like I was when we won the title two years ago.'

However, with injuries mounting up, Rocastle's weight had become an issue. Reporting back for pre-season, he had tipped the scales at close to 13½ stone. If he was ever going to get back to the dynamic winger who had been a regular for England little more than a year previously, then he would need to shed at least half a stone.

Rocastle's battle with his weight, together with the fact that Graham thought that his long-standing knee injury had curtailed his mobility, also meant that there were questions being asked about where his best position might now be. Over the last few seasons Rocastle had built a reputation as one of the most exciting wingers in the country, but even he was feeling the pressure to prove that he could still be effective in such a role.

'I'm not a person who loses confidence,' he said. 'But after what's happened in the last two years, I've started feeling nervous when I never used to be. I feel the pressure because people are wondering if I can still do what they expected two years ago. I know I can still go past people, and get in crosses and shots like I used to. It's a case of showing that again at a top level.'

With the subject of his best position up for discussion, Rocastle revealed that he simply wanted just to play football: 'I'll play wide right or switch to the centre if that gives me another chance. I'd just like a run to prove myself again.'

Working his way back to full fitness, Rocastle spent most of pre-season coming off the bench in a low-key tour of Sweden, followed by games against Plymouth Argyle and Celtic. By the time the Makita tournament came around, Graham felt Rocastle was ready to start, albeit in central midfield, a position he had not played in regularly since his first season under Don Howe.

However, with his ability to read the game, quick feet, imaginative penetration of passing and tenacity in the tackle, Rocastle proved against Panathinaikos that a return to this role might now suit his declining powers. But then yet another injury struck. A badly broken finger forced him to leave the field after 66 minutes in the following game against Sampdoria. Requiring an operation just when he was desperately trying to concentrate on his new role and get fully fit, it was a source of yet more frustration and inconvenience.

Despite this minor setback Rocastle had delivered another encouraging display from the centre of the park, which led *The Times* to state in its match report that he had put in an 'impressive showing'.

With his hand still in a cast, he returned to action for the Charity Shield against Spurs, with the game offering the opportunity for Arsenal to avenge some demons following the shock FA Cup semi-final defeat the previous season. But as is so often the case in this season curtain-raiser, the game that transpired was a drab affair, ending in a 0-0 draw, with not even the excitement of extra time or penalties to get pulses racing. Instead, the teams shared the trophy, which only served to highlight the relative worthless nature of the contest.

While the season began in worrying fashion, with a draw at home to QPR followed by two away defeats, to Everton and Villa, things soon picked up, as did Rocastle's form. His performance against FK Austria in the European Cup was certainly a reminder that he still possessed the quality to play at the top level. On the night Arsenal were sensational, winning 6-1. Rocastle's economic distribution from the middle of the park, supplemented by his unerring understanding of the rhythm of the game, had seen him instinctively know when to play it short, hit it long or drive forward, creating a succession of chances for his team-mates in the process.

Heralded by the Arsenal match programme as 'one of our greatest heroes on Wednesday night, with a display of tigerish tackling and accurate passing', Rocastle emphasised how pleased he was with his new position: 'I'd always turned out in the centre until the last five years. That's where I began. That's where I made my first league appearances. But we had Paul Davis and Stewart Robson for the central midfield positions when George Graham came here, so he moved me wide right. I'm reverting to old habits – though I was a little rusty to start with. It's a different game to playing wide, where I'm expected to take on defenders and fire in shots and crosses. We have four forwards who are all capable of scoring regularly. Sometimes that means the central midfield players have to sit in there and play a holding role, because you don't want to get caught too far forward and let your immediate opponent run past you into a dangerous position.

Some of the fans shout at me to go forward. I'll do so whenever I can. That's what I enjoy. That's not what the job is all about, though. On the wing, you depend on other players bringing you into the game. In the centre, you're much more involved. But the game isn't about frills. It's about two-touch football, winning the ball, using it accurately to start attacks, and making sure you keep on top of the player you're facing.'

Following the 6-1 demolition of FK Austria, Arsenal put five past Sheffield United, with Rocastle's deflected shot marking his first league goal of the season. Scoring goals was certainly not an issue for the team, but George Graham still made a surprise move for a new frontman, which delighted not only the Arsenal faithful but David Rocastle too.

Having become Crystal Palace's record post-war goalscorer, Ian Wright was now a man in demand. A legend at Selhurst Park, he was nevertheless unable to resist a move across London when Arsenal offered £2m for his services, especially as it gave him the chance to finally play alongside his old friend David Rocastle.

'Signing for Arsenal Football Club – and playing with my best pal, David Rocastle – was a dream come true,' Wright told Arsenal's official magazine. 'Rocky and I had known each other since we were kids in south London. Arsenal meant everything to him. When I first arrived at the club, I remember going round his house and we stayed up all night talking Arsenal. I think we got to bed at about 5am. But I could have carried on listening to David telling me just how great this football club is for even longer. He stressed the club's tradition to me ... Rocky would say things like, "Make sure you tuck your shirt in" and "If Tony Adams wants to wear long sleeves then we all wear them – no arguments". It was those little things that set the club apart.'

Just a day after signing, Wright and Rocastle finally got to play alongside each other for the very first time, in a League Cup tie at

Leicester. While the game ended in a disappointing draw, the standout moment of the game was Wright's debut goal, a low drive from the left-hand corner of the box. As Wright wheeled away in celebration, Rocastle held his friend's face in his hands and smiled, wide-eyed. It was almost too good to be true that two boys from the same council estate, both the offspring of immigrant parents, could now be living out their dream together.

Things got even better in the next game, as Arsenal made the trip to the Dell and Rocastle and Wright truly lived out all of their childhood footballing fantasies. Running the length of the field, Rocastle had put Wright through on goal, only for his shot to be saved. But Rocastle followed up to slam in the rebound and give Arsenal the lead. Soon afterwards it was Wright's turn. Racking up the frenetic excitement surrounding his arrival, he scored a brilliant hat-trick, showing the thousands of fans who had made the journey to Southampton just why he was their club's record signing.

If Arsenal had looked formidable before Wright's arrival, they now had another dimension altogether. Indeed, by the end of September they had climbed to third place, although they still lagged nine points behind leaders Manchester United. However, as Arsenal progressed in the European and League Cups, a trip to Old Trafford was looming. In the build-up, Wright predictably attracted most of the headlines, but some also complimented Rocastle on his brilliant form since his friend's arrival, with critics even tipping him for an England recall.

When questioned on his form, and change of position, Rocastle said, 'The way it is in football these days you've got to have more than one position under your belt. I prefer the centre because you're more involved, even if you don't get to show your skill factor as much as you do on the wings. The way the manager wants me to play, I have become a two-touch player. With the front players we've got now, the midfield doesn't have to do anything spectacular, just get the ball to them quickly. I can appreciate that because as a wide player I often feel I don't get the ball early enough.'

Arsenal's trip to Old Trafford not only gave them the opportunity to cut their opponents' lead at the top, but it also provided Rocastle with a chance to prove his international credentials against the likes of Bryan Robson and Paul Ince. However, Old Trafford had not been kind to Rocastle on previous visits. He had earned the only sending-off of his career after a tussle with Norman Whiteside in 1987 and, of course, in 1990 there had been the infamous battle of Old Trafford, which saw Rocastle not only fined but dropped from the squad for a number of weeks.

On this occasion, Rocastle emphatically banished all of his Old Trafford demons once and for all. With *The Times* proclaiming that he had been 'exceptional' in the 1-1 draw, it went on to say, 'He illuminated the afternoon with flashes of brilliance which prompted his manager, George Graham, to describe him as man of the match.'

Despite Rocastle's all-round performance, putting former England captain Robson, as well as the likes of Ince and Webb in the shade, there was one moment of brilliance that had lit up one of the world's greatest stages.

Right back Lee Dixon had hoisted a long ball forwards, which was left to bounce on the halfway line. Seizing on the loose ball, Rocastle used all of his tenacity to nick it away from the outstretched boot of Neil Webb, and then drove into the Manchester United half, where he faced a wall of red shirts. Holding off the backtracking Paul Ince to his left, Rocastle saw Robson coming in to sandwich him from the right. A lightning-quick stepover saw him shift in an instant towards Robson before his body snapped back to face Ince. The shift in body weight was over in a split second but it opened up a small gap between the two United players which had previously looked to be closed. A double tap of the ball, with his right and then left foot, was followed by a surge of acceleration as he drove through the middle, leaving them both dazzled like children witnessing a magic trick.

With United's back four back-pedalling, it seemed that Rocastle's only option was to hold the ball up and wait for help to arrive. However, as he glanced up he spotted the huge frame of Peter Schmeichel a few yards from his line. After displaying his tenacity, sleight of foot and speed, all that was now left was for Arsenal's number 7 to show that he also possessed vision and precision. Thirty-five yards from goal, Rocastle dug his right foot under the ball and lifted it over Schmeichel's despairing dive and into the goal via a combination of the underside of the bar and the back of the Manchester United goalkeeper. While the noisy enclave of travelling supporters let rip a belligerent roar, United fans clapped in appreciation of the talent that had just been paraded before them.

To have scored such a goal in a top-of-the-table clash, after beating a renowned midfield trio and then one of the best goalkeepers in history, illustrated that David Rocastle was indeed a special player. Even Alex Ferguson could not fail to acclaim the goal. 'I don't think the goalkeeper had any chance,' he said. 'You've got to hand it to Rocastle. That was a brilliant piece of imagination and improvisation.'

While Steve Bruce would equalise and maintain Manchester United's unbeaten record, the plaudits were all Rocastle's. As always, despite earning rave reviews, he remained magnanimous. 'I got a lot of praise after the game,' he told Kevin Connolly. 'But how can anyone say you've dominated a competitor like Bryan Robson? You have to compete and compete against him. None of the midfield players had a moment to spare on the ball that afternoon. But so much good football was played and that's a credit to the players' quality.'

After a nightmare two seasons Rocastle had again proven his worth. 'In hindsight, I wasn't doing the business for Arsenal when I was left out of the World Cup squad, especially after a knee injury cost me a bit of edge,' he admitted. 'Personally, last season was all a bit of a nightmare amid the club's success. I lost form and was dropped. Every time I came back I got injured again.'

Following his scintillating performance at Old Trafford, Sven-Göran Eriksson's Benfica awaited in the European Cup. In a noisy and intimidating atmosphere, Arsenal acquitted themselves well in the early stages, with Rocastle looking especially comfortable in the slower pace of European football. However, after star player Isaías gifted the Portuguese side the lead, it looked like a 1-0 defeat beckoned.

But with a crucial away goal up for grabs, Rocastle once more displayed his immense worth from a central position. Picking the ball up midway in the Benfica half, he span away from his opposite number and, with seven defenders in front of him, somehow possessed the poise and vision to slot the ball through to Kevin Campbell, who emphatically finished from a tight angle. The subsequent 1-1 draw made Arsenal favourites to progress to the next round, while the all-round performance proved that the team were a match for Europe's finest.

However, the season was about to take a turn for the worse. After a solid home win against Notts County, Arsenal then suffered an appalling month. Crashing out of the League Cup to Coventry, a winless spell in the league followed, which saw them lose to West Ham and draw with Oldham and Sheffield Wednesday. With their title challenge evaporating, Arsenal turned their attention to the European Cup.

Despite holding an away-goal advantage over Benfica, Arsenal slumped at Highbury. While Colin Pates had opened the scoring, Isaías had responded with a long-distance rocket, which took the game into extra time. Chances to win the tie were squandered, with Smith shanking a gilt-edged chance wide and Adams missing an open goal. In contrast Benfica were clinical, with Isaías again proving to be the difference, helping to seal a 3-1 win on the night and a 4-2 victory on aggregate.

The result and performance left Rocastle reeling: 'We had our chances all right. They played well that night and we took stick for being unimaginative. But what really hurt was that they were stronger than us in extra time. We were straining after a lot of hard matches. They don't face anything like that gruelling programme in Portugal and that lifted them as the game went on. It was a big blow. I felt deflated for a long time after that defeat. We all did. But we also learnt a lot.'

The season quickly lurched from bad to worse, as Rocastle's close friend Michael Thomas was allowed to leave the club and sign for Liverpool. Thomas had barely played after falling out with Graham but it was still a move that upset the squad. Indeed, Thomas was also quick to voice his displeasure at Graham's tactics following the move. 'I found his style of football so unattractive,' Thomas told the press. 'It was too direct. I might as well have been a long-distance runner rather than a first division footballer.'

Graham's record of winning matches and trophies meant that attacks of this nature by disgruntled players could usually be swiped aside. But with results continuing to slip in the league throughout December and going into the New Year questions were suddenly being asked.

The one chance for redemption came in the FA Cup. With Arsenal drawn to play fourth division Wrexham on 4 January 1992, a club that had finished bottom of the Football League the previous season, it offered the tantalising opportunity to see the league's best team against the league's worst.

Goalscoring talisman Ian Wright might have been suspended for the trip to the Racecourse Ground, while Graham had recently made the curious decision to bench Anders Limpar in favour of new signing Jimmy Carter, but the team was still brimming with quality. In the circumstances, the pundits predicted an easy victory.

While the ramshackle Racecourse Ground was supercharged with roaring Welshmen, they had been all but silenced by half-time, as Arsenal's clear superiority was rewarded with a 1-0 lead, courtesy of Alan Smith. Over steaming cups of tea in the cramped dressing room, Graham urged his players to keep playing as they had been. There certainly didn't appear to be anything to be concerned about. As Paul Merson revealed in his autobiography, 'I've never been in a more one-sided match. Even George didn't seem that arsed in his team talk; he knew we were bossing it. "Right, no silly injuries," he said. "No sending-offs. Let's just get this game out of the way and get out of here." Then Wrighty started gobbing off. He'd come along to watch the tie. "Fucking hell, if I'd been playing I'd have scored 20 by now," he moaned.'

As the second half progressed, Arsenal still appeared relatively comfortable, despite not adding to the scoreline. Nothing whatsoever indicated that a shock might be in store, not even when Wrexham won a free-kick, 25 yards from goal, with just seven minutes remaining. Even when Mickey Thomas, the ageing former Manchester United midfielder, stepped up, the Arsenal players weren't concerned, knowing it would take a supreme effort to defeat David Seaman, the best goalkeeper in the country.

Taking three steps back, the curly-haired Thomas wiped sweat from his brow and exhaled in the brisk air before striding forward and pile-driving his foot through the ball. In a flash, it tore past the wall, past the outstretched hand of Seaman, and crashed into the top corner. It was the goal of a lifetime. While it looked an aberration in the overall scheme of the game, Wrexham's players, and fans, suddenly had a new-found belief.

Resigned to a replay the following Tuesday, Arsenal's shell-shocked players argued among themselves, knowing that Tuesday Club activities would have to be suspended. Meanwhile, Wrexham piled forward, smelling blood.

Sitting deep, Arsenal intended to soak up the pressure of their inferior opponents, and hopefully hit them on the counterattack with the pace of Groves, who had now replaced Campbell. That was the plan anyway. But as the game entered its final minute the ball broke to Wrexham's Steve Watkin, who improbably prodded the ball past Seaman to put the Welshmen 2-1 up. As delirious scenes broke out around the Racecourse Ground, half of Arsenal's team dropped to their knees. Cajoling and screaming at them to regroup, Rocastle knew there were a few minutes of injury time remaining and he wasn't prepared to concede defeat just yet.

Roaring up the field in search of a desperate equaliser, it appeared that the game had been salvaged when Jimmy Carter dramatically tapped home at the near post. To Graham's disgust, the linesman had raised his flag for offside. It was an extraordinary decision, as replays showed that Carter had clearly been onside. Nevertheless, soon afterwards the final whistle blew. Arsenal were out of the cup in the most humiliating of circumstances. And now the season really did look all but finished.

'You had to play in that match to realise how crazy the scoreline was,' Rocastle later said. 'The result hinged on two refereeing decisions. I've replayed them over and over in my mind – and I still can't understand how we lost. But we took it with dignity and got on with our jobs, which says a lot about the club.'

Crossing his arms and looking down his line of silent players, Graham calmy but sternly told them some home truths: 'We've had a great run of success but it hasn't just happened by magic. We've earned that success by hard work that has enabled you to make the most of your ability. Now you must question your application and your attitude. You have stopped doing all the good things that got us to the top. Nobody has a God-given right to succeed. If you're not willing to put in the work that is required then I shall start looking for players who are. Let me see the pride back in your performances, or else.'

The rest of January went by in a darkened haze. It was almost as if Arsenal had been on a big night out, only to emerge the next morning hungover and full of regret. Unable to shake the mental scars of the Racecouse Ground, goalless draws against Villa and QPR were followed by a 2-0 defeat to Liverpool and a 1-1 draw with Manchester United. In this spell the team went eight games without a win and were marooned in eighth spot, 20 points off the lead. This was not how the champions had envisaged defending their title.

As February commenced, a 1-0 win at relegation-haunted Notts County, followed by an uninspiring draw at Norwich, somewhat steadied the ship before the Arsenal juggernaut suddenly powered back to life against Sheffield Wednesday. With Arsenal struggling to create and finish chances, this was the game where everything came right. Wonder goals from Limpar and Merson were supplemented by clinical strikes from Campbell and Wright, as Arsenal ran out 7-1 winners.

'I don't think we've been playing as badly as our critics suggest,' a defiant Rocastle said after the game. 'A lot of frustration built up, though. We took that frustration out on Sheffield Wednesday. If we hadn't spent so long hugging each other we could have scored 10 in that last half-hour.'

Displaying new-found confidence, Arsenal ended the season in style. As George Graham has said of this period, 'We went through the last 17 matches of the season undefeated and climbed from eighth to fourth. During that late run we produced some of the most blinding football I had ever seen from an Arsenal team, and that includes my days as a player at Highbury.'

Whether it was professional pride kicking in, or the realisation that a UEFA Cup place was still up for grabs, the performances at times were breathtaking. There was also the lure of the European Championship that summer, with Arsenal's England contingent anxious to avoid the disappointment of missing out again. 'No way will we lay down and just play out the season,' Rocastle said in the middle of this resurgence. 'We have a lot of pride at stake. We have so many players bidding for places in the European Championship finals too. There should be a good few Gunners in Graham Taylor's squad, plus Anders for Sweden.'

In a remarkable run of results, Liverpool were demolished 4-0, Palace 4-1, and on the final day of the season Southampton were subjected to a 5-1 hammering. On the day Ian Wright scored a hat-trick to clinch the golden boot ahead of his rival, Gary Lineker, and Arsenal were also crowned top scorers in the league. Graham believed that if the season had been just six weeks longer then Arsenal would have clinched the title. The team's mid-season jitters had cost them dearly. Despite such a glorious run they still didn't secure a UEFA Cup spot, as they finished in fourth place, 10 points off champions Leeds United.

As for Rocastle, he still saw his future very much at Arsenal. When asked how he felt the team would fare the following season, he declared, 'The title race will be wide open. We've had a disappointing season. Liverpool have been rebuilding, and struggling with injuries. But we'll be there next season, and so will they. Manchester United will challenge too, if they carry on sneaking results the way they've done this season. Leeds are developing all the time. Manchester City and Sheffield Wednesday could cause some upsets. Bluntly, though, there are only maybe 10 teams with a realistic chance of winning honours – and some of them are cup teams rather than league teams. That's the beauty of Arsenal when we play to our potential . . . we can do well in any competition.'

Having made 47 appearances in a season in which he had emphatically proven he still had the ability to deliver at the top level, Rocastle had every right to envisage that he would again be a key part of the Arsenal team the following season. Already looking forward to the new season in the fledgling Premier League, he now concentrated on his outside chance of avenging some demons and making England's 1992 European Championship squad.

CHAPTER 12

THE GOOD, THE BAD AND THE UGLY

Just four substitute appearances after his exciting first-team debut, David Rocastle was shocked to find himself back in the reserves. The promise he had shown against Newcastle had failed to flourish in a series of cameo appearances and, as such, Don Howe thought the starlet wasn't ready for the big time on a regular basis.

Initially taking his demotion well, scoring in two consecutive reserve games, Rocastle hoped that Howe might perhaps look at him again, especially after the first team suffered the ignominy of a 6-1 defeat at Goodison Park. However, with Howe continuing to overlook the youngster, Rocastle's impatience turned to dismay. Ineffectual and uninterested in the following reserve game against Portsmouth, Burton had no choice but to haul him off at half-time. Suddenly it looked as if he was back at square one, with his professional career hanging in the balance.

'I think that the worst thing from my point of view was being put in the team so early and given too much exposure,' Rocastle told Arsenal columnist, Fiona Cohn. 'All I could think about after was when I would be playing for the first team again. I didn't lose my enthusiasm for playing in the reserves but it was much more difficult to motivate myself. I lost form badly, and I had to work hard to get it back again. It was very frustrating but I learnt from the experience.'

Indeed, while he might have lost his focus, he was also struggling to adapt to the new-found demands of fame. Rocastle had confided to Cohn that he had been 'disturbed' by acquaintances' attitudes towards him since he had his name in print. However, Rocastle was keen to emphasise that the change was certainly not due to him. 'I know that if I was changing, there are plenty of people to stop me and give me a good kick,' he said, 'but that isn't likely to happen. It's very nice to taste some of the good life, but there's no reason to go overboard, it's not in my nature.'

Those who knew Rocastle best testified that there was certainly no change in him after he had reached the big time. 'He was never one of those guys who became famous and threw it in your face,' Junior Hamilton told me. 'He never cut his mates off from back home. He was always out with us all. And while he would often buy the drinks it was always done in a quiet manner, not like he was showing off. We always appreciated it and made sure we returned the favour. He was always just "Dave" and we were proud of him.'

Errol Johnson told me that his friend was never flash. Indeed, as he was without a driver's licence, in part because he couldn't afford to pay for lessons, he still caught the tube to training, as well as to first-team games. Rather than buy himself a swanky pad, he even continued to live at home, where he tried his best to look after his mother and siblings. 'He was always spoiling us all,' Karen Rocastle told me. 'One of my treasured possessions is a teddy-bear cushion he just came home with one day for me.'

Rocastle showing youthful signs of pace and balance (left), while his musical tastes were given an early chance to blossom (above).

The only picture the Rocastles have of the family all together, in 1970.

Rocastle on a cruise with lifelong friend Jenny Fraser. *(Jenny Fraser)*

Relaxing at home.
(Jenny Fraser)

Rocastle holds 11-month-old Sasha at her first Christmas, while doting grandmother Eva looks on.

Rocastle was just 18 years old when he made his first team debut in a drab 0-0 draw against Newcastle – he even needed to ask for a lift to the ground! *(Getty Images)*

A young Rocastle poses by the Highbury trophy cabinet, ready to help add to the collection. *(Jenny Fraser)*

In his debut season for Arsenal, Rocastle made an instant impact. Watched on by team-mates Steve Williams (left) and Kenny Sansom, he challenges West Ham's Mark Ward. *(PA/Empics)*

Because of his remarkable promise, Rocastle won the Arsenal Supporters' Club Player of the Year award – 'one of my proudest moments'.

It was for his tricky wing play in his early days that Rocastle was well known. Here he's just too quick for the Reading defence in the third round of the FA Cup in 1987, and the referee points to the spot. *(Mirrorpix)*

But sometimes Rocastle lost his cool when fouled. George Tyson sends him to the dressing room after the young Arsenal star retaliated against Norman Whiteside in January 1987 – it was the only red card of his career. *(Mirrorpix)*

Action from the Littlewoods Cup final against Liverpool in April 1987. *(Getty Images)*

Rocastle joins in the celebrations after Arsenal secure their first trophy since 1979. *(PA)*

North London rivals in action. Rocastle battles with Ossie Ardiles of Spurs.

(Getty Images)

Holding off Millwall's Teddy Sheringham as Arsenal close in on the title in 1989.

(PA/Empics)

That winning feeling! After the most dramatic climax to a league season, Arsenal secured the title with virtually the last kick of the match. *(Getty Images)*

Dancing on the balcony – Rocastle leads the celebrations from Islington Town Hall after Arsenal claimed their stunning title triumph. *(PA)*

Even at the height of his career Rocastle never considered himself a star. Indeed, his brother, Steve, has previously recalled his excitement at spotting Charlton star, Carl Leaburn, out shopping one day, when he was already a first-team regular at Arsenal.

Yet with the pressures of professional football, and fame, threatening to overwhelm him, Rocastle went back to basics. Firstly, he stayed behind for extra training with Terry Burton, hoping to get his confidence back. 'It can happen to young players,' Burton told me when we discussed Rocastle's struggles. 'That excitement of first playing football and the build-up, and the thinking you've made it, maybe your game disappears a little bit. Maybe you stop doing the things that you were good at. It's a case of getting back down to it and working at the basics again. The ones with good character come through. And thankfully Rocky did.'

While Burton helped to take care of matters on the pitch, Charlie Nicholas also had a word of advice: 'Speak to my agent. He'll take good care of you.' The agent in question was Jerome Anderson.

Anderson had been working in finance when he was introduced to Charlie Nicholas early in his Highbury career. Having struck an instant rapport, Nicholas subsequently asked him to look after a few matters, which eventually led to Anderson becoming his full-time agent. With Nicholas endorsing Anderson to all of his team-mates, it was only a matter of time before he represented the vast majority of the Arsenal team, and in the process became one of the most powerful agents in the country.

When I spoke to Anderson he remembered the day that Nicholas first brought a shy teenager to see him: 'Charlie was the one that introduced us. He brought him into my office one day and I remember Rocky was sporting an Afro. Charlie just said, "Look, this is David Rocastle. He is a very big talent and he needs some looking after."'

As Anderson spoke to Rocastle, he immediately warmed to him. 'He was just a nice, fantastic, young man,' he told me. 'Honourable. Honest. Very appreciative. He told me he wanted to be the best he could be at football and he wanted me to do everything else for him so he could concentrate on maximising his ability as a player.'

And that is just what Anderson did. Immediately lifting a load from the young starlet's mind, he took care of arranging interviews and looked after his day-to-day life, organising his driving lessons, helping him to buy a car, as well as a small home in Barnet. In time there would be a high-profile boot deal with Nike, as well as the first VHS video ever dedicated to a footballer, *The Rocky Road to Success*.

Ensuring that he never had to worry about anything, Anderson became much more than an agent to Rocastle. 'He used to call me "Dad",' Anderson told me. 'This was more than a business relationship. The business was almost secondary. We were proper family. While David was obviously younger than me, we used to go out socially. We'd go out for lunch or see each other at the kids' birthday parties. We had a special relationship. One of the most special I've known. He was a fantastic guy.' Such was the strength of their relationship that Rocastle even became godfather to Anderson's children.

Feeling more settled, Rocastle was soon back in the groove, starring in a 5-0 reserve team win against Palace. Continuing to train well, Howe soon took notice, particularly as his experiment of playing centre back Chris Whyte as a forward had failed to yield any real success. However, it would take another Stewart Robson injury for Rocastle to finally be invited back into the fold.

Unbelievably, the match in which Rocastle made his return was on New Year's Day, against north London rivals Spurs. Furthermore, he was picked to play in central midfield, where he had caught the eye in his youth-team days. While the 0-0 draw wasn't particularly memorable, Rocastle recalled that he spent half the game blind. 'One of my contact lenses fell out,' he laughed. 'I somehow managed to cope, and the lenses have not been any trouble since. I suppose they gave me a new outlook on the game!'

Despite his vision being limited, Rocastle was ecstatic to be back. 'I'm glad I got that second chance,' he said. 'I was pleased with my debut match – but most players seem to look good on their debuts. I wanted to show that I wasn't just a one-off player.'

As 1986 commenced Howe suddenly felt it was time to unleash more of his young stars. In the weeks ahead Adams, Keown, Hayes, Quinn and Caesar would all have a taste of first-team action. Rocastle was particularly pleased to be joined by his friends, especially as it meant that he got to room with Gus Caesar. While the two were always on their best behaviour in their early days together, Caesar confided that there was a tiny hint of rebellion. 'Sometimes we'd have a cigarette in the room,' he laughed. 'I was a big smoker and if Dave saw me having one he'd usually join me. We'd be lying in our beds watching the TV, trying to find a film to watch. Every so often he'd even bring out the Baileys. It helped us sleep, to be fair, as I suffered from insomnia, and Dave was always up late as well.'

The emergence of youth certainly bought Howe and Cartwright some much-needed goodwill from the terraces, with crowds having slipped to just 16,000 for the home game against Birmingham, which Nick Hornby called 'surely the worst game of football ever played in the history of the first division'.

'The North Bank loved this new wave of Highbury kids,' Jon Spurling remembered in his book *All Guns Blazing: Arsenal in the 1980s*, 'because they were keen, fresh and anxious to stake their claim to a pace in the side. They coped superbly in these high-octane games and we were prepared to forgive them for their occasional mistakes and teenage impetuosity.'

Fast becoming a fixture in the team, Rocastle scored his first goal on 15 February 1986, on Luton's plastic pitch in the fourth round of the FA Cup. 'The game was one each,' he later recalled. 'Tony Woodcock did a great cross to me and I scored with my head. Michael Thomas was in the crowd and he couldn't believe I scored with my head.' Indeed, as seen by Thomas' reaction, Rocastle's heading accuracy was a frequent source of amusement to some members of the squad. So it was somewhat ironic that he should break his duck for Arsenal in such circumstances.

However, his well-directed header failed to make the headlines. Instead, the newspapers focused on yet another outbreak of trouble as three fans were stabbed in the ground, and 32 arrests were made for violent disorder. It is hard to imagine in these more sanitised times that something like this could occur at an English football ground, but such was the regularity of these events in the 1980s that there was no real outcry. It was almost accepted as par for the course.

The 2-2 draw at Kenilworth Road was then followed by a 0-0 draw at Highbury in the replay, which meant a return to Luton where a dire performance culminated in a 3-0 defeat. This result saw many fans finally tire of Howe's long-ball tactics and call for a change.

Even though the team's league form picked up dramatically, with Rocastle grabbing his first league goal in an emphatic 4-1 defeat of Aston Villa at Villa Park, it was said that the directors at Highbury were again sounding out Terry Venables about the prospect of him succeeding Howe. Subsequent wins against Ipswich, West Ham and Coventry, which took the team to within just 10 points of the top of the league with four games in hand, might have led many managers to dig in, but not Howe. Just 15 minutes after the win against Coventry he handed in his resignation.

'I had had a few differences of opinion with Peter Hill-Wood,'

Howe later told the Arsenal match programme. 'I felt from experience that the club was looking for a change and I'd heard that he'd been talking to Terry Venables. I then discovered that they'd approached Terry behind my back and I felt I had to make a stand about that. I didn't object to them approaching Terry but I felt I deserved more honesty from the club. But that's the way football is sometimes.'

If anyone had been sad to see Howe and Cartwright depart, it would have been Rocastle. Howe had given him his chance, while Cartwright had nurtured him. Many don't look back on this period of Arsenal's history with misty eyes but there is no doubt that the two were instrumental in introducing the likes of Adams, Rocastle and Keown to the first team. In time they would all of course deliver in abundance.

With Venables ultimately turning down the position, Steve Burtenshaw reluctantly took the helm until the end of the season. While on paper it had appeared that Arsenal still had an outside chance of winning the title, true Highbury connoisseurs were never convinced. In any event, with Howe gone, the team crashed to three consecutive defeats, leaving them with nothing left to play for.

For Rocastle, the season at least looked to have ended on a high note. Before the home game against Nottingham Forest, he was informed that he had been called up to the England Under-21 squad to face Italy. Amazingly, this was his first ever England call-up, having never even been invited for so much as a training session as a schoolboy.

Understandably, he was thrilled, but the game against Forest would not only prevent his involvement, it would also have tremendous consequences for his future career. Launching himself into a tackle he was never destined to win, his knee suddenly buckled. As he tried to get to his feet, he found that he couldn't bend his leg and subsequently crashed back to the floor. Rushing from the dugout, Gary Lewin took one look at the injury before frantically waving for the stretcher to be brought on. 'I can still remember that cold, awful feeling washing over me when he didn't get up,' his friend Jenny Fraser told me. 'It was horrendous because no matter what he always got up, but this time he stayed down.'

Rocastle's season was over. He had torn his cartilage and required an operation. Although today such an injury might be seen as relatively minor, usually treated via keyhole surgery to repair, or remove, the damaged part of the cartilage, back in the 1980s it was major. Moreover, removing the cartilage, while perhaps not causing any immediate issues, would in time lead to arthritis, due to the bone now rubbing against bone.

Nevertheless, Rocastle was not feeling too downhearted. 'After the operation I thought I'd be feeling more sorry for myself than I am,' he told Kevin Connolly. 'The whole cartilage was removed and the first 48 hours after the operation were agony. I was in bed for two days and I could hardly move. I was lucky that my family kept my spirits up. But over the past week I've had time to look back on what's happened to me this season – because I haven't had time to take it in while it's been going on.'

In plaster, Rocastle was forced to spend the next few weeks confined to sleeping on the living-room sofa. As he slowly recovered, it was announced in May 1986, following the lowest home crowd in 20 years, of just 14,486, that the strict disciplinarian George Graham would be taking charge the following season.

Rocastle's injury could not have come at a worse time. Not only would he have to quickly gain fitness to impress the incoming manager, but his contract was also due to expire. And as he and his team-mates would soon find out, Graham was certainly not a man to let his heart rule his head.

CHAPTER 13

ENGLAND REDEMPTION

If David Rocastle's form had returned during the 1991/92 season, then England's had plummeted since the halcyon days of Italia '90. With Bobby Robson triumphantly vacating the manager's post, Aston Villa boss Graham Taylor had taken over the hot seat. Although Taylor had never won a major honour, his record was still impressive: five promotions, two first division runners-up spots as well as an FA Cup final appearance, he had also played a major role in the development of John Barnes and David Platt. However, despite this success, there were still some concerns about his suitability for the top job.

Unlike most of his predecessors, Taylor had no direct experience of international football, either as a player or as a manager. His involvement in European club competition was also limited to just three rounds in the UEFA Cup. Another source of concern was his direct style of play, which some said was not suited to the demands of the free-flowing international game.

Despite these apprehensions, there was certainly a strong base on which Taylor could build. Although stalwarts Terry Butcher and Peter Shilton had now retired, taking 200 caps' worth of experience with them, players like Platt, Gascoigne, Des Walker, Parker and Stuart Pearce were in their prime, while established stars such as Gary Lineker, Peter Beardsley and Bryan Robson continued to make themselves available for selection.

In addition, there were numerous players who had failed to make Robson's World Cup squad, but who certainly had a case for inclusion. At Arsenal alone there was Rocastle, Adams, Smith, Merson, Dixon and Seaman, while the likes of Alan Shearer, Matthew Le Tissier, Teddy Sheringham, Ian Wright and Les Ferdinand had started to emerge as players of huge promise.

Despite this array of talent at his disposal, Taylor immediately sparked controversy with some of his selections. A 2-0 win against Poland in his first competitive test was straightforward enough, but in the following game, against Ireland, he dropped star player Gascoigne to the bench and replaced him with Gordon Cowans. The ensuing drab performance in the 1-1 draw in Dublin certainly didn't help Taylor's cause, with some critics already questioning his suitability as England boss.

For the vital trip to Turkey, with three teams locked on four points at the top of the group, Taylor made another curious decision, this time dropping Bryan Robson in favour of Dennis Wise. Yet while the critics sniped at the former Wimbledon player standing in for the United legend, it was Wise who was to score the winner, putting England top of the group.

England may have extended their lead by again beating Turkey, in the home tie at Wembley, regarded by many as one of Gascoigne's greatest displays, but some of the performances in the intervening friendly games, as well as the players selected, gave rise to further unease. Struggling against teams like Australia, New Zealand and Malaysia, caps had been awarded to David Hirst, John

Salako, Brian Deane, Earl Barrett, Mark Walters and Gary Charles, while Beardsley, Waddle and Robson were shunned.

In his autobiography, Paul Merson discussed his bewilderment at some of Taylor's decisions: 'England had a lot of quality players, it was just the manager who wasn't up to much. And the more I played for Graham Taylor, the weirder it got. Tactically, he was all over the place. Before a game we'd often have to sit in the video room and watch an hour of the opposition taking throw-ins. Graham's thinking was that the team taking the throw was weakened, they only had 10 men on the pitch and we should take advantage. It all seemed a bit Mickey Mouse to me.'

With just one game to go to secure qualification, and England still unbeaten in the qualifiers, Taylor could however point to his record as proof that he knew what he was doing. But with Poland and Ireland just two points behind England, Taylor also knew that his team could not afford to slip up for their visit to Poznań.

By this stage, loss of form and injury had meant that Rocastle hadn't been near an England squad in over 18 months. But with him now earning rave reviews for his performances in central midfield, journalist Clive White, for one, was certainly keen to see Rocastle make a return to the national side. 'One would not have to stretch the imagination half as far as a *Rocky* film script to foresee a comeback next week of the kind Sylvester Stallone himself would approve,' he wrote in *The Times*. 'This is one comeback that, should it receive the England manager's blessing, could not be viewed as a retrograde step. Arsenal have only just relaunched Rocky's club career, at the ripe old age of 24, but the player's form has been such a revelation that Taylor would be foolish not to consider him for his squad.'

As talk of a recall gathered pace, Rocastle couldn't contain his excitement. 'England? You hope, don't you?' he said. 'Until a few weeks ago, I hadn't even thought about England again. I had enough to do holding my place in the Arsenal side. But I'd hate to think I made my last England appearance when I was 22. It's reassuring to know that Graham Taylor hasn't closed that door.'

Rocastle certainly hadn't done his cause any harm when, just before Taylor announced his squad, he had starred at Old Trafford, dominating Bryan Robson and scoring an outrageous 30-yard chip over Peter Schmeichel. To the delight of Rocastle and his supporters, this was enough to see Taylor recall him for the vital qualifier against Poland.

When discussing his reasons for bringing Rocastle back into the fold Taylor said, 'The balance and the shape wasn't right . . . We've been disappointing in terms of creativity in the middle of the park. I'm looking to get more from that department.'

But when Taylor announced his team to start in Poland, it was greeted with raised eyebrows. For such a vital game, his five-man midfield had fewer international caps between them than left back Stuart Pearce. In the middle, there was Andy Gray, Geoff Thomas and David Platt, while Andy Sinton was on the left and Rocastle on the right. It was hardly a midfield that looked international class, even back then.

Rocastle's recent run of good form had also been with him playing in the middle, so it was a curious decision for Taylor to put him out wide, especially when he had admitted he was brought into the squad to add creativity from central midfield. In the circumstances, it was of no surprise to anyone but Taylor that England's midfield was consistently overrun, with Rocastle ineffective on the flank. One goal down at half-time, it looked like England could be crashing out, until Rocastle finally made a vital impact on the game. Swinging in a corner, Gary Mabbutt headed it on for Gary Lineker to acrobatically volley home. The 1-1 draw was enough for England to qualify for Euro '92 in Sweden, but again the manner of the performance and the manager's selections were ripe for criticism.

Nevertheless, England had reached a major tournament, and, with Rocastle playing regularly for Arsenal, there was still every chance he could make up for his Italia '90 disappointment. Expected to start the subsequent friendly match with France, he twisted his ankle in training and had to withdraw from the squad.

While he started the 2-2 draw with Czechoslovakia in Prague, he was, to the amazement of many, selected in the unfamiliar position of right back, the first time he had ever played there. For some reason, Taylor seemed incapable of giving him an opportunity in a central position and, unsurprisingly, he was nowhere near his best.

When asked about his favourite position for the national team, Rocastle was diplomatic but his preferred choice was clear. 'It doesn't bother me,' he said. 'As long as I'm in the team! However, I think I'm more involved in the centre, whereas on the flanks you rely more on other players to bring you into the game.'

Competition for places was hotting up, and with the tournament just two months away, Rocastle was becoming increasingly anxious to avoid the let-down of two years previously. 'I've been through all that, so I'm really keyed up to make sure I go to the European Championship,' he said. 'I desperately want to be there in Sweden in June. After 1990 I'll never take anything for granted in football again. The memory still haunts me.' But with chances to make an impression running out, Rocastle had to ensure that he delivered if given an opportunity.

That opportunity came in May when he was called up to face Hungary for what was essentially a final audition. Once again, things didn't go entirely to plan. A bad bout of gastroenteritis meant he had to withdraw. As he was already an outside bet to make the squad, members of the press were now all but writing him off. His form was good. His reliability was not.

Rocastle's final chance to gate-crash the party came on 17 May

1992, in a glamour game against Brazil. Apart from Gary Lineker spurning the chance to equal Sir Bobby Charlton's England goalscoring record, the 1-1 draw was largely forgettable. Late in the second half, Rocastle made an appearance, but he once again found himself stuck out on the right wing. His once unshakeable assurance when one on one with a fullback had apparently deserted him. Preferring to pass the ball rather than explode to the by-line, he was a benign presence.

It therefore came as no great surprise when Rocastle found himself left out of England's Euro '92 squad. What might have astonished many, however, was that, at just 25 years of age, he had played his last game for England. During an injury-disrupted period, he had won 14 caps and had never been on the losing side. There is no doubt that he never really showed his true talent over a consistent period on the international stage, but he had still played a key role in helping his country to qualify for two major tournaments. Sadly, he played in neither. And while his England career was set to end, so was his time at Highbury.

CHAPTER 14

'STROLLER'

Ironically, one of the perceived greatest disciplinarians in Arsenal's history had been nicknamed 'Stroller' in his time as a player at Highbury. Between 1966 and 1972, George Graham had graced the club 308 times, and was never seen as a player with a bent for hard work, discipline or bone-crunching tackles. Rather, with his debonair good looks and love of the high life, he was renowned as a graceful goalscorer, as well as someone who could unlock a defence with his eye for a pass, all done without breaking sweat.

Graham's time as a player was certainly remembered fondly by the Highbury faithful. Not only had he helped Arsenal claim the Inter-Cities Fairs Cup in 1970, but he had also been an integral part of Bertie Mee's double-winning side of 1971. His performance at Wembley in their historic 2-1 FA Cup final victory over Liverpool had even seen him named man of the match. Some believe that he might even have had a claim to scoring Arsenal's equaliser in the game, although Eddie Kelly was officially credited with the goal.

In any event, following his successful spell at Highbury, Graham moved to Manchester United in 1972, and from there he went on to play for Portsmouth, Crystal Palace and California Surf with mixed success. Highbury was where his heart had always remained, as evidenced by the fact that, at his home in Hampstead, he boasted an extensive collection of Arsenal memorabilia.

After retiring in 1978, a career in management certainly didn't look likely for a man better known for his Frank Sinatra impressions in London piano bars than for his desire to become a coach. To the surprise of many, he returned to his old club Crystal Palace to assist his former Chelsea team-mate, and then Palace manager, Terry Venables. The two were an instant success. Leading Palace to the first division, their potential was such that Palace were christened the 'Team of the Eighties'. In 1980, Graham followed Venables to Queens Park Rangers, where more success followed, before Graham eventually decided to go it alone, being appointed Millwall manager in December 1982.

At the time Millwall were bottom of the third division, with dwindling crowds and little money. On the face of it, Graham's playing style and high living would seem to render him totally unsuitable for a career as a manager, let alone one in the basement of the rough-and-ready third tier. Frankly admitting in his autobiography, 'I'd never have picked myself for one of my teams,' Graham immediately installed structure and discipline in the Millwall squad, and saved them from relegation.

Building on this team ethic, he subsequently led the club to promotion the following season. And after a steady season in the second division, he looked set to mount yet another promotion challenge before Arsenal came calling.

To most seasoned pundits, it was clear that Graham was on the verge of creating something special at Millwall, particularly with a young, improving Teddy Sheringham leading the line. However, for an Arsenal fanatic, the lure of a return to Highbury was too tempting, even if the club had drifted far from its double-winning heyday of the early 1970s.

While he had already enjoyed some success, not everyone cheered his arrival. 'Our new manager, George Graham, was a mystery to me,' Paul Merson admitted in his autobiography. 'I didn't know him from Adam.' Indeed, while the vast majority of Arsenal fans were great admirers of Graham from his playing days, his appointment was certainly not thought of as heralding a new era.

With the culture of the club seemingly based around signing, or at least trying to sign, superstars such as Charlie Nicholas, it was hoped that a big-name manager would be brought in. The pragmatic Graham was far from that. But it was clear to some that the superstar experiment had been a bitter failure. Not only had it not resulted in any silverware, but the style of football had also kept the fans away. Moreover, it had resulted in a damaging divide in the squad, disrupting team harmony in the process.

Therefore, while Graham was not a universally popular choice, the decision to hire him proved to be an inspired one. Adept at working on a small budget, and imposing discipline and structure, he was the perfect man to reinvigorate the club.

When the players reported back to Trent Park for pre-season, Graham immediately set out his intentions. 'The boss got us all together,' David O'Leary revealed in his autobiography. 'Without holding a gun to anyone's head, he laid down the law. He said he would treat us like men, but discipline would be tight. He didn't expect us to behave like saints ... but he made it clear he was concerned about some of the bad publicity the club had been getting off the field. There was no room for any doubt on that score ... things had to change.' And change they would.

The first item on the agenda was instilling team spirit. Image was a big part of this, and so he banned the likes of Charlie Nicholas and Graham Rix from wearing earrings. He also demanded that players wear club blazer, tie and trousers to all matches, declaring, 'The casual days are over' and 'I've never liked players to look slovenly'. This even applied to players tucking in their shirts when playing, always wearing shin pads and not gaining any unnecessary weight.

However, living up to the Arsenal image did have some benefits. All the tables on the team coach were suddenly laid out with place mats and cutlery, while waiters in black trousers and white coats would serve a post-match meal, which could be salmon and melon to start, followed by chicken, fish or pasta for the main course, a crumble and custard for dessert, and then, finally, a cheeseboard. It was a far cry from a greasy bag of fish and chips wrapped in old newspaper.

Being late to training was frowned upon, with players fined £10 each time they were so much as a minute overdue. However, Graham did have some sympathy. He allowed each player to be late once a month, before the fines would kick in.

The drinking days were also apparently over. Summoning Charlie Nicholas into his office, Graham made sure that his star player was aware of the new guidelines. 'You're a super player,' Graham told him, 'but if you continue to live a faster life off the pitch than on it, I shall come down on you like a ton of bricks.' As a result, all players were banned from drinking two nights before a game, while the gambling culture at the club was similarly put to a stop, with Graham banning card games on the coach.

Those who didn't fall into line with the new regime were swiftly told they could go. Paul Mariner was subsequently given a free transfer, while Tony Woodcock was allowed to return to Germany.

'When I first arrived at the club,' Graham later said, 'I had a look at the staff and decided there were a lot of prima donnas who'd probably seen their best days, so it was time to get the broom out and start sweeping a few out of the door and give the youngsters a chance.'

Thankfully, there was an abundance of youngsters at Arsenal who were willing and waiting for Graham to put his faith in them. One of those was, of course, David Rocastle. However, he was still recovering from knee surgery and was also out of contract. When he reported back for pre-season, his cause wasn't helped when he weighed in a stone too heavy.

'Before that summer he had always been quite skinny,' Gus Caesar told me. 'But after his operation I remember he came back for pre-season and he had turned into another person. It was like a total metamorphosis. I'm not sure if it was a case of overeating, or lifestyle, because I never saw him overindulging, and he wasn't a big drinker, but he had really bulked up. His thighs were huge. That's when we first really started to call him "Rocky".'

His weight gain was understandable yet still not ideal, especially as Graham wasted little time in assessing his squad and deliberating over who deserved a new contract.

While Rocastle fretted about the situation, he was not to know that Graham was just as concerned about getting him to sign. 'Howard Wilkinson, then in charge at Sheffield Wednesday, telephoned in my first week to casually enquire about David Rocastle,' Graham revealed in his autobiography. 'This set the alarm bells ringing in my mind because I knew Howard had been impressed by Rocastle when he was handling the England Under-21 team. David was on holiday in the Caribbean, and I ordered that he had to be met at the airport on his return and brought straight to my office at Highbury. If necessary I was prepared to lock the door so that he could not leave without signing a new contract. As it turned out, I found him the easiest person in the world to deal with and he willingly signed himself to Arsenal, and he became one of my favourite people.'

Just like Graham, Rocastle was an Arsenal fan. He wasn't concerned with using Wilkinson's interest to drive a hard bargain. All he was worried about was signing the contract and playing for his club.

Not everyone found Graham's contract talks quite so agreeable. When Martin Keown asked for a mere £50 a week increase he was turned down. Soon after, he was shown the door and sold to Aston Villa for just £200,000, although six years later Graham would re-sign him for £2m. Even the likes of David O'Leary, who had given the club 11 years of sterling service, weren't given a pay rise. It seems that Niall Quinn was one of the few who managed to get any sort of increase out of Graham – just £7 a week!

With contracts finalised, Graham scoured the transfer market for new additions to bolster his squad. Anticipating a star signing, Perry Groves' £50,000 transfer from Colchester United was one that underwhelmed many fans. But Groves was young, talented and hungry, not to mention cheap. As such, he was the archetypal Graham purchase.

'When I signed Arsenal were historically a big football club who hadn't won a trophy for eight seasons,' Groves told me. 'There were a lot of excellent players there already but the team structure wasn't right. I think George had looked at the personnel and he thought it might need some more desire and intensity in the team. You can coach people. You can make people have that touch. You can edu-cate people more on where to run, when to run. But one thing you couldn't put into a player is desire and heart and that's what he looked for.'

Groves had come from Colchester, where he had been a big fish in a small pond. At Arsenal he was suddenly surrounded by renowned international players and star names, one of whom was David Rocastle, who Graham had earmarked for a right midfield role, the same position as Groves.

'I had my first training session at taking corners with David Rocastle,' Groves remembered. 'I didn't really know him but he couldn't have been more welcoming. Obviously, he didn't know who I was but he found out that I was a right-winger and that I was obviously coming in to try and take his place. But he was such a nice kid. I can remember trying to get on his good side. He took a few corners, and he duffed a few by the near post, and I was trying to be like his best friend, saying, "Great ball, Rocky!"'

The difference between Graham's training regime and Howe's was also soon made clear. 'With Don, pre-season was a time when you'd be puking up,' Gus Caesar winced. 'He'd run you so hard you'd go home and you'd be knackered. You couldn't do anything. It was very different with George. I remember his first day; we were at Trent Park and after 45 minutes of light stretching and jogging he told us we could go home. We couldn't believe it. The following day we did the same but he threw in some hill runs. Every day it went up in intensity but his philosophy was that he didn't want to burn us out. We never really did any long-distance running. Everything was short and sharp, just like in a game. It was great for Rocky as he was such a skilful player it meant his legs weren't heavy by the end of the summer. In the afternoons we would concentrate on technical play, so even that was quite static. I think most of us felt the fittest we had ever been after George's first preseason, yet it almost felt as if we hadn't really done much.'

While physical fitness was a necessity, Graham's primary focus was on the team structure. 'I wanted a team that could pull back,' he revealed in his autobiography, 'and then rifle forward on the counterattack.'

To be able to pull back, Graham concentrated on building his defence, which when he arrived consisted of Viv Anderson, Tony Adams, David O'Leary and Kenny Sansom, a foursome O'Leary later declared was 'as good as any defensive unit I have played in'. Graham certainly had the raw materials to work with, but now he had to take all that talent and harness it as one.

'I would sometimes use a pitch-width rope,' Graham revealed, 'that the players would hold on to as they tugged and pulled each other while they disciplined themselves to staying in their zone. Then I would release one of the fullbacks, and the remaining three players had to stay attached to the rope and take on responsibility for covering a wider zone with lateral movement.'

One of the great images of Graham's Arsenal team was the sight of the back four moving up in unison, as the opposition played the ball beyond them, with one of the centre backs holding his arm aloft, claiming offside.

Defending and attacking set pieces was also an obsession. 'We always used to work on set pieces, free-kicks and corners,' future signing Brian Marwood told me. 'I can't remember the number of corners I took where Bouldy flicked it on and there was Tony Adams diving in to get on the end of it.'

As for Rocastle's responsibilities, Perry Groves told me what Graham expected from his right-wingers: 'First and foremost the job was to protect the fullback. That's why Lee Dixon and Nigel Winterburn probably played over 600 games. The back four quite rightly got a lot of credit but we gave them a lot of protection. It was our job to ensure the opposition's wide player didn't get a kick. When we had the ball, the gaffer wanted us to give the team width. When you took the fullback on, nine times out of 10 he'd want you to go on the outside to get your crosses in because it turned their back four to face their own goal. He hated it if you came inside. Nowadays managers want their wingers coming inside, and playing little one-twos, but under George, if you kept going inside he would take you off! We always played 4-4-2 as well, so when the winger on the other side got a cross in it was your job to get on the back post and be the third striker in the box. Without the ball there was a lot of shuffling across; you had to tuck in and be no more than 10 metres away from the central midfield player on your side.'

Rather than shrink from this new training regime, Rocastle loved it. 'It was as if it was a cup final for him every day,' Groves smiled. 'He was just as intense, and showed the same dedication as he showed on a Saturday.'

Brian Marwood also recalled Rocastle's love for the game, and for life. 'He was a special character,' he said. 'Always full of energy. Always the first to training. You'd hear his laugh before you'd see him. Then you'd see his big smile. He lit up any room or training session. He just loved his football.'

Yet Graham certainly didn't take it easy on Rocastle. 'He was always on at Rocky,' Groves remembered. 'He would say, "David, you're keeping hold of the ball for too long." George just wanted to make him as good a player as he possibly could. He knew he was tough. He knew he could tackle. He knew he could run. He knew his desire. He knew he could score some more goals. He wanted to be damn proud of him but he wanted him to play in the right areas, not dribble in defensive areas, and not to dribble when we were under pressure. He would get it in his head that he wanted to play one- or two-touch. The gaffer would be like, "David, pass the ball. Pass the ball, David!" And Rocky would be like, "Fuck off. Leave me alone."'

For his first pre-season Graham took his squad to Portugal, Scotland and Ireland. During their time in Scotland Groves recalls a particularly embarrassing incident, one that also emphasised Rocastle's likeable and forgiving nature: 'It was pre-season and we were up in a place called Largs. Rocky was obviously the first choice right-winger but he'd played in a pre-season game and he didn't have a particularly good game. It sounds terrible, but I was quite pleased, because he was playing in my position. That's just the ruthlessness of being a professional. Anyway, I played the next game and I think I scored. Back at our training base, everyone had to use the payphone to call home, because, remember, there were no mobile phones back then. I was talking to my old man, and I was telling him about Rocky's performance, and about how well I had played in comparison. Anyway, I put the phone down and to my horror Rocky was standing behind me. He'd heard everything I said! It was a total nightmare. I turned around and I just went, "Oh, shit." And he said, "You weren't that fucking good today either," and then he walked off. When I walked in to our evening meal I was a little apprehensive, when suddenly he shouted, "Oh, there he is. There's Buzby." Buzby was a big thing on British Telecom adverts at the time. All the lads cracked up. He could have been difficult but he was good as gold.'

Graham's squad was assembled, drilled and ready to make their mark on the 1986/87 season. And it would prove to be one that would see David Rocastle become a Highbury legend.

CHAPTER 15

A WHOLE NEW BALL GAME

In the summer of 1992, thousands of people seemed to be placing Chinese woks on the front of their houses. To many, these huge white dishes were an eyesore, but to the average football fan they were a pass to an exciting new world. The 1992/93 season heralded the inaugural season of the Premier League, and along with it Sky TV, which would be broadcasting what they proclaimed in their adverts as 'a whole new ball game'. No more was football the province of free-to-air TV and the working man. It was now big business.

Football during the 1980s had hit rock bottom. With dwindling crowds and crumbling infrastructure, a series of hooligan-related incidents, and disasters such as Hillsborough, had led many to believe that the status quo needed urgent reassessment. Lord Justice Taylor's subsequent report had scoured the wasteland of English football for a solution. At the top of his list was the edict that all first division clubs must invest in all-seater stadiums.

However, this required a significant financial outlay, beyond the means of most clubs. In the terms of the pre-existing TV deal with ITV, signed in 1988, its £44m was shared equally between all clubs in the Football League. To add insult to injury, it was doled out over a four-year period. This therefore left the clubs with as little as half a million pounds each. Arsenal's total turnover at this time was just £1.5m a year, which meant that paying for stadium upgrades, as well as attracting top players to the club, would be very difficult.

As English football died a slow, bloody death, Arsenal director David Dein instantly grasped what needed to be done. On 16 November 1990, he attended a dinner in London with other representatives of the so-called 'Big Five' – Noel White of Liverpool, Sir Philip Carter of Everton, Martin Edwards of Manchester United and Irving Scholar of Tottenham Hotspur, as well as Greg Dyke, then a senior executive at ITV. The main topic of discussion was their frustration at having to share the TV revenue with those outside the first division, with Mansfield Town receiving as much as Manchester United, as well as their belief that the Football League had not been getting sufficient value for the broadcast rights in the first place. As the talks progressed, the notion of breaking away from the Football League started to formulate.

Yet it took almost two years of frantic negotiations for such an idea to become a reality. Dein and White first had to persuade the FA's Graham Kelly to support the proposal, following which the Big Five then had to coax the rest of the first division to go along with them. Unsurprisingly, this gave rise to a number of issues. Of most concern was the Big Five's plan for this new league to consist of 18 teams, rather than the existing 22. Indeed, even when all of the clubs were finally on board it took a High Court ruling in the summer of 1991 to decree that the FA could indeed oversee a breakaway from the Football League.

So, with the new league scheduled to commence for the 1992/93 season, the rights to the FA Carling Premiership were made available for television companies to bid for. While the usual suspects, such as the BBC and ITV, showed considerable interest, there was a new player in town, one that realised how live football was essential to its then failing business model.

BSkyB, owned by Australian media tycoon Rupert Murdoch, had struggled in its first few years to pick up subscribers. With Murdoch describing live sport as a 'battering ram' for pay television, conditions were ripe for change. Murdoch needed a competitive advantage over terrestrial TV that would attract subscribers, and the fledgling Premier League desperately required someone to give it a much-needed cash injection. A perfect match, Murdoch stunned the football world when he paid £305m for live rights to the Premier League over a five-year period. To truly appreciate the scale of this monumental deal, just seven years previously consultants had valued first division television rights at just £12m.

Live football had been a luxury for most football fans up until this point, with coverage limited to just a handful of games a season. With Sky now calling the shots, there would be at least two live games a week, on a Sunday afternoon as well as the new *Monday Night Football*. To most football fans this was sheer nirvana, as coverage also changed beyond all recognition.

Not only was there a glitzy Americanised studio, where presenters such as Richard Keys and Andy Gray could analyse the games in never-before-seen detail, but there were also fireworks and cheerleaders, as well as half-time entertainment, all accompanied by a booming voiceover and garish graphics. I can remember the sheer excitement at watching Richard Keys, resplendent in his trademark canary yellow jacket, introducing the half-time act of The Shamen, who performed their number one hit, 'Ebeneezer Goode', on the pitch. This was certainly not to everyone's taste, but to millions of youngsters getting into the game for the first time it was as if the glamour of the American Super Bowl had invaded and blown away the crumbling grey of the eighties.

Some of it worked. Some of it didn't. But the influx of money and publicity certainly gave the game a sorely needed boost, and would set the Premiership on its way to becoming one of the most successful sports leagues in the world, watched in over 200 countries and with TV rights worth over £5 billion by 2015.

Gearing himself up for the fledgling Premier League, David Rocastle returned to London Colney desperate once again to prove a point. The previous season he had delivered some of the best displays of his career, yet this had still not been enough to see him force his way into Graham Taylor's squad for the 1992 European Championship. While he was shattered to miss out, England hadn't made it out of the group stages, and returned home in disgrace.

Keen to prove Taylor wrong, Rocastle also looked forward to mounting a title challenge with his old friend Ian Wright alongside him. After all, Arsenal had finished the previous season so strongly that many pundits certainly thought the title was a realistic ambition.

As always, there was the usual transfer talk, insinuating that a number of clubs were interested in Rocastle. Not only was he uninterested in moving, he also thought Arsenal would have no intention of selling him. By this stage he was a double title winner, and England international, who at 25 years of age had just played 47 games the previous season.

However, when Rocastle arrived for training on the morning of 22 July 1992 he was surprised to find George Graham waiting for him in the car park. 'David, can I have a word?' his manager asked, ushering him towards his gold BMW 7 series. Climbing into the passenger seat, Rocastle had no idea that the conversation that was about to follow would prove to be one of the most traumatic of his life.

Watching his team-mates jog out to the training pitches, some of whom were looking on curiously at the scene in the manager's car, Rocastle was stunned when Graham said, 'David, the board has accepted a bid for you from Leeds United. Howard Wilkinson is waiting to speak to you.'

The words must have felt like a sledgehammer to someone who was an avid Arsenal fan. He had never shown the slightest inclination to play elsewhere, not even when clubs from France and Italy were circling with big-money offers. As far as Rocastle was concerned, he would happily see out his whole career at Arsenal, and go on to win numerous trophies alongside his friends. Now, in an instant, it all seemed to be over.

Respectful of the decision, but rocked all the same, Rocastle replied in a faltering voice, 'Okay, boss. I don't want to leave Arsenal, you know that. But if I'm no longer wanted here I suppose Leeds is as good a place as any to go.'

Graham later said that this conversation was among the most difficult of his career. 'I was so full up with emotion that I could not say what I wanted to say: that he was one of the nicest people I have ever come across in the game, and that he had always been a wonderful advertisement for Arsenal Football Club and for football in general. He had been a class act.'

'I cried,' Rocastle later confessed. 'It was like leaving one big happy family. I had been around Highbury for nearly 13 years and I knew everyone from the tea lady to the chairman. It was an extremely emotional moment when George Graham told me he had agreed a deal with Leeds United. We sat and talked in his car – the first time I'd ever done that – and he said that Howard Wilkinson wanted me. I could see a few Arsenal lads walking by and, when it hit me that I wouldn't even have time to say goodbye, I shed a few tears.'

The move didn't just cause distress in his professional life, it affected his personal life as well. He now had two young children, Melissa and Ryan, with Janet. Moving up north, away from their family and friends, at such a time was a decision not to be taken lightly.

While Rocastle pondered all of this, a frenzy ensued in the press. No one could quite believe that Arsenal, who had been hoping to challenge for the title, would be willing to sell one of their star players to the current league champions. However, in an interview with the *People*, Tony Adams agreed with Graham's stance on selling both Rocastle and Michael Thomas. 'I do think George Graham was right to sell Michael Thomas and David Rocastle,' he said. 'They were not as sharp and as hungry as they'd once been. You never saw any more of those great runs when David would dip his shoulder and go past a player.'

When I asked Perry Groves about this he disagreed. 'I don't think he lost his hunger,' he said. 'He wasn't as fit because his knee injury wouldn't let him train to the required intensity. I don't think he had that physical capability in him any more.'

Rocastle's knee had certainly given him plenty of cause for concern in recent years. Forcing him to miss large chunks of previous seasons, it had also clearly had a debilitating effect on his dynamism. In later years, Graham gave an interview on talkSPORT in which he confirmed that this was why he felt it was time to move him on: 'It was really because of the problem he had with his knee. He had difficulty [in training]. He would put on weight. If he put on weight he couldn't do the power work we were doing at the time. It was a chicken and egg situation. He had to train hard but his knee blew up. And if you didn't train him hard then he put on a lot of weight.'

In hindsight, Rocastle's agent Jerome Anderson agrees that the knee had become a problem. 'I think he lost something,' he told me. 'If you get any small hindrance at the level these boys are playing at it can show. Because of the knee issue he lost a little bit of pace.'

To many observers, it had seemed that his knee was no longer really an issue, as evidenced by the 47 games he'd played the previous season, games in which he'd earned high praise for his performances. However, Graham had clearly seen that the knee was deteriorating and the opportunity to sell him for £2m was too good to turn down.

The move was so sudden that even Jerome Anderson was taken aback. 'I remember receiving a call from Rocky,' Anderson told me. 'He was very emotional because it had come as a shock. He was Arsenal through and through. I was very surprised but I had known that Howard Wilkinson had liked him as a player for a long time, and at the time Leeds United were the champions, so I decided to focus on that. I told David it could be a wonderful opportunity. He was extremely disappointed to leave his spiritual home but to go to the league champions at that particular time, and be their record signing, was something he was very proud of.'

At the time, Wilkinson had actually been in the process of trying to sign England international Trevor Steven from Marseille, but as soon as he had heard Rocastle might be available he called it off. 'I decided to go for David before I lost him,' Wilkinson told the *Sunday Mirror*. 'I have been chasing him [Rocastle] since May. His pedigree, his two championship medals and his England caps speak volumes for his quality.'

Once Graham had him given permission to speak to Wilkinson, Rocastle flew to Dublin, where Leeds were on a pre-season tour. Over drinks, Wilkinson outlined that he saw Rocastle as the natural replacement for his midfield linchpin, Gordon Strachan. At 35, Strachan was not only in the twilight of his career but he had also undergone an operation on his back. As such, he was likely to be out for a period of time and there was even the prospect that he might not return at all. 'Gordon went on forever,' Wilkinson told me, 'but at that point you couldn't be sure for how much longer. We were honest with each other about that.'

Wilkinson's close relationship with his captain meant that they had even discussed his potential replacement, with Strachan fully endorsing the choice of Rocastle. 'We talked about it,' Wilkinson confirmed. 'Gordon was more than just a player. He was a very good captain and you could talk to him as if he was a member of staff. You knew that whatever you were saying would be between you and him.'

Strachan's time in the team appeared to be coming to an end but the Leeds United midfield was still formidable. Containing the likes of Gary Speed, Gary McAllister, David Batty, Steve Hodge, Rod Wallace, new signing Scott Sellars and up-and-coming young-ster Mark Tinkler, it was the envy of the first division. However, with European Cup football to look forward to, and a gruelling title defence, Wilkinson feared it might still not be enough. 'I was trying to build on what was a good team but not necessarily a good squad,' he told me. 'I realised that if we were to maintain our momentum, we needed more quality players to add to the excellent group that we had. Obviously David was a quality player.'

Although Rocastle was set to join the champions as their record signing, Wilkinson stressed that he would be one of the first man-agers to really implement squad rotation. 'That was made very clear,' he told me. 'You could see that that was on the horizon. The demand became so great and we knew we had a lot of hard games to come.'

Wilkinson might have been an admirer of Rocastle, but there still remained the problem with his knee. Graham had been honest with Wilkinson about this, as he privately doubted whether the player could even pass a medical.

The Leeds United physio at the time was Alan Sutton. When I

spoke to Sutton, he told me that the results of Rocastle's medical did raise a few eyebrows. 'I remember that the cartilage operation did leave damage to his knee,' he said. 'He had a permanent swelling on it. There was a lot of arthritis. Looking back, we possibly should not have signed him. Even the surgeon queried it. He asked if we knew about the knee and we said we did. I think Arsenal were surprised we signed him. Anyway, we did, and believe it or not the knee was never really an issue in his time at Leeds.'

Having passed his medical, on 24 July 1992 David Rocastle tearfully severed his ties with Arsenal Football Club and officially joined Leeds United. 'The idea of leaving, having grown up at Highbury, hit me hard, very hard,' he told the press. 'But then when I realised it was the champions of England who wanted me, it suddenly all got a lot easier. Then, when I joined up with the Leeds lads in Dublin where they were playing a friendly, I realised that this was a big and homely family too. And I realised that a similar spirit and camaraderie exists at Elland Road. I got that family feeling all over again – and that's important to me. This is one truly great club. I've signed a four-year contract and I couldn't be happier. I realise I'll be playing in Europe with the champions.'

Even with such a prospect on the horizon, Rocastle was keen to emphasise that he still needed to prove himself. 'The first thing I want to do is get in the team,' he said, 'as just because I've come down here on a big fee doesn't mean I'm going to walk into the team. I'm going to knuckle down, get down to work, and prove to the boss I'm worthy of a place.'

Just two days later, he made his Leeds debut against Stuttgart in the Makita tournament, which had moved up north following Leeds' championship success. While this was a pre-season friendly, Stuttgart would also be Leeds' first opponents in the European Cup. The match therefore represented an opportunity for the

Elland Road faithful to observe their future opponents, as well as see their record signing in action.

The fans would no doubt have been pleased with what they saw. Leeds won the game 2-1, with Rocastle scoring the winner and also being named man of the match. However, there were warning signs of what was to come, when Wilkinson brought him off early. 'Compared to a few of our lads I thought David was flagging in the last 20 minutes and that is why I brought him off,' Wilkinson explained. 'I thought he did very well and he scored a very good goal, but he started training with Arsenal four or five days later than us and, what with the transfer, he hasn't had much time to prepare.'

Happy to support Wilkinson, it was also clear in Rocastle's post-match comments that he would have liked to stay on. 'No player ever wants to be taken off,' he said. 'But for the sake of the result and keeping the shape of the team I thought it was the right decision. It was great to score a goal and get the team through to the final. I know now I have to get my head down and work to earn a regular place.'

A few days later Rocastle would again be substituted, this time at half-time, as Leeds lost to Sampdoria in the Makita final. In the great scheme of things, his being replaced was not yet something to be overly worried about. Of greater concern at this point was Gordon Strachan's announcement that he was miraculously on course to be fit for the start of the season. Competition for places was already fierce enough, with Wilkinson having added Rocastle and Scott Sellars to the championship-winning midfield over the summer.

In his autobiography, *More Than a Match*, Leeds striker Lee Chapman questioned the wisdom of Wilkinson signing both players: 'While both were recognised as talented players, the Leeds players themselves wondered about the manager's intentions. The club now boasted seven international midfield players, at least three of whom would have to sit out each game. Who would be left out and would anyone be leaving the club? The speculation mounted.'

Such speculation was answered before the Charity Shield game against Liverpool. Picking a midfield four of Speed, Batty, McAllister and Wallace, Wilkinson left Rocastle, Hodge and Strachan on the bench, while Sellars sat in the stands. Despite being expected to play, as the club's record signing, Rocastle nevertheless backed up his manager. 'I have not completed a full game yet,' he said, 'but my fitness is coming along. I know I will have to work hard to earn my place and Gordon's availability won't make things any easier.'

Indeed, while Leeds won the game 4-3 thanks to a brilliant hat-trick by enigmatic Frenchman Eric Cantona, Rocastle watched it all from the bench. It was no doubt disappointing not to get a run-out at Wembley but he was aware that the real business would begin the following weekend, when Leeds commenced their title defence at home to Wimbledon.

Most respected figures in the game had predicted that Leeds would retain the title, particularly with their reinforcements. 'Leeds are the champions,' Alex Ferguson said on the eve of the season, 'and they will be in there fighting for the title again ... And they have added quality with David Rocastle. If we finish above them we won't be doing so badly!'

Rocastle was also in bullish mood. 'We can rule for another five years,' he predicted. 'A lot of people make out that you're there to be shot at as champions and that everything suddenly becomes so much harder. But I don't go along with that. If you play for Leeds or Arsenal you are a big scalp for most teams whether you've just won the league or not. The lads here were up at the top all last season and handled the pressure brilliantly. When you look at what the squad achieved last season, the way it has been improved during the summer and the number of young players still developing, you've got to fancy us to challenge for all the top honours for years. You won't win the title with 12 or 13 top-class players. You need about 18, and that's the strength in depth the boss has created here.'

However, as the new Premier League season kicked off on 15 August 1992 most were shocked to find that David Rocastle wasn't even named in the Leeds squad. Even more perplexing was that Wilkinson confirmed that his record signing wasn't injured. 'I just picked what I thought was the best team for today,' Wilkinson told the press after the 2-1 win. 'I am sure David will be disappointed, but so will Steve Hodge and Gordon Strachan to have only been substitutes. Players will have to get used to disappointments like that.'

And get used to it he would, as in the following game against Villa Rocastle again found himself out in the cold. 'I was under no illusions I would walk into the team here,' he told the *Daily Mirror*. 'I knew the position when I arrived. It's all about having quality players and a big squad. That's what I'm part of here.'

With David Batty struggling with a calf injury, Rocastle might have hoped that this would at least give him an opportunity to be in the squad for the trip to Middlesbrough. Not only did Rocastle miss out once more, but Leeds slumped to an emphatic 4-1 defeat.

While Leeds' form would improve, with a 5-0 win against Spurs in the following game, Rocastle was still unable to find himself as much as a seat on the bench. Despite this, he finally earned his first start in the European Cup, away to Stuttgart, with Wilkinson believing that his composure on the ball was more suited to the European game.

Lining up on the right side of midfield, Rocastle was back to the position in which he had enjoyed so much success with Arsenal, albeit a slower, less mobile version. All the same, he enjoyed plenty of the ball and was often Leeds' most creative attacking outlet, with his rapier runs forward offering respite for his defenders.

Goalless at half-time, Rocastle had every right to feel as though he had proved a point. Indeed, the *Sunday Mirror* said in its match report that he had 'acquitted himself superbly despite his glaring lack of match practice'.

As a result, when Wilkinson chose to make a substitution in the 46th minute, Rocastle might have been perplexed to see his number held up. Clapping the Leeds fans, who heartily sang his name, Rocastle high-fived his replacement Steve Hodge and sat on the bench, where his team-mates patted him on the back for a job well done.

It seemed that Wilkinson had opted for caution. Rocastle's attack-minded runs had caused Stuttgart problems but his opposite number, Thomas Strunz, had also been a constant menace. Earmarking Hodge's more defensive nature as the key to stifling Strunz, Wilkinson could only look on in disgust as the German brilliantly set up Ludwig Kögl for the first goal, with Stuttgart going on to win the game 3-0.

'This is an absolutely crazy result,' a confused Wilkinson told the press after the game. 'From looking as though we were going to win it at half-time, we let the convicted men out of jail. And we all know what happens when you let them escape like that.'

With his substitution against Stuttgart having backfired, Rocastle might have felt he would return to the starting line-up in the following league game, against Southampton. Unbelievably, he didn't even make the squad. It wasn't until 3 October that he would actually make his first league appearance for a stuttering Leeds side, when he came off the bench in a 4-2 away defeat to Ipswich.

If Leeds had been playing well then Rocastle's absence might have been understandable, but their form had been indifferent. Failing to pick up a single away win, they had also lost 2-0 to title rivals Manchester United.

Although Rocastle had earned much praise for his first-half performance against Stuttgart, he didn't feature in the return leg, which Leeds won 4-1, their best display of the season. However, it still wasn't enough to progress, as they crashed out on the away-goals rule. But there was to be a dramatic reprieve. Charged with fielding an ineligible player, Stuttgart were ordered to contest a replay at the neutral Nou Camp. In front of a half-empty stadium, super-sub Carl Shutt memorably scored the winner to set Leeds up with a battle of Britain clash against Glasgow Rangers. All the while, Rocastle continued to be missing from the action.

In such circumstances, Rocastle's absence became all the more curious. Unsubstantiated rumours started to swirl around the football world, with some even suggesting that Wilkinson and Rocastle had squared up to each other on the training ground.

In an attempt to show solidarity, the pair held a joint TV interview alongside the Elland Road pitch. 'There seems to be this assertion that David and I have fallen out, and have thrown fists at each other, as a result of which I don't pick him,' Wilkinson said. 'The facts are that during the summer Gordon looked very, very unlikely to be ready for the start of the season. It looked very unlikely he might play again at the top level, so I went out and tried to get the best around, and David is the best around. Fortunately for me, and the fans, but not for David, the wee man is back playing the best he's played for five or six years. So I don't know what people want me to do. Play 12 players? I don't think me leaving David out has warranted some of the insinuations and innuendos reported in the press at the moment.'

As the interviewer turned to Rocastle and referenced the fact that his manager was beside him, Wilkinson laughed and jokingly made an aggressive move towards him, clearly showing that there had been no breakdown in their relationship.

'It's the way the gaffer is with all the players,' Rocastle explained.

'It's more like a father and son relationship. If you've got a problem you can obviously go and see him. Y'know, I'm laughing at the moment because I can't believe the fuss that is being made. At the start of the season I was under no illusions that I was going to be walking straight into a championship-winning side. I knew I was bought for the future. I think people are maybe thinking I'm 32, 33, coming to the end of my career, but I'm not. I'm 25. I've got time on my side and the club has invested money in me to produce over the next four or five years.'

When the interviewer then asked if Rocastle had knocked on Wilkinson's door to demand an explanation, he smiled and shook his head. 'No,' he replied. 'I've never done that. Maybe I will in 1995 if I'm still in the reserves.'

To all intents and purposes the matter seemed to be dealt with. Yet closer examination of Rocastle in the interview might have revealed that all was not well. While there was a smile permanently etched across his face, as it always seemed to be, his eyes told a different story. Puffy, with dark circles encompassing them, they told of a man who had been having sleepless nights. Although Rocastle had said that Wilkinson's door was always open, this was not something he could go to him with, particularly after just joining the club. It was a secret that hardly anyone was aware of, not even his own family, and it was eating him up.

CHAPTER 16

CENTENARY

Arsenal has certainly had a few explosive moments in its history, which is perhaps no surprise when you learn of the origins of the club. In the 1800s the Royal Arsenal, based in Woolwich, had carried out armaments manufacture, ammunition proofing and explosives research for the British armed forces, as well as supplied arms for the battle of Waterloo and the Crimean War. In 1886, with the new football leisure craze sweeping the country, its workers decided to set up a football team, which they called 'Dial Square', after one of their workshops. However, they soon changed the name to 'Royal Arsenal', creating a legend in the process.

Playing their fixtures at the Manor Ground in Plumstead, they happened upon their official club colours by accident. Having moved from Nottingham to Woolwich for work, players Fred Beardsley and Morris Bates wrote to their former club, Nottingham Forest, and asked if they might be able to help the new club out with some equipment. Soon after, they received a box containing old redcurrant shirts and white shorts and socks.

By 1888, the redcurrant shirts had a new addition to them. Inspired by the Metropolitan Borough of Woolwich's coat of arms, which included three cannons, the Royal Arsenal had its first club crest. In time, the adornment of the cannon on the shirt would also lead to the club's nickname, the 'Gunners'.

Subsequently renamed 'Woolwich Arsenal' in 1891, the team went on to become the first southern member of the Football League. However, with dwindling attendances and perilous finances, the club was effectively bankrupt by 1910, until they were saved by businessmen Henry Norris and William Hall.

Unable to prevent the struggling club from being relegated to the second division in 1913, Norris advocated a move across London, to a site in Highbury, and also shortened the club's name to just 'Arsenal'. When competitive football resumed in 1919, following the First World War, Arsenal were elected to rejoin the first division, where they continued to be a middling club of little consequence. But then, in 1925, Herbert Chapman was appointed as manager. The rest, as they say, is history.

Having already won the league twice with Huddersfield Town, Chapman revolutionised the club. Signing Cliff Bastin and the mercurial Alex James, Chapman's Arsenal dominated the 1930s, winning the FA Cup in 1930 followed by two league titles, in 1931 and 1933. Yet this period of dominance threatened to come to a dramatic halt in the wake of Chapman's sudden death from pneumonia in early 1934.

Nevertheless, Joe Shaw and George Allison ably took up the reins. Under their guidance, Arsenal won three more titles, in 1934, 1935 and 1938, as well as the 1936 FA Cup. Such was the team's dominance on, and off, the pitch that Arsenal was soon christened the 'Bank of England club'.

The out break of the Second World War might have stemmed the club's progress but under Allison's successor, Tom Whittaker, things were soon back on track. Winning the league in 1948 and 1953, and the FA Cup in 1950, another period of dominance seemingly beckoned. However, it would be another 17 years before the club again added silverware to its trophy cabinets.

After the surprise appointment of club physiotherapist Bertie Mee as manager in 1966, he led the club to its first European trophy, the Inter-Cities Fairs Cup, in 1970. The following season he improved on this, as the club memorably won the league and cup double. But more disappointing campaigns followed, with only the 1979 FA Cup added before the club celebrated its centenary in 1986.

For such a historic season, the club launched a new kit, aided by a new manufacturer. Since 1965 Arsenal's shirts had been manufactured by Umbro, but the centenary season saw the club move to adidas, whose proposed kit caused some controversy. Not wanting to be seen to be pandering to commercialism, Arsenal had initially refused the addition of adidas' famous three stripes on their shirt sleeves. Thankfully, in the end a compromise was reached.

The red shoulders of the new polyester shirt remained stripe-free, while the white sleeves and white shorts would have the new addition of the three red stripes. Subtle adidas stripes were also incorporated in the red body of the shirt itself, although these were hard to detect and so unlikely to upset the purists.

In any event, the club's concern at not being seen to be overtly commercial was misguided, as in 1981 it had happily accepted £400,000 from electronics giant JVC to have its name plastered across the front of the team's shirts. Still, while there had been opposition on both counts, the adidas shirt, with JVC on it, would in time become one of the most iconic football shirts in English football history.

Following years in the relative wilderness, marked by unattractive football and failed star signings, optimism was not particularly high that the good times at Highbury were just around the corner. However, the fans certainly expected a better start than losing two out of their first three games. Murmurs that former North Bank favourite George Graham might be out of his depth only grew as three goalless draws, against Spurs, Luton and Oxford, were followed by defeat at Forest.

When regulars Rix, Robson and Nicholas succumbed to injury some felt that Graham's small squad could even be facing a relegation battle. As such, there were critics who urged him to buy more players, while others encouraged him to change his rigid style of play.

'By the middle of October he was in a little trouble,' Nick Hornby wrote in *Fever Pitch*. 'There was a nil-nil draw at home to Oxford which was as poor as anything we had seen in the previous six years, and already the people around me were yelling abuse at him, outraged at his perceived parsimony.'

In the face of fierce criticism, Graham remained unmoved. He was steadfast in his belief that champagne and caviar would come after the bread and butter. And so it proved.

With the team winning just three times in its opening nine games, and with injuries crippling the squad, the trip to Goodison Park on 4 October looked to be a daunting one. However, this was truly the day when Graham's tactics fell into place. What's more, they were carried out to the letter by unheralded stars such as Steve Williams, and hungry youngsters like Rocastle, Adams, Quinn and Groves.

Having spent most of the game pegged back, Williams' bludgeoning shot from all of 30 yards saw Arsenal seal all three points. It was a classic smash-and-grab, which in time would become Graham's hallmark.

The win at Everton was, however, only a brief glimpse of things to come. The following game at Highbury saw a return to the dire displays that had characterised the season thus far. Drawing 1-1 with Huddersfield in the League Cup, Graham finally exploded. 'For the first time we experience the fierce side of George Graham,' Kenny Sansom remembered in his book *Going Great Guns*. 'He is disgusted with the performance and lets us know it. He says afterwards that the commitment wasn't there and I disagree. We had words and there was a lot of shouting and moaning . . . It was only the boss's frustration coming out and he said that we showed too many bad habits. "Good teams don't play like that," he shouted and it was an evening to forget. But as captain I could not tolerate him saying that the players were not giving commitment.'

In time, such 'insolence' would see Sansom sold, but for now Graham called his team back to the training ground, on their day off, to work over team shape and set pieces.

It seems that this approach worked. Suddenly possessed by an unshakeable assurance, the team went the next 20 matches undefeated in all competitions, and all without their supposed 'stars'. 'Boring, boring Arsenal' came the chant from Chelsea fans at Stamford Bridge, but they proved they were anything but. Winning 3-1, the effervescent Rocastle grabbed a goal in a thrilling display on the right wing.

Yet even when the team won, Graham was not always satisfied. Following a 3-1 victory over Manchester City in the League Cup, with Rocastle scoring once again, Graham was furious with the defensive display. 'Trained hard today,' Sansom recalled, 'our punishment for the second-half performance against City. More defending, more talking, more physical work.'

Graham was obsessed. Any mistake was leapt upon and analysed before being corrected in a lengthy training exercise. Day after day, week after week, there was never any respite from his fanatical attention to even the smallest of details. Some of the players might have believed that his drills had been merely for pre-season, yet they were now learning that this was a full-time affair. 'Surprise, surprise, more defending today,' Sansom wrote of yet another defensive training session. 'It has become a joke with the players. David O'Leary and I are pulling [coach] Theo Foley's leg about it before every training session. "Tell you what, Theo, isn't it about time we did some more defending?"'

On 15 November 1986, a 4-0 win at Southampton sent Arsenal to the top of the league. The team may have been shorn of its stars, but Graham had finally fashioned it into a unit. Nick Hornby wrote of this dramatic turnaround, 'He turned Arsenal into something that anyone under the age of 50 could never have seen before at Highbury, and he saved, in all the ways the word implies, every single Arsenal fan. And goals ... where we had come to expect 1-0 wins at Highbury, suddenly fours and fives, even sixes, became commonplace.'

Suddenly, Arsenal looked genuine title contenders, and one of the main reasons for their lofty position was the form of their right-winger. Meeting compliments about his form with a grin and a shrug of his shoulders, Rocastle said, 'I'm not playing too bad. But the team's playing well and when the team's playing well you don't want to be the odd one out playing badly. There is so much competition here for places you have to be on your toes all the time. You just can't afford to let your game drop. There is no room to slacken off; you have to keep doing your job otherwise someone else will be wearing your shirt.'

And Rocastle was also keen to acknowledge the help of his team-mates: 'They've all encouraged me and geed me up. Viv Anderson and I form a partnership on the right – and Viv is always talking to me, using his experience to help me through the game. Likewise with Steve Williams and Paul Davis in midfield. They give me a boost when I need it – and they tell me straightaway if I ever get sloppy.'

The Anderson–Rocastle combination on the right-hand side had been one of Arsenal's most dangerous weapons. When I spoke to Anderson, he remembered it fondly. 'It was a great little partnership,' he said. 'Under George we had learnt it was a team game, so communication was vital. If I told Rocky I was bombing on he would sit, and if he was bombing on I would do likewise. He was great for tracking his runner as well. The two of us used to gang up on wingers. I think they would be surprised that it wasn't only me they had to deal with. There weren't too many skilful wingers around like Rocky who were also great defensively. And, of course, we scored a lot of goals going down the right-hand side.'

While this partnership reaped dividends on the pitch, Anderson also had some sage advice for Rocastle off it. Having been one of the most prominent black footballers in the game, Anderson had had to deal with the worst forms of racist poison which all too often dripped from the dregs of the terraces. Arsenal had a high proportion of young black players, and Anderson made sure to pass on some advice. 'I told him what Brian Clough had once told me,' Anderson said. 'If you're going to let people in the stands upset you then you're never going to make it as a footballer. You need to dismiss it and concentrate on your game. That's what I tried to say to David. He was a very talented lad but had had to learn to keep his focus at times because some of the things he heard were shocking. David was always a good listener and quick learner, though. He soon caught on.'

It also helped Rocastle that he had the support of fellow black team-mates Michael Thomas, Gus Caesar and Paul Davis. 'The fact we had all come through the youth team, and were now in the first team together, was a big help,' Caesar told me. 'It gave us strength. If you were the only black player at a club I think it could have been difficult but we all looked out for each other.'

Sadly, Caesar recalled that it wasn't just the terraces that were an issue. 'There was an incident on the training ground where Rocky had a dust-up with one of the boys,' he told me. 'When we pulled them away the player in question cracked some comment about his race. To be fair, this was completely out of character for the player, and I knew that he wasn't racist, but it still must have hurt. The player apologised and Rocky accepted it. It didn't seem to affect him. I think he knew it was something stupid said in the heat of the moment.'

In any event, Rocastle continued to be in stellar form, with the 3-0 win against Luton in December showcasing him at his very best. Built like a middleweight boxer, and with the speed of an Olympic sprinter, his turns were quick and sharp, his pace was electric, while his tackles were uncompromising. It seemed there was nothing the 19-year-old winger couldn't do. Unsurprisingly, most of the top clubs in Europe were now taking note.

By the end of the year, the 'Rocky Rocastle' chants regularly rolled off the North Bank as the Highbury crowd took the young winger to their hearts. 'The crowd have been marvellous to me ever since I made my debut against Newcastle last September,' Rocastle smiled. 'They've stuck by me even when things were not going the way I'd hoped. They've helped give me the confidence not to be afraid to try something different. If I make a mistake, they don't get on to me. They know I'll try and make up for it next time.'

When asked by Kevin Connolly about his thoughts on why he had struck up such a rapport with the fans, Rocastle replied, 'I think they know that I always give 100 per cent, that I've come up through our junior ranks and that I'm Arsenal through and through. I also reckon it's easier for a young player to be accepted than, say, a big-money buy. The fans don't expect so much to start with, and if you have a run they really get behind you – like they've got behind me.'

In spite of a serious injury, and a change of position, Rocastle's impact in 1986 was such that the Arsenal Supporters' Club voted him their Player of the Year. 'David is a very popular winner,' Supporters' Club secretary Barry Baker said of the award. 'He's quickly made a great impression with the fans.'

Typically, Rocastle refused to believe the news: 'At eight o'clock one night the Supporters' Club secretary rang me up and said I'd won Player of the Year. I didn't even know I was in the running. I thought it was one of the lads messing about so I said, "Yeah, all right," and put the phone down. He rang me back and said it was true, though. It was one of my proudest moments. The supporters are the people who matter. They are the ones who pay their money and support you rain or shine.'

Rocastle was also honoured that he had now joined some of the most illustrious names in Arsenal's history. 'I'd seen the Player of the Year plaque on the wall at Highbury,' Rocastle proudly recalled, 'with great names like Liam Brady and Kenny Sansom. To think I was going to be up there with them was amazing.'

On 27 December 1986, Rocastle helped mark Arsenal's centenary celebrations with yet another mesmeric display, at home to Southampton. On one occasion he beat the same player three times in the same move, eventually causing him to fall over. The crowd roared its approval as he nonchalantly passed the ball back to Anderson. The only person who wasn't pleased to see such showboating was George Graham, who ran to the sideline and hollered, 'David! Two-touch!'

The New Year's Day defeat of Wimbledon was distinguished by more outrageous Rocastle skill, as well as the return of Charlie Nicholas. Nicholas had actually been fit for a few weeks but had been unable to force his way back into the team. But with Rocastle and Nicholas in tandem, the North Bank was in for quite a treat.

Controlling the ball in his own half, Rocastle invited two

defenders towards him like a snake charmer. As he stood still, the defenders warily approached, aware of his quick feet yet also still believing that they could rob him of the ball. When they finally made their move, Rocastle was already gone. Slipping a delicate pass to Steve Williams, he had left them both standing.

Sprinting into the Wimbledon half, he watched on as Williams passed the ball to Paul Davis, who sprayed it out to Quinn on the left wing. Without the need to control it, Quinn played a first-time pass to Nicholas, who darted into the jam-packed penalty area from the left-hand side. As the Wimbledon players were attracted to Nicholas, no one had picked up Rocastle's rampaging run, which saw him now standing directly in front of the Wimbledon goal-keeper, Dave Beasant.

Ignoring Rocastle, Beasant charged out of his goal to narrow Nicholas' angle. In a flash, Nicholas slipped the ball to Rocastle and made a move towards the centre of the goal. Just five yards out, most players would have chosen to have a shot, but with Nicholas' run taking Beasant out of the picture Rocastle instantly returned the ball to him, which the Scotsman proceeded to tap into an empty net. It was a sensational goal, one that the current Barcelona squad would be proud of, and all achieved on a pitch that was only fit for Sunday league football.

A 2-1 defeat of Spurs saw Arsenal continue their remarkable unbeaten run, but there were some warning signs that the hectic Christmas schedule had started to take its toll. Playing on heavy pitches, and with the same 11 players usually turning out, the team was beginning to look jaded. This became evident to captain Kenny Sansom and manager George Graham in the training session following the win at White Hart Lane.

'We are still affected by the Spurs victory,' Sansom remembered. 'The players are tired and jaded in training and the boss asks us all the time: "What's wrong, lads?" George and I had a chat and I told him that I thought the youngsters were sluggish and that they were not responding because their minds were still on Tottenham. The boss agreed and we cut short the rest of the morning. A few sprints and training was called to a halt. It was a sensible decision because we are all super-fit and there is no need to push the kids if they don't want to at this stage. The boss was calling instructions but some of the minds were not alert enough.'

Graham was so concerned not to burn his team out that, in an unprecedented move, he also gave his players the following day off. It is no surprise that some of the younger players were starting to feel the pace. At the start of the season, the likes of Quinn, Hayes, Adams, Groves and Rocastle had only played 68 games between them. To date, they had exceeded all expectations, but was it really possible for them to maintain such high standards?

While Arsenal would spend the rest of January preserving their unbeaten record in the league, as well as progressing in the FA Cup, it was a trip to Old Trafford that finally provided evidence that the youngsters were reaching the end of their reserves. Showing clear signs of fatigue, Arsenal lost the game 2-0. However, exhaustion wasn't the sole reason for the loss. Rocastle also had to accept his fair share of the blame.

From the first minute, United's bustling centre forward, Norman Whiteside, had set the tone, going through his repertoire of tricks. Late tackles and insults were all doled out, as he unsettled Arsenal's young players. Rocastle eventually reacted after a high and late tackle, crashing into Whiteside and sending him sprawling to the floor, which saw the Manchester United forward retaliate by kicking Rocastle in the chest. Losing his cool, Rocastle kicked him back, in full view of the referee. Ignoring Whiteside's kick, referee George Tyson instead issued Rocastle with the only red card of his career.

George Graham confided afterwards that, while Alex Ferguson

was a close friend, they almost came to blows in the tunnel over this incident. In hindsight, even Ferguson had to admit that Rocastle had been hard done by. 'It was one of those games when big Norman did about 45 fouls and never got booked,' he said. 'How he got away with it I'll never know.'

Captain Kenny Sansom certainly had a lot of sympathy for Rocastle. 'We were furious because Norman didn't go with him,' he said. 'And the fact that we believed that David didn't deserve to be sent off. He had learnt his lesson, however; he was softened up by Whiteside and fell for the trap. Rocastle is an aggressive little player, very exciting on the ball and fights like a tiger to win it back. At Old Trafford he discovered that he should have walked away from provocation.'

Rocastle would, of course, never walk away from any provocation at Old Trafford. When questioned about this incident, he said, 'I think I lost my rag a little because I was so involved in the game. I did something out of character. I went to swing a kick at a certain player and the referee sent me off. I thought I should have been sent off, but the other player should have come with me. I'll never forget the referee's face when he sent me off. Very stern. He just said, "Get off." There was nothing I could do about it. I remember going back to the dressing room, and it's a lonely feeling because you're there on your own, and all your team-mates are trying to salvage something because you've been sent off. I said to myself, "Never again will I let that happen to me."'

While Arsenal's unbeaten streak was at an end, there remained everything to play for. Sitting at the top of the table, they were also still in the FA Cup and through to the semi-finals of the League Cup, where they would face old adversaries Spurs. If ever there was a chance for Rocastle to redeem himself then this would be it.

CHAPTER 17

THE ABYSS

'Karen, I've got a problem.'

Karen Rocastle had never heard her brother's voice sound so shaken. He was also not a person who readily admitted that he had any problems. David Rocastle was still very much seen by his family as the father figure, always responsible, always mature, always in control. The way he saw it, he was there to look after everyone else, not the other way around. Those who were close to him said he never opened up. Everything was always 'good' and there was always a smile on his face, but not now.

'What's wrong, Dave?' Karen asked, hearing the sound of traffic on the other end, which meant he was on the car phone.

'There's something I've got to tell you,' he replied, his voice faltering, as he tried to tell his sister a secret he had kept for over three years.

'What is it?'

'I've been having an affair.'

'What? Who with?'

'A girl from London. Her name's Sharon Edwards.'

Hearing this came as a surprise to Karen, but not as a complete shock. While her brother and his girlfriend Janet were in a long-term relationship, he had always been very popular with the opposite sex. With his clean-cut good looks, easy smile and charming manner, he would have been a hit whatever profession he had ended up in. However, all of those attributes, together with the fact that he was a famous professional footballer, had made him even more desirable.

Rocastle certainly wasn't part of the group of players at Arsenal who purposely went out looking for 'birds'; the girls just happened to come to him. Always polite and happy to talk to anyone, he was also never rude enough to turn them away. Regarded by all who knew him as the perfect gentleman, he was also prone to temptation like anyone else.

Attending a north London house party in 1989, Rocastle's eyes had immediately fallen on an attractive girl surrounded by admirers. Beautiful and bubbly, Sharon Edwards lit up the room. As everyone gravitated towards her, Rocastle asked one of his friends to introduce him. Seeing the attraction writ large across Rocastle's face, his friend instead gave him a warning, 'Dave, she's not very well. She's got sickle-cell anaemia.'

Having been born with the hereditary condition, Sharon had spent much of her young life in and out of hospital. Despite having a reduced life expectancy, she never let it stop her. Over the years she overcame major ankle and hip operations to make a career for herself in HR, while she was always the first to accept an invitation to a party, never wanting to miss out. Taking pride in her appearance, Sharon lived for the moment.

Unperturbed by his friend's warning, and captivated by Sharon's lilting laugh, Rocastle soon made his way across the room to say hello. Before long the pair were talking and laughing like old friends. Sharon didn't know who he was, but it was clear the attraction was mutual. Soon they were involved in a full-blown relationship, which not everyone approved of.

'At the time, I didn't like him,' Sharon's cousin Michelle Edwards told me. 'I knew he was in another relationship and I felt he was taking advantage of my cousin. But Sharon would never hear a bad word said against him.'

While the pair got on well, there was perhaps another reason for Rocastle's apparent fascination with Sharon. 'I think there was some connection because of her illness,' Michelle continued. 'She was open about it and I think he felt protective of her, maybe because of what had happened with his own father dying young.'

However, as their relationship progressed there came another complication. Something Rocastle was now telling his sister for the very first time.

'Listen, Karen,' Rocastle continued. 'Sharon and me, we had a baby daughter around a year ago. Her name is Sasha.'

Karen stopped for a moment, stunned. 'Does Janet know?'

'I just told her.'

'Why only now?'

'Because I've got a problem.'

Karen had thought that the problem was the affair and subsequent child. She could only imagine how Janet would be feeling at hearing such devastating news. Indeed, Karen and the Rocastle family had grown very fond of Janet over the years. Karen and her boyfriend, Junior, had gone out frequently with her and David, and only a few weeks before had visited them in Leeds, where they had gone to the cinema to see *The Bodyguard*.

As Karen thought this, she suddenly became conscious of her brother's deep breaths on the other end of the phone, which told her he was trying to prevent himself from crying. 'David, what is it? What's wrong?'

'Karen . . .' he said. 'Sharon's dead. She died this morning.'

Suddenly everything became clear.

'What? How?'

'She's been ill for a while, but she's always been all right. But she went into the hospital yesterday and . . . and she didn't come out.'

'David, where are you now?'

'I'm in the car. I'm coming to London. I need to go and see her in the hospital mortuary. Will you come with me?'

'Of course,' Karen said, realising that for the first, and only, time in his life her older brother needed her.

An hour later, Karen got out of her car and saw her brother waiting for her. No words were said. A hug was all that was needed. When they pulled away, Karen could see from his puffy, bloodshot eyes that he had been crying.

Together they walked into the mortuary, where Rocastle told the receptionist they were there to see Sharon Edwards. Shown to a darkened room, they could see that Sharon's body was already laid out. At seeing her, Rocastle finally broke down. Karen also became upset. She had never seen her brother like this before.

Holding Sharon's hand he turned to his sister and said, 'All she wanted was to meet Mum. I couldn't even do that for her. She could have made a lot of money selling the story to the papers but she didn't. She really loved me.'

Putting her arm around his shoulders, Karen could only offer him the comfort of being there. In the circumstances, she didn't have the words.

Back in the car park, as her brother dried his eyes, Karen decided to ask the one question that was now bothering her. 'David, what's going to happen to your daughter?'

'I want to look after her, but I don't know if Janet can handle it.'

Karen nodded. It was a tricky situation. Her brother was clearly determined to do the right thing, but at the same time she really felt for Janet, appreciating what a huge shock this must have been for her. 'Look, Dave,' Karen said. 'I'll take her. Let me look after her for you.'

Her brother shook his head. 'Thank you, Karen, but I couldn't let you look after my child. Sharon's mum is going to take her.'

He was distraught that this would mean he wouldn't get the chance to play a big part in her upbringing, but, caught in terrible circumstances, he didn't have a lot of choice.

While he sent money every month to help pay for Sasha's food, clothes and education, he never felt it was enough. Whenever he was in the south with Leeds, he would ask Karen if she could pick Sasha up from her grandmother's in Essex and take her to the team hotel so they could spend a few hours together. He never tried to hide her, or deny that she was his daughter, often playing with her in full view of his team-mates.

Less than a year later, Sasha's grandmother, Eva, decided to return to Jamaica, and took Sasha with her. Rocastle was devastated but was at least comforted by the knowledge that Eva doted on and cared for his daughter like no one else. However, one person who struggled to come to terms with the situation as she grew older was Sasha Edwards Rocastle.

'There were times I was so mad at him,' Sasha told me. 'I missed him so much. And, of course, I missed my mum. I never got to know either of them properly. I've only really got two memories of my dad. Sitting on my nan's step with him, and going to a hotel with him. It was tough. I wish I had got to really know him.'

Although the situation tore Rocastle apart, he also faced trouble at home. Having just moved to Leeds, Janet Nelson had to deal with this news away from the immediate support of her family and friends. In those first few weeks their relationship was on the brink, with the added pressure of having two young children to raise, and Rocastle being in the spotlight as Leeds United's record signing.

'There was clearly stuff going on under the surface,' Junior Hamilton told me, 'but he somehow managed to conduct himself publicly as he had always done. It was eating him up but he kept his self-respect. He was never rude to anyone, or showed anyone that he was suffering. That was Dave.'

Rocastle and Janet must have talked it through long into the night. While he may have made it to training and flashed a smile, there was too much on his mind to really exert himself. In time, this had a detrimental effect on his fitness and meant that he couldn't last 90 minutes, something that Wilkinson and Alan Sutton both told me was a factor in him not playing. Wilkinson certainly wasn't aware that his new signing was having to confront such personal difficulties so early into his time at Leeds. He merely put his poor fitness down to adapting to a new training regime and culture.

Of course, another issue Rocastle battled was homesickness. 'I don't think he ever really settled,' Karen told me. 'He was down in London a lot and I think it says something that he never bought a house up north. He was always renting.'

Rocastle actually loved living in Leeds, but during a time of extreme stress he needed to be around those who loved him. At Leeds, he knew John Lukic and Chris Whyte from his Arsenal days, while he would also grow very close to Chris Fairclough, but at this moment in time he needed his family, as well as old friends. As such, during those first few months, he took every opportunity he could to drive back home. The trip usually took three hours and sometimes he might only be back for the day. His family remembers that he would even drive home just to get his hair cut in the local barber's in Brockley before going straight back to Leeds. Again, this amount of travelling, when he was trying to find his fitness, took its toll.

While the football world was full of frenzied speculation that

Wilkinson and Rocastle had fallen out, everyone missed the real issue. At this time Rocastle was more concerned with saving his relationship, and making sure that Sasha was well looked after, than worrying about football. He knew he wasn't fully fit. He knew he wasn't fully focused. Gordon Strachan's return merely provided him, and Wilkinson, with a convenient explanation for his absence.

Yet as Rocastle tried to concentrate on football, the situation with Sasha continued to have an impact. Understandably, his mother Linda treated Sasha as a grandchild. As such, her picture was proudly displayed on the wall in her living room, alongside photos of her other grandchildren, Melissa, Ryan and, in years to come, Monique. However, to avoid any upset, Rocastle asked his mum if, at least at first, she could temporarily take Sasha's picture down whenever he and Janet came to visit.

It appears that the affair, and child, were proving difficult for her to move on from, and she didn't need any reminders. Sadly, the effect of this was that Rocastle was torn between his family and his partner and children, and Karen believes that it kept them from seeing him as much as they might have. It was a tremendously distressing and stressful situation for all involved.

Dealing with the fallout from his private life, Rocastle eventually had to get to grips with his professional one. Sinking without a trace at Leeds, there was at least some motivation on the horizon to focus his mind. His old team Arsenal were coming to Elland Road.

CHAPTER 18

HIGHBURY HERO

The last time Arsenal had won a major trophy had been the famous 1979 FA Cup win over Manchester United. For a club of Arsenal's size, it had been a barren eight years since that glorious day. But by mid-Feburary 1987, the domestic treble was suddenly looking very possible, and all in George Graham's first season in charge.

However, with games in three competitions coming thick and fast, the first hurdle Arsenal needed to overcome was Spurs in the League Cup semi-final. And their north London rivals were certainly formidable opposition.

Boasting the likes of Glenn Hoddle and Chris Waddle in midfield, as well as free-scoring striker Clive Allen, who was on his way to 49 goals in all competitions, Tottenham had won far more silverware than Arsenal in recent years. FA Cup winners in 1981 and 1982, they had also won the UEFA Cup in 1984. As such, Spurs had every right to feel confident going into the two-legged tie, particularly as Arsenal's Player of the Year, David Rocastle, was not available due to suspension.

With the first leg at Highbury, it was hoped that the team could secure a good result at home, with Rocastle then able to play in the return at White Hart Lane. So good had Arsenal's form been going into the game, with just one loss in the last 24, that this certainly seemed more than achievable.

Therefore, the 1-0 defeat that followed came as a hammer blow. Kenny Sansom called his team's performance 'bitterly disappointing'. Clive Allen's winning goal might have been offside, but he had been a constant menace throughout the game, dragging O'Leary and Adams all over the pitch. Much of Arsenal's success had been built on playing the ball out of defence but even this was lacking on the day, and, despite Graham's frustration, they had continued to play high balls to Niall Quinn.

'In the players' room after the game it was clear that the Tottenham boys thought they were at Wembley,' Sansom said. 'They believed that they had done the hard work and, with a home leg to come, they were through. And who could blame them? An away goal is so vital in these semi-finals.'

Before the crunch second leg at White Hart Lane, Arsenal had three games to negotiate in order to keep their treble challenge on track. A 2-0 win against Barnsley saw them progress in the FA Cup, while two draws, against Sheffield Wednesday and Oxford, still kept them top of the league.

Their confidence knocked, the team travelled to White Hart Lane on 1 March to play their foes under the rain-specked floodlights. Rocastle was back but the team had now lost Steve Williams with a broken arm. In his place, reserve-team right back Michael Thomas lined up in the unfamiliar position of central midfield.

In an intimidating atmosphere, with both sets of fans noisily defending their corner of the city, Arsenal started the game where they had left off at Highbury, outshone, outrun and outthought. Time and time again, Clive Allen was allowed to breach the

Arsenal defence with only the heroics of John Lukic limiting him to just the one goal in the first half. Dejectedly making their way towards the dressing room, it seemed that the tie was effectively over. Spurs would be going to Wembley once again, while Arsenal would have to hope they could sustain their challenge in the league and FA Cup.

However, as the players slumped against the white-tiled walls, they heard the muffled sounds of the Spurs Tannoy providing fans with information on how they could purchase their tickets for Wembley. Graham told his players to be quiet and listen. Suddenly, the sound of their archrivals' 1981 hit, 'Ossie's Dream (Spurs Are on Their Way to Wembley)', filled the stadium. Charlie Nicholas later said of this, 'George didn't need to say anything after that. We just nodded at each other and went out, ready for battle.'

They might have been two goals down, away from home, facing their free-scoring enemy, but suddenly the players were on their feet. Rocastle was feeling particularly enraged. Clip-clopping his way down the tunnel, the roar of the crowd welcoming the teams back on to the pitch, he cajoled and coaxed his team-mates, working them into a frenzy. Clapping his hands together, gritting his teeth, his body was taut with intent as he emerged into the rain.

As the game restarted Arsenal looked a team transformed, rediscovering the vigour that had made them a formidable force for so much of the season. Rocastle motored up and down the right flank, assisted by the overlapping Anderson, while Thomas, meek and overawed in the first half, suddenly started to snap around Hoddle, frequently regaining possession and turning defence into attack.

Finally the pressure told. A Rocastle long throw was headed towards goal by Quinn. Ray Clemence clawed it away but the ball fell at the feet of Viv Anderson, who scrambled it into the net. In a businesslike fashion, the players trooped back to the halfway line, the job only half complete, defiance still burning in their eyes.

As the minutes ebbed away and the desperation increased, Graham marauded to the touchline and waved his team forward in search of an equaliser. This left gaping holes at the back, which Clive Allen was quick to exploit. But despite numerous gilt-edged chances to seal the tie, John Lukic stood firm, making save after save in what must have been his finest performance for Arsenal.

The red neon clock on the scoreboard flickered to show that the 90 minutes were up. At this the decibel levels increased but it seemed Arsenal's efforts had been in vain. However, Rocastle refused to concede defeat. A constant menace on the right flank, he went on one final lung-busting run, jinking past his marker to whip in a low cross between the defence and keeper. Quinn was first to react. Poking the ball past Clemence, the big Irishman sprinted towards the Arsenal end, his arms aloft.

Celebrating like a man possessed in front of a bubbling sea of joy, Rocastle jumped on Quinn's back and clenched his fist towards the fans. They were still in the cup. The treble was still on.

While these days there would be a penalty shoot-out to split the teams, in this instance it was on the toss of a coin to decide where a replay would be held. The loss of the toss determined it would be White Hart Lane. Usually this would have been met with dismay, but after a thrilling second-half display the Arsenal players felt they had the measure of their opponents. 'I could sense from their players when we met again after the game that they were worried,' Kenny Sansom said of the atmosphere in the players' lounge. 'They were too quiet.'

So, on 4 March it was a return to White Hart Lane, with a place in the League Cup final still up for grabs. In the dressing room Graham made sure each of his players knew their responsibilities. Meanwhile, Theo Foley reminded them of the half-time Tannoy announcement in the previous game. Last but not least, captain Sansom stood tall and told his team-mates of the haunted look in the Spurs players' eyes as they had trudged off the pitch. This was their time. Their moment. Don't let it pass.

With Sansom's words ringing in their ears, and having already won at White Hart Lane twice, the players ran down the tunnel full of confidence. 'Players like Rocky and Niall knew they could "do" players like Gough and Waddle 'cos they'd "done" them on Saturday,' Charlie Nicholas later told Jon Spurling.

Once again, though, Clive Allen was to prove the difference. With just 15 minutes remaining he scored what looked to be the winning goal. Soon after, Charlie Nicholas was stretchered off and replaced by perennial reserve Ian Allinson. A goal down, Arsenal were now deprived of the player many perceived to be their match-winner. Suddenly, the Tottenham fans started to chant 'Spurs are going to Wembley'. And once again, this spurred the Arsenal players on. Indeed, Kenny Sansom recalls that referee Joe Worrall even said to him, 'Come on, Ken, you can still do this.'

Surging forward, Arsenal cast aside all thought of defending, as Spurs suddenly resembled a punch-drunk boxer, resorting to desperate tackles and clearances to save the day. But on the 82nd minute they could hold out no more, as Ian Allinson, the most unlikely of scorers, mishit the ball to wrong-foot Clemence at his near post. A further replay seemingly beckoned but one look at the Spurs players might have told you that the fight in them had gone. Some had sunk to their knees, while Chris Waddle trudged back to the halfway line, his head slumped into his chest. Only Glenn Hoddle seemed to realise that there was still all to play for.

As both sets of fans roared their team to the finish line, the referee looked at his watch. The game was in the 89th minute but with Spurs camped in their own half, Arsenal were intent on settling the tie once and for all.

Rocastle, with the capacity to excel in the most inhospitable conditions, dug deep to make a final surge into the penalty area, his marker too tired to follow him. Meanwhile, out on the left wing the ball broke to Allinson. Firing a mishit volley into the penalty area, the ball suddenly arrived at Rocastle's feet. Unmarked, he tried to bring it under his control but it wasn't as crisp as he would have liked. With the ball getting away from him, Clemence rushed from his goal line to try to smother it. His eyes widening, Rocastle stretched, mud flicking off the grass and spattering his shirt as he managed to stab the ball with his weaker left foot.

For a moment everything seemed to go in slow motion. Falling to the floor, he saw the ball go beyond Clemence, trickle through the mud, and then . . . a roar!

Holding his arms aloft, almost in shock, he was mobbed by his team-mates. Suddenly realising the magnitude of the goal, he screamed in delight, beads of sweat reflecting off his forehead, steam wafting from his curly locks.

'I was with the Arsenal fans,' Jerome Anderson told me. 'I remember he was celebrating and he was looking for me. He always used to look for me because he knew I would be there. That goal was really the start of his rise to superstardom. The next day was the first time he really had to do a lot of press.'

The scenes in the Arsenal end are hard to imagine in modern football. With terracing still in place, the crowd was almost as one, rocking back and forth in unison, huddled tight together. It is also hard to imagine the Arsenal team today celebrating quite so enthusiastically at reaching a League Cup final, even if it was at the expense of rivals Spurs. This was truly one of those occasions that can never be repeated. A perfect storm of years of underachievement being blown away by a last-minute goal, by a favoured player, against bitter adversaries.

There was to be no comeback from Spurs. Just three minutes later, the shrill sound of the final whistle signalled a famous victory.

Joining the fans in singing Wembley songs, a suitable riposte to the Spurs fans who streamed out of the stadium, the normally reserved Graham ran to his players and enveloped Rocastle in a hug.

'It was the second of three or four lifetime moments where my delirium was such that I had no idea what I was doing,' Nick Hornby remembered, 'where everything went blank for a few moments ... The depression that I had been living with for the best part of the 1980s packed up and started to leave that night.'

Back in the changing room the celebrations continued. 'I have to admit that I have never experienced such excitement before,' Kenny Sansom said. 'It was fantastic. In the dressing room two crates of champagne went in minutes and the lads took great delight in singing "Spurs Are on Their Way to Wembley" at the top of their voices.'

As for the match-winner, he was happy to joke with his team-mates that despite their criticism of his shooting, particularly with his left foot, he had still scored three goals in the last six matches. 'The lads have been giving me some stick in training because I've been having some really bad shots and headers,' Rocastle told Kevin Connolly with a grin on his face. 'I just point to my record in recent matches.'

When discussing the fact that it was his weaker left foot that scored the vital goal, he laughed: 'That's the one I usually use for standing on. After the game Steve Williams told me that when he saw me about to shoot with my left foot he shut his eyes and hoped. I know how he felt!'

Happy to jest about his own shortcomings, he was also quick to praise his team-mates. 'The lads' determination was fantastic,' he continued. 'But as time ticked on, our chance was going. Ally's goal really turned the game. He got a couple of bad bounces and had to wait a long time for the ball to come down – then he stuck it away superbly.'

With Wembley awaiting, there was still the small matter of the league to concentrate on. Since the loss to Manchester United, Arsenal had failed to win a game. The fixture list was also congested following the three cup games against Spurs. Still, Rocastle was confident that the team had what it took to continue challenging on all three fronts. 'We've lost a little ground since the turn of the year,' he said. 'But we're still in contention for the title. If we get the odd setback, I don't think it will affect us too much. In fact, I think it would make us more determined. We know we have a good side here and we're capable of beating anyone.'

While that might have been the case, the team had been running low on reserves even before the marathon effort against Spurs. Facing league games against title rivals Liverpool and Everton, as well as a Wembley final, Rocastle and Arsenal would have to dig deep if the season was to end with silverware.

CHAPTER 19

MAKING A POINT

After heartache, drama and fitness concerns, Leeds United's record signing finally made his first Premier League start four months into the season. The devastating situation with Sharon had continued to plague him, but over the previous few weeks he had managed to get down to business and concentrate on his fitness. While not at 100 per cent capacity, he had certainly done enough for Wilkinson to trust him with a start, and, what's more, it would be against Arsenal.

Arsenal came into the game on the back of six straight league wins. In contrast, Leeds had won just four league games all season. Rather than exhibiting the form of defending champions, they were looking like relegation candidates. The European Cup had certainly been a distraction, but after being knocked out by Rangers in early November it at least gave the team a chance to focus on their dreadful league showing.

Under the floodlights on a miserable day in Yorkshire, the rain was relentless. While the waterlogged pitch hindered most players, it seemed to bring out the best in Rocastle. Determined to take his chance, his hunger to be involved in all aspects of the game saw him motor through the mud. Tackle after tackle was won. Passes were hit long and short. Dribbles were quick, sharp and destructive. Awarded man of the match for his efforts in the incredible 3-0 win, the *Daily Mirror* proclaimed, 'David Rocastle directed operations', and that he was at the 'centre' of all that was good, as he 'splashed through endless puddles'.

Such was Leeds' dominance that the only real opportunity of note for Arsenal came courtesy of a Rocastle back pass. Playing the ball back to Lukic, it had got caught in a puddle which provided Wright with a chance. Thankfully, Lukic saved the day. 'It just shows how bad the pitch was,' a relieved Rocastle said afterwards, 'because I did hit the ball back fairly firmly. As soon as I saw it went to Ian I thought he'd put it away no problem, but I think the fact he was staying with me for the weekend made him feel sorry for me.'

Despite this one error Rocastle had every right to feel happy with his day's work. 'The team performance was nearly perfect,' he enthused. 'We could have won by five or six. That's no disrespect to Arsenal. That's just how we played that day. I had nothing to prove to them. Maybe I might have been trying harder because I've got everything to prove to the Leeds fans.'

The Leeds fans were certainly satisfied. Rocastle's name had echoed around Elland Road after the game, as the travelling Arsenal contingent had also joined in. Applauding all corners of the ground, Rocastle had stood drenched in sweat and euphoria. He felt that he had finally arrived.

Given the magnitude of the win, and that his record signing had made an encouraging full debut, Wilkinson might have chosen this moment to issue him with some praise. However, when asked how Rocastle had performed, all he said was, 'We kept a clean sheet, and always looked to keep a clean sheet until David made a mistake on the back pass and Lukic got us out of the muck.'

While Wilkinson might have wanted to focus on the team, it would no doubt have been disheartening for Rocastle to hear that the only thing his manager had highlighted was his one mistake. Despite this, he at least found himself in the starting line-up for the following game at Chelsea. Up to that point Leeds had not won an away game all season, but after the Arsenal result confidence was running high.

However, a 1-0 defeat was followed in quick succession by a catastrophic 4-1 trouncing at the hands of relegation-threatened Nottingham Forest. To make matters worse, just two days before the game Wilkinson had opted to sell star striker Eric Cantona to rivals Manchester United for the paltry sum of £1m. Wilkinson justified the sale by asserting that it was a good fee and claimed that Cantona had become disruptive. Despite this, Cantona would go on to become a Manchester United legend, propelling the club to its first title since 1967.

Without Cantona the team's form continued to be erratic, and once again Rocastle found himself on the sidelines. By January, he had still only completed three games for Leeds and was linked with a move away, with West Ham, Everton and even Liverpool said to be monitoring him. 'I'm just keeping my head down, training hard and hoping things improve for me,' he said when questioned about a potential move, tiring of the constant speculation.

Spending more time with the reserves than the first team, he would be forgiven for feeling downcast after what had been a horrendous few months on a professional and personal level. However, his reserve-team colleagues recall that, far from throwing a tantrum, he was actually the one player who kept it together.

'David and I were roommates,' Scott Sellars told me. 'He was just what I needed because, I must admit, I was finding it tough being out of the team. But he kept me going. He kept all of us going.'

Mark Tinkler, the young midfielder trying to break into the first team, also recalled Rocastle's positive influence. 'He always took time out to speak to the young players,' Tinkler said. 'We couldn't get enough of him. He was a fantastic guy to be around. He'd make you feel great.'

While I interviewed Sellars and Tinkler separately, they both used the same words to describe their former team-mate – 'bubbly', 'positive', 'upbeat' and 'always with a smile on his face'.

Leeds' first team may have struggled in the Premier League but the reserves were a different proposition. With a midfield of Rocastle, Sellars, Hodge and Tinkler, they could have been more than a match for most Premier League teams.

However, Rocastle had come to Leeds to compete for trophies. As much as he tried to keep his head, it must have been incredibly frustrating to be restricted to a series of cameos. Even when he did come off the substitutes' bench and make an impact, such as against Southampton, where he turned a 1-0 defeat into a 2-1 win, he still found himself left out of the squad for the following game against Everton.

The season was fast turning into a total disaster. Some newspapers even printed stories that he had walked out of Elland Road after a furious showdown with Howard Wilkinson. This only made matters worse. Rocastle was so upset at the story that he threatened to sue the newspaper involved. 'I want our supporters to know they can totally discount some of the articles that have been written about me recently,' he said. 'I had nothing to do with any of them, and they were well wide of the mark to suggest that I'd had enough and wanted away. The thing that upset me the most was the headline that tried to make out I'd been in to see the gaffer and told him, "Let me go." Anyone who read that would think I'd told the paper I'd actually asked to leave, and I really took exception to that. I haven't spoken to him and I most certainly haven't asked for a transfer. This is still the place for me. As the boss says, no one who's out of the team is going to be totally satisfied but the answer is to battle your way back in. That's a challenge, and I'm not going to walk away from it.'

Rocastle continued to remain dignified in testing circumstances, but Leeds legend Billy Bremner did the opposite and hit out. In an interview with the *Sunday Mirror*, he questioned why the likes of Rocastle hadn't been given more game time when the Leeds midfield had been so poor. 'Howard has made errors this season in his choice of sides,' he said. 'That has stemmed from the dropping-off in performance standards of Gordon Strachan, David Batty, Gary Speed and Gary McAllister in midfield. Last season they were the strength the championship-winning team was built on. Every one of them produced superb, seven out of 10 performance averages. This season it has been down nearer four or five out of 10.'

Just as it seemed Rocastle's chance of a first-team recall was all but gone, Wilkinson surprisingly reinstated him for the visit of Manchester City on 13 March. On the day, Rocastle's venomous volley was enough to separate the sides, as well as mark his first Leeds goal. As the *Independent* said afterwards, 'Rocky's horror show may be over, at least temporarily.'

And it certainly was a temporary reprieve. Starting in the subsequent draws against Forest and Chelsea, he was then dropped for the defeat to Sheffield United. Having kept his own counsel up until this point, he finally snapped. 'I'm absolutely gutted about this and don't know where to turn or what to do,' he told the press. 'Being told I was out of the side for Bramall Lane after playing in the last three matches – all unbeaten – felt terrible. This was a very big derby occasion and a very important match for Leeds, and it's just awful that I wasn't wanted for it. I'm not saying that I'm going to steam in and ask for a transfer. But if the manager feels I've got no part to play in matches like these, then it's hard to believe I've got a future here.'

Such was the furore surrounding his being dropped for the second match running, this time against Blackburn, that at the Supporters' Club annual dinner his arrival was greeted by fans chanting, 'Rocky! Rocky!' Proving he had a sense of humour about the situation, when Wilkinson got up on stage he pointed to Rocastle and said to the crowd, 'Leeds United's answer to the Invisible Man is here – David Rocastle. Actually, I love him dearly. The chairman told me not to leave you out tonight, Rocky.'

Typically, Rocastle laughed. He may not have been happy with the lack of playing time but, contrary to reports, he and Wilkinson respected one another. As Wilkinson said when I spoke to him about their relationship, 'David was a nice lad. He was shy. I never had a problem with him. I just think that there were some short-comings in his actual physical fitness and that's why he didn't play as much as we would have liked, that and of course the form of Gordon Strachan. At Arsenal he was a few pounds lighter, lean, fresh and fit. I don't think we ever saw that side of him at Leeds.'

The season had not only been disastrous for him, it had also been one to forget for Leeds. Finishing in 17th place, the defending champions were only two points off the relegation zone. It is still considered the worst title defence in recent years, although at the time of writing Chelsea were in a similar tailspin. Amazingly, Leeds had the best home record in the league but also the worst away record, failing to win a single game.

For Leeds, and Rocastle, there needed to be a dramatic upturn in fortunes if they were both going to return to former glories the following season. But once again, things didn't turn out as planned.

CHAPTER 20

WEMBLEY GLORY

The monumental efforts of the Arsenal players in the three cup games against Spurs had come at a cost. While a Wembley cup final against Liverpool was on the horizon, the club's league form all but collapsed. Following the semi-final victory at White Hart Lane, Arsenal failed to win in the next six games, not only losing to title rivals Liverpool, but also being knocked out of the FA Cup by Watford.

Suddenly, from having three trophies to play for, there was now only one, and that would be against one of the best teams in the country. Would Arsenal finish yet another season trophyless?

As it became clear that the League Cup final was going to be absolutely crucial, Graham opted to rest some of his key players. For the league game against Watford, he left out Viv Anderson and David Rocastle, who would have been suspended from the final if he were to pick up another booking. Kenny Sansom said of this, 'Rocky looks tired anyway; he has had a long season.'

Unsurprisingly, a weakened Arsenal team lost the game 2-0.

What was just as worrying, however, was the fact that Arsenal had scored just one goal in seven first division matches. And it wasn't as if the team was actually creating any chances for Quinn, Hayes or Nicholas to score. If they were going to stand any chance of beating a strong Liverpool team then something needed to change – and urgently.

With this in mind Graham had decided that his depleted players could do with a break. As such, on Sunday, 22 March the team flew out to the Algarve to spend a few days in the sun. Graham would prove to be a fan of such mid-season breaks in years to come, with Marbella becoming a particular favourite. While the locations might have been glamorous, Graham usually insisted that the team still be put through their paces. But on this occasion, Graham let his players take it easy. Spending most of the week soaking up the sun, a football was rarely seen as they sat by the swimming pool, enjoyed a few beers, as well as an occasional walk or light run along the beach.

As the team took time out to relax, Graham remained hard at work. Eager to address his side's goalscoring deficiencies, he bought Leicester City striker Alan Smith for £700,000. Smith had struck up a prolific partnership with Gary Lineker at Leicester, and while Graham admired his goalscoring record – 84 goals in 217 appearances – it was his ability to hold up the ball, and bring others into play, which really excited him.

However, Graham would have to wait until the following season to unleash Smith, as he would not be allowed to join the club until pre-season. While this addition was certainly something to look forward to, it didn't solve the team's immediate goalscoring problems, with the League Cup final less than a week away.

Of further concern to Graham was his Player of the Year's sudden lethargy. Having left Rocastle out of the team to play Watford, and then given him a few days to relax in the Algarve, he had hoped that his star man would come roaring back to life. But in the last league game before the cup final, Rocastle was again listless in the 1-0 defeat to Everton. Repeatedly failing to get past his man, while also not providing any ammunition for the forward line, he spluttered his way to the final whistle.

Something clearly wasn't right. Rocastle knew it. Graham knew it. Still, there was that nagging feeling that he had already proven himself to be a man for the big occasion. Maybe, just maybe, his first appearance under the famous Twin Towers might invigorate him. That was all Graham could go on if he was to name Rocastle in his team.

The build-up to the game dominated the press all week. On paper it was presented as Liverpool, serial trophy winners, against Arsenal, also-rans in recent years. That storyline alone spiced up many headlines. However, it could be said that, below the surface, this game was really a battle of the 1980s. Northern socialism versus southern capitalism. While the city of London was booming, thanks in no small part to Thatcher's pro-business policies, the north of the country was in serious decline. Liverpool was at the forefront of this, with its docks hit particularly hard.

Regarded as the game's aristocrats, Liverpool Football Club was viewed by many as standard-bearers for their demoralised city. In contrast, Arsenal epitomised Thatcherism at its worst, or finest, depending on your point of view. Led by millionaire businessman David Dein, the club was upgrading its infrastructure, putting in place a bond scheme to redevelop the ground, while also considering the addition of corporate boxes to the Clock End.

As the newspapers covered all angles on the clash, George Graham did likewise. On 2 April he named his starting line-up: Lukic, Anderson, Sansom, Williams, O'Leary, Adams, Rocastle, Davis, Quinn, Nicholas and Hayes. On the substitutes' bench were

Thomas and Groves, with no place for semi-final hero Ian Allinson. Rocastle was at least in. Graham had decided to trust that on the day he would come good.

More than that, Graham had actually earmarked Rocastle as the potential match-winner. Due to injuries, Liverpool midfielder Ronnie Whelan was set to line up at left back. Playing out of position and not renowned for his pace, Graham hammered into his team the importance of getting the ball to Rocastle at every opportunity, so that he could run at Whelan.

With everything taken care of, the team spent the night at the Noke Hotel in St Albans. Waking early the next morning, to be met by a grinning Paul Davis, who was filming the day on a huge camcorder, there was a relaxed atmosphere among the squad, with no hint of nerves. This was helped in part due to Kenny Sansom settling the team down with his mixture of mickey-taking and impressions, for which he was renowned.

After breakfast, the players, dressed in club blazer and tie, were ushered on to the team bus to make their way to Wembley. Taking their usual positions, with Rocastle and Michael Thomas next to one another, they suddenly saw the Twin Towers in the distance. As some of the younger players craned their necks to get a better look, the likes of Sansom, O'Leary and Anderson quietly began to focus their minds on the task ahead.

With wailing sirens, the police escort helped to guide the bus through the stagnant traffic, and announced the team's arrival on Wembley Way. 'Georgie Graham and his red-and-white army!' the thousands of buoyant Arsenal fans suddenly chanted. Looking out of the window, Rocastle flashed his trademark smile and gave a thumbs-up to the fans, who cheered in return.

As a child Rocastle had loved watching the coverage of Wembley cup finals. He knew that back home in Lewisham many of his old friends would be watching the team bus snake its way into the belly of Wembley Stadium, just as he had done a few years previously. Today would be his chance to finally grace the pitch itself.

Yet despite the goosebumps of excitement and the crowd breaking into chants of 'Oh, Rocky, Rocky, Rocky, Rocky, Rocky, Rocastle', he was concerned. For the last few weeks he hadn't felt himself. Sluggish, tired and feeling heavy, the zip seemed to have gone from his legs. Something wasn't right. But today he needed to perform. To perform for the fans who had been so welcoming towards him. For his family who had given him their love and support. For his friends Errol Johnson, Gary Hill and Kevin Arnold, who would have killed to swap places with him. And, of course, for Micky Cheeseman and Terry Murphy, who had given him the chance to be there. Today all thoughts of lethargy would have to be pushed aside.

Following Graham from the coach to the changing room, the players found their shirts were already hanging up on pegs. Getting undressed, flicking through the match programme and applying rub, the chants of the two sets of fans from outside filled the room, as they geared themselves up for the game ahead. Liverpool were always in good voice but on this day they were more than matched by the Arsenal fans, who were situated above the tunnel and could be heard loud and clear in the dressing room.

Following the warm-up, Graham sat his team back down for last-minute pieces of advice. 'The first 20 minutes are vital,' he told the silent dressing room. 'Molby and McMahon will strangle the midfield if we let them.' At this, Graham turned to Paul Davis and Steve Williams, indicating that it was their job to get a hold of the game early on. 'Tony, David,' Adams and O'Leary looked up. 'Watch Rush, don't give him a moment.' They nodded in return, knowing the incredible statistic that Liverpool had never lost a game in which Rush had scored. Then it was back to Rocastle. 'Get the ball to David quickly,' Graham ordered, again emphasising how the key to victory would be for Hayes, Rocastle and the overlapping Anderson to gang up on Whelan in a pincer movement. With that, the buzzer rang throughout the dressing room. It was time. 'Best of luck, lads,' Graham said, as Sansom led the way out towards the tunnel.

By now, even experienced campaigners like Kenny Sansom were nervous. He may have been an England regular but as of then he had never won a major trophy. He knew this could be his last chance. Charlie Nicholas was also feeling the pressure. He was bought for moments such as this and, up till that moment, had not delivered. With Graham clearly not a fan of his lifestyle, and the newspapers predicting he would be sold in the summer, he also recognised that this was his big chance.

The youngsters – Rocastle, Adams, Hayes and Quinn – were balls of nervous energy. They had proven during the season that they could beat the best, yet as they looked across at their opponents they were suddenly struck by who they were up against. Dalglish, Hansen, Molby, McMahon and Rush, to name just a few. All looked relaxed. And all looked across at the Arsenal team with no sign of nerves whatsoever. They had all been here before, and more often than not they had triumphed.

Finally, the referee, a Torquay policeman, led the teams on to the pitch. Suddenly, the muffled chanting became an explosion of noise. As Graham and Dalglish took their teams to meet the guest of honour, Sir John Moores, 40,000 Arsenal fans cheered in the sunshine, waving red-and-white banners, scarves and flags, while releasing hundreds of red-and-white balloons into the clear blue sky.

With the pleasantries out of the way, it was time for battle. After creating half-chances early on for Quinn and Nicholas, Arsenal soon found themselves on the back foot. Sensing the game slipping away, Graham swiftly emerged on to the touchline to scream instructions at his players, ordering them to push up. However, with Molby dictating the play this was easier said than done. Despite the Dane's ample frame, Davis and Williams struggled to get close to him as he sprayed passes all over the pitch. Rush was also causing problems, coming short and then going long. O'Leary and Adams argued with each other, and then berated the midfield for not picking him up. And on the brief occasions when Rocastle did get the ball, McMahon was quickly across to shepherd him away from the exposed Whelan.

On the 23rd minute the pressure finally told. Molby split the Arsenal defence with a probing pass which set McMahon through on goal. Lukic rushed out to narrow the angle but, rather than shoot, McMahon squared the ball to Rush who finished off the move. Arsenal were a goal down, and the Rush statistic went through the heads of all the fans and players. Graham looked on from the sidelines, exasperated. The three players he had identified as the primary danger men had just waltzed through his team unhindered.

Frustrated at their inability to get out of their own half, Sansom suddenly started to bomb forward, which left gaps for Liverpool to exploit. 'Kenny! Kenny!' Graham screamed at his captain from the touchline. 'Keep the shape!'

The first half-hour was all Liverpool. Nothing Arsenal did seemed to come off. But a free-kick on the edge of the Liverpool penalty area raised some hopes.

As the ball was tapped to Davis, he comically shot straight into Quinn's groin. With the ball ricocheting around the penalty area, blind panic suddenly took over. For a second, an uninitiated observer might have thought this was a pub match rather than a cup final between two of the best teams in the country. Just yards from the goal, Nicholas somehow contrived to hit the post. He raised his hands to his head, thinking his big chance had gone, but Anderson was first to react. Pulling the ball back across the goal, this time the Scotsman made no mistake, tapping the ball past Grobbelaar and into the empty net.

Arsenal had been poor. The goal was against the run of play. But somehow they were back in the game, and, what's more, they also had belief.

Stunned, Liverpool sat back to regroup, letting Arsenal have more of the ball. But Rocastle still stood out on the right wing, cutting a frustrated figure. It was clear that Dalglish had ordered his team to stop the ball getting out to him and, if it did, then two players were to be on him as quickly as possible. It was perhaps the first time that a team had identified him as a danger man, and he was struggling to come to terms with the added attention. When he did get the ball, more often than not he was forced to turn infield and play a square pass to Davis. Every time he did this, the red-faced Graham hollered, 'David! Outside!'

All square at half-time, the game was very much in the balance. Again, as the players drank cups of tea in the dressing room, Graham reiterated, 'Stop Molby and McMahon playing. You stop those two. You stop Liverpool.'

And this time the team listened. In the second half, Williams and Davis hounded Molby and McMahon, winning the ball back quickly and then using it diligently, passing wide to Rocastle, who now looked re-energised, or through the middle to Nicholas, playing with new-found confidence, happy to show off his repertoire of flicks and tricks. Sansom and Anderson were also suddenly bombing on, overlapping the wingers and creating new angles. Up against Whelan, Rocastle now had three options, to beat him, or pass to Anderson on the outside or Hayes on the inside. Time and again Arsenal went down the outside, creating opportunities for Nicholas in the process.

Liverpool started to look tired as the youth of Arsenal's team began to tell. Graham noticed this and decided to bring on Groves for Quinn, knowing that his pace might make the difference in the final 20 minutes. Meanwhile, Liverpool brought on player-manager Dalglish for Paul Walsh, in the hope that experience would triumph over youth as the game came to a close. With Dalglish, a legend of the game, next to Groves, a £50,000 signing from Colchester, it summed up the difference in the clubs' status in recent years. But the balance was about to shift.

Groves, a blur of motion, suddenly had the Liverpool defence frantically back-pedalling. They started to sit deeper, to counter this menace, which only encouraged Arsenal on to them.

With just eight minutes remaining, Sansom's long ball to Groves set him up against Gary Gillespie. Using sheer pace, Groves steamed past the Liverpool fullback, leaving him in a heap, as he broke down the left flank. Looking up, he spotted Nicholas on the edge of the penalty area and cut the ball back. It seemed that Nicholas just needed to sweep the ball home to put Arsenal into the lead, but as it came to him he was off-balance. Swiping wildly with his right foot, he didn't connect cleanly. However, with Whelan having anticipated a clean strike, his haphazard attempt to block the weak shot deflected it past his wrong-footed goalkeeper and over the line. GOAL!

The Arsenal half of the stadium erupted. A jolt of frenetic excitement surging through his body, Nicholas jumped over the hoardings and raised his arms victoriously at the fans, letting their cheers wash over him. It may not have been textbook, but Nicholas was bought to be a match-winner and, with just over five minutes to go, it looked as if he might have delivered.

Predicting a final Liverpool assault, Graham swiftly swapped Thomas for Hayes, to shore up the midfield, while he screamed at Groves and Rocastle to protect their fullbacks. Unable to play through the congested middle, Liverpool had no choice but to launch long balls to Rush, which Adams and O'Leary happily headed away to safety. Rather than just sit back, Arsenal now felt that Liverpool were out of ideas and began to play some of their best football.

Davis and Rocastle toyed with the Liverpool midfielders before Nicholas' back-heel almost put Groves through. The fans roared their approval, while Graham was apoplectic on the sideline. It was no time for fantasy football. It was time to shut up shop. Fearing the wrath of their manager, his players did just that, keeping possession when possible and launching the ball downfield for Nicholas to chase when there was no other option.

Whistles from the Arsenal end filled the air as the Wembley clock showed time was up. Graham jumped up and down, frantically pointing to his watch. The referee looked down at his own. Then he lifted his head, put the whistle to his mouth and blew. Game over! Arsenal had won the cup. It was their first trophy in eight years, while they had also consigned the famous Rush statistic to history.

As the Liverpool players dropped to their knees, Rocastle and his team-mates climbed the famous 39 Wembley steps so that Sansom could lift the trophy. All Rocastle could think in the circumstances was, 'This is just like being on the television!'

After lifting the cup, to the deafening applause of the Arsenal fans, and enjoying a lap of honour, the players returned to the changing room to continue the celebrations. 'It is difficult to describe the dressing room,' Sansom said. 'It is like the inside of one of those parties you wished you hadn't visited. Bottles everywhere, kit strewn around ... This is the happiest dressing room I have ever been in.'

With the cup filled to the brim with champagne, it was passed around the dancing and whooping players so that they could savour the taste of victory. Yet as Rocastle smiled and celebrated, he reflected on his performance. 'I wasn't pleased with my display,' he later recalled. 'I didn't play to my potential. I did perform a useful role, making runs inside and taking defenders away, so Viv Anderson had space to attack down the right. I'd like to have shown more of my creative qualities.'

But Rocastle also had other concerns. As Arsenal's season all but crumbled following this victory, winning just five of their remaining nine games, he asked to have a blood test.

'After the Littlewoods Cup win over Liverpool I found I had trouble breathing,' he confided. 'I thought it was the sheer effort that went into beating Liverpool at Wembley. I was totally drained. Tests showed I was suffering from exhaustion and a blood complaint. I was ordered to take a complete rest.'

All in all, the season had been a roaring success, with a trophy won and a top four finish in the league. Sadly, the same could not be said for the 1993/94 season . . .

CHAPTER 21

MAKE OR BREAK

At the crack of dawn every morning, David Rocastle softly kissed Janet on the cheek, looked in on the sleeping Melissa and Ryan, before leaving the house just as the milk float was trundling down the road. Pounding the streets in the early morning sunshine, Rocastle went for long runs around Leeds, not only to burn off his excess fat but to banish all negative thoughts from his mind.

'There were whispers I wasn't fit enough,' he later told the *Sunday Mirror*, 'and on reflection it was probably true. So for six weeks I worked on my fitness, went on four-mile runs and reported back eight pounds lighter.'

Trim, rejuvenated and feeling more like his old self, he scored 'a stunning goal', according to the *Mirror*, in a 3-0 win at Cork where he 'danced through the Cork defence and played a neat one-two with new signing Brian Deane before firing a shot past the goalkeeper'. The previous season hadn't gone to plan but Rocastle was doing absolutely everything to ensure that this time around Wilkinson couldn't ignore him.

His pre-season form was certainly enough to catch the eye of other clubs. Liverpool were again being linked with Rocastle, this time in a potential swap deal with Paul Stewart, while a host of Serie A giants such as Roma, AC Milan and Juventus were also said to be keeping a watching brief. Continuing to be hot property in the football world at large, he remained *persona non grata* at Leeds, despite all of his hard work.

Left out of the team to face Manchester City on the opening day, Rocastle continued to be overlooked. After a 4-0 home defeat to Norwich City he might have expected to be in contention for the trip to Highbury but still found himself frozen out. Slowly but surely he was reaching breaking point. He had knuckled down, got fit, and done everything that had been asked of him, yet even with the team playing poorly there still seemed to be no way back. In an interview with *Match* magazine, a trim Rocastle was pictured wearing boxing gloves and appeared to be in a combative mood.

'It's been a difficult period for me,' he said. 'I spent seven years working hard to build a decent reputation in the game only to find it's taken a knock back. My family have helped me through all the hurt and frustration. If I'd been single, I would have cracked up by now as it's been that rough. I try not to bring it home but it's not been easy. It's the lowest I've ever been in my career. Some days I wondered whether I would ever play first-team football again. What really hurts me most is the names I've been called. People have labelled me a flop and a misfit and it's unfair. I've not had enough games to be called a flop. They only have the right to call me that if I have a lengthy run in the side and still don't produce my best. If that happens I'll be the first to hold up my hands and say I've failed. But until then they should shut up.'

Underlining his frustration, and feeling perhaps there was nothing left to lose, Rocastle chose to take on Wilkinson. 'I've never wanted anything from the management except to be given a fair chance,' he continued, clearly desperate to get his feelings off his chest. 'It was really hard to take when, even though we were struggling and not winning games last season, young kids were being put in ahead of me. When you cost £2 million and sit on the bench, it hurts. When I have played in the first team the critics say I'm not fit. Well, I won't get fit in the reserves. But those people don't understand because they've never played the game.'

Continuing in the *People*, he stressed that he felt his career was passing him by. 'Every week I switch on *Match of the Day* and realise it's another Saturday gone,' he said. 'I feel I'm playing well but until the manager puts me in the team there's nothing I can do. I don't mean just one or two games – I need a run of about 10 to get me going but I've never had that. I've heard it said I was bought for Gordon Strachan's position but when he was injured I didn't get a sniff. I don't want to leave, but I've been in the game 10 years now and I want first-team football.'

Rocastle did, however, manage to show a sense of humour at his situation. Once, when he was followed by a pack of journalists, he found he had been locked out of the Elland Road dressing room. As he knocked on the door, he smiled to the press pack, 'Is someone trying to tell me something?'

Such was Rocastle's lowly status that he was only named on the bench for a League Cup tie with Sunderland. While he made his first appearance of the season, coming on in the 66th minute, Leeds conspired to lose 2-1, as their form lurched from bad to worse.

However, when Strachan was ruled out for at least a month with a knee injury, it finally looked as though Rocastle might have the opportunity for an extended run. Starting in the 0-0 draw with Ipswich, he was solid, if not spectacular. Building on this, he kept his place in the side for the 3-3 draw with Blackburn, followed by the same result against Sheffield Wednesday, where he won the man of the match award after providing assists for Chris Fairclough and Gary Speed.

Gaining match fitness and sharpness, Rocastle then delivered his best display in a Leeds shirt. Starring in a 4-1 demolition of Chelsea, he had scored the fourth goal in the process. In its match report, the *Independent* said, 'The re-emergence of David Rocastle has invigorated the team where it was strongest in their championship year. Rocastle had been a £2m misfit after his transfer from Arsenal, unable to dislodge Gordon Strachan but, as Wilkinson has had to tell him on more than one occasion, everything comes to those who wait. Peter Pan's injury has finally given Mr Impatience his chance, and he could hardly have done more to take it. A model of diligence and enterprise on the right, he also scored the goal of the game, when he shimmied one way and then the other, bemusing Johnsen, before driving the ball in from the edge of the penalty area.'

The Times was equally effusive, stating that he 'could be forgiven a small smirk amid the flood of outrage . . . and revived memories of the darting skills that earned him a championship medal at Highbury'.

Faced with a grinning Wilkinson after the game, some reporters enquired why Rocastle had been left in the cold for so long. 'It happened because of a player who is not bad called Strachan,' he smiled, 'but David Rocastle is a magnificent human being. If I had a daughter free . . .'

Following this performance, and Wilkinson making it clear that he had no issue with Rocastle, he continued to deputise for the injured Strachan, not losing a game during his time in the team. Yet as soon as Strachan was fit again, Rocastle found himself sidelined for the visit of Swindon Town. If he had struggled to contain his frustration before, then this perceived slight brought it all tumbling out.

'I am devastated,' he told the press after the game. 'There's nothing else I can do. Maybe I should ring Graham Kelly at the FA and ask if there's a law against me and Gordon Strachan playing in the same side. I played the last six matches, four of which were hard away games. I was looking forward to two home games where I could express myself. Instead I was dropped. I knew I was not playing on Friday when the boss told us the team and I wasn't in it. But he didn't speak to me. I have a contract here for two years but if they don't want me they should tell me. I don't want to leave. I only want to play for Leeds. But I don't know what the manager expects of me. I don't think it's anything personal – at least I hope not. I'm not a prima donna. I'm a good pro. I have not been outspoken but this has really blown me . . . Two weeks ago I won the man of the match award, now I am not even on the subs' bench.'

Some might say that Rocastle's outburst was unprofessional. Perhaps it was, but in the circumstances it was hard not to empathise. Even on the back of an unbeaten run, and with him showing signs of his old form, this still wasn't enough for him to keep his place ahead of Strachan.

When Wilkinson was asked about the situation with Rocastle, he launched a stinging response. 'He may be disappointed, but I can assure you he's not half as disappointed or annoyed as I am,' he snapped. 'I can understand his frustration up to a point, but not his outburst. If he seriously thinks he has no future with this club then he is entitled to move on. In the old days, players as cheesed off as David would knock on the manager's door and ask to go. Not any more. Now you suddenly get veiled threats appearing on the back pages of newspapers. If David wants to talk over his future he should do it with me in person.'

Rocastle wasn't the only player at Elland Road who now broke ranks. Just a week later, Steve Hodge issued his own blast against

Wilkinson. 'No player can go through 18 months of frustration and not come out blowing his top,' he complained. 'I am not being big-headed but I could play in any Premiership side tomorrow. Before joining Leeds I was sub no more than four times in nine years. Now I have been sub 47 times in the last two years. It's soul-destroying. Things haven't worked with Howard. I can be stubborn and he can be just as stubborn but he's the manager.'

Hodge and Rocastle had arrived at Elland Road as high-profile England internationals. If only one of them had been missing out, then you might draw the conclusion that it was down to that individual's temperament or loss of form. But a scenario in which players like Hodge, Rocastle and Sellars were continually excluded, even with Leeds losing games, tells its own story.

Such had been the success of the midfield quartet of Speed, Strachan, Batty and McAllister during the team's championship-winning season that Wilkinson no doubt found it hard to let go. While he had signed the likes of Hodge, Rocastle and Sellars with squad rotation in mind, that ideal never came to pass. Instead, it was the old quartet who continued to start game after game. Even when some had suffered a loss of form, Wilkinson continued to stand by them, in the belief that they would in time come good again. Only when they were injured would a reserve get an opportunity.

The time had clearly come for Rocastle to depart if he was going to have any chance of kick-starting his stuttering career. Thankfully, Manchester City swooped in December 1993, offering their striker David White in a swap deal to take Rocastle to Maine Road. The nightmare looked to be coming to an end, as long as he passed a medical – not an easy task with his ravaged knee.

Wilkinson was sorry that it had not worked out but he also felt the time was right for Rocastle to move on. 'People have to recognise that they can't play every week,' he said. 'But there's a period of time where it becomes counterproductive for the player and the club. David Rocastle had got to the point where he saw he had no future with Leeds. In business they say it's nice when both parties get up from the table smiling. I think we had that here.'

Just 18 months previously Rocastle had joined the champions for a record fee, hoping to win the title. Now he was preparing for a relegation fight at one of football's most dysfunctional clubs.

CHAPTER 22

THE CULL

George Graham's high standards meant he was satisfied, if not entirely happy. Having had a real opportunity to assess his squad during his first season in charge, a big issue still remained – eliminating the drinking clique. As far as Graham was concerned, this group needed to be culled if he was to stand a chance of truly fashioning a team that would be in his own mould. As such, the 1987/88 season saw a long list of star names depart.

First up was Viv Anderson, who while not part of the drinking clique, joined Manchester United for £250,000. Next was cup final hero and terrace favourite Charlie Nicholas, who first faced the ignominy of the reserves before being sold to Aberdeen mid-season. Also living on borrowed time were Graham Rix and Kenny Sansom, particularly as Graham had bought fullback Nigel Winterburn from Wimbledon, and during the season would add midfielder Kevin Richardson.

While striker Alan Smith finally joined the club in pre-season, and was seen as an upgrade on the raw Niall Quinn, some fans still urged Graham to go out and spend big. Young, cheap and hungry was his preferred market, but some fans were still mystified when former target John Barnes signed for Liverpool from Watford, without Graham even making an enquiry. Barnes would go on to be a huge success, but Graham remained confident that in David Rocastle he had potentially the best winger in the country.

Rocastle may have ended the season out of sorts, but with a few weeks' rest it was felt that he would return to his best. 'I'm breathing OK after my worries at the end of last season,' he confided. 'So there can be no excuses. It's up to me.'

However, whenever Rocastle had any time away from training he seemed destined to put on weight; a pattern which came to haunt him throughout his career. On this occasion there was at least half a stone to lose when he returned. This problem was not something he chose to hide behind a team of PR specialists and spin. He quite openly admitted it in an interview with Kevin Connolly: 'When I reported back for pre-season training I was overweight.'

Losing the weight was not the only issue. It would take so much running to get it off that by the time the season came around he was already feeling heavy-legged. To make matters worse, Arsenal could not have had a tougher start, facing Liverpool and Manchester United in their first two fixtures.

When over 57,000 fans flocked to Highbury for the opening game of the season, they might have been hoping for a repeat of the League Cup final result. Indeed, they certainly took every opportunity to mock the away fans with their triumph. However, Dalglish had been busy during the summer. Ian Rush might have left to join Juventus, but John Barnes and Peter Beardsley had been brought in to support John Aldridge. In tandem, the three would form one of the most potent attacks in English football.

But Arsenal also had every reason to feel confident. New signing

Alan Smith was now leading the line, alongside the mercurial Charlie Nicholas and the previous season's top scorer, Martin Hayes, with Rocastle behind to provide them with excellent service.

Despite this, none of the new signings made the headlines, as Aldridge and Nicol scored for Liverpool, with just Davis responding for Arsenal. The result may have been disappointing but of greater concern to any right-minded fan was the hail of bananas being thrown on to the pitch by the Liverpool supporters, something that also perturbed Nick Hornby: 'Banana after banana was being hurled by the away supporters' enclosure. The bananas were designed to announce, for the benefit of those unversed in codified terrace abuse, that there was a monkey on the pitch; and as the Liverpool fans have never bothered to bring bananas to previous Arsenal matches, even though we have always had at least one black player in the side since the turn of the decade, one can only presume that John Barnes was the monkey to whom they were referring.'

Once again Rocastle was left ruing his display against Liverpool. Struggling to get into the game, he had been subbed for Groves. A mixture of not being match fit, as well as having to contend with increased attention, saw him say, 'Marking has got even tighter now that opponents have become aware of what I can do ... I've seen enough of the game already to be well aware of the downside as well as the cups and awards. Fitness isn't a worry. The challenge is picking up from last season. Yes, I'm under pressure – but that's what we get paid for.'

The subsequent 0-0 draw at Old Trafford, followed by a 2-0 defeat at QPR, had not only left Arsenal winless after three games, but had also seen Rocastle replaced again. 'Being subbed is not a nice experience,' he admitted. 'That's the manager's job. All I can do is try and prove I'm too valuable an asset to the team to be subbed. I've got to shrug off the last few matches. I've come through difficulties like this in the last couple of years, and I can do it again.'

In what was virtually a mirror image of the previous season, Arsenal and Rocastle soon came roaring back to life. Dropping Nicholas, Graham brought Groves into the team, as Arsenal beat Portsmouth 6-0, with Rocastle back in fine form, not only scoring but playing a part in Alan Smith's hat-trick. Showing the grace and flexibility of a gymnast, his body twisting this way and that, he had tormented his fullback, whipping in an array of crosses for Smith to attack.

This result set Arsenal on the way to another lengthy unbeaten run lasting 15 games in all competitions. Rocastle's travails in August suddenly looked to be behind him. The first name on the team sheet, he won the Barclays Young Eagle Player of the Month award for September, in recognition of his barnstorming displays. Despite this, he was still not entirely satisfied. 'I think I'm playing better than at the start of the season,' he said. 'That was a really hard opening – Liverpool, Manchester United and QPR in the first week. I was glad to get them out of the way. But I know I can produce a lot more. I need to start going past players again – the way I was last season. I haven't been doing it lately. I need to regain the confidence and the will to take on defenders, instead of looking to pass the ball when I get it.'

Anyone who had been watching Rocastle might have been surprised at his comments. Some of his football had been scintillating in this spell. Not only had he found the net against Portsmouth and Wimbledon, he had again been on the scoresheet in a 2-1 win at White Hart Lane, which further cemented his status as terrace favourite, while his two goals at Norwich, in a 4-2 win, saw Arsenal go top of the league.

His performance at Norwich prompted the *Sunday Times* to comment that it was 'remarkable by any standards'. Norwich, it said, 'were destroyed mainly by Arsenal's right-side England U-21 midfielder, David Rocastle. It left Norwich's captain, Steve Bruce, wondering how long it will be before Rocastle takes over from England's Trevor Steven in the senior England team.'

'Whereas Steven possibly has the edge defensively,' Bruce later told the press, 'I feel Rocastle has that little bit extra in terms of attacking flair.'

Just as Arsenal, and Rocastle, hit the heights, with a club record 10 straight league wins, they were brought down to earth with a 1-0 home defeat to Southampton. This supposed aberration was followed by a 2-0 defeat at Watford. After a record-breaking winning streak, Arsenal would now win only three of their next 13 games. The major cause of this was a goal drought by Alan Smith, who had been so prolific in the first few months of the season. While some of the crowd criticised him, others had sympathy, pointing out that the service to him was non-existent. Forced to live off hopeful long balls, it was no wonder that Smith's chances to score were now so rare.

Again, Rocastle's form had also faltered. Over the busy December period he resembled the tired player he had been at the end of the previous season. Frustratingly inconsistent, he was seemingly incapable of maintaining his good form over the course of a full season. To compound matters, John Barnes had displayed exceptional form for Liverpool, who now topped the table. Some fans again questioned Graham's judgement for overlooking the man from Watford, as by the end of the year Arsenal had slipped away from any chance of being in contention for the title.

Surveying his faltering team as the New Year approached, Graham decided it was once again time to take some hard decisions. Prepared to wield the axe on those who had failed him, Rocastle hoped to escape another cull.

CHAPTER 23

THE MAINE MAN

'The club of cock-ups.' That is how the *Independent* described Manchester City in the autumn of 1993. While Manchester United swept all before them, and the city rocked to the sound of the Stone Roses and acid house, City was seen by many as a laughing stock.

After years of underachievement, they were floundering in the relegation zone, with an acrimonious takeover battle tearing the club apart. In one corner was former crowd favourite Francis Lee; in the other, chairman Peter Swales. Sinking deeper into the mire, optimism and enthusiasm were at an all-time low, and many were already calling for manager Brian Horton's head, although he'd only taken over from Peter Reid in September.

Despite all of this, two-time title winner and England international David Rocastle was desperate to join the sinking ship. The only potential stumbling block was his medical. With his long-standing knee issue – George Graham had been surprised that he'd passed his medical at Leeds – and an additional 18 months of football on the clock, there was a good chance that things could have deteriorated further.

The Manchester City physiotherapist Eamonn Salmon was in charge of overseeing the medical and, while it was nowhere near as comprehensive as you might get today, it still revealed a problem. 'The X-ray revealed a worn knee,' he told me. 'But we didn't really have scans then so we couldn't take a proper look. However, an X-ray of the knee can look as if it is perfect, and a person can hardly walk, and an X-ray can also look absolutely awful, and the person can still play football. So in that respect, back then, you didn't weigh your decision solely on the basis of the X-ray. I do recall that we met with the manager, Brian Horton, and said, "Look, we're a bit concerned with his knee," but it came down to the fact that he had been playing recently at Leeds, and playing well.'

Brian Horton recalls that he wasn't unduly concerned about the knee. 'With most footballers when they have a medical there will be some kind of issue,' he told me. 'They play football all their life since they were a kid so they pick up knocks along the way. Rocky was 26 at the time and at that age you can have some wear and tear. You can have a bit of arthritis. You can have a bad injury somewhere along the line. Players have all these issues and they come back and play fantastic.'

Putting his Elland Road nightmare behind him, Rocastle couldn't hide his delight. 'This is a fantastic move for me considering I have been out of the limelight for the 18 months I've been at Leeds,' he said. 'To get the opportunity to show I can play football with a big club like City is an early Christmas present for me.'

Such was Rocastle's desire to make an impact at Manchester City that even when his partner Janet opted to return to London with their two children, he still went ahead with the move. Staying in a hotel in Manchester would be lonely, but after almost two years of personal issues, and not playing, Rocastle knew that it was vital he was 100 per cent focused on the job at hand.

Having prepared himself for a relegation battle, he was pleasantly surprised by what he found at the Platt Lane training ground. 'What I have seen at City so far revives memories of when I joined Arsenal,' he told the press prior to his debut. 'Just as we had at Highbury, City have a blend of youth and experience and it only has to be channelled in the right direction. Here at City there are superb young prospects like Richard Edghill, Garry Flitcroft and Steve Lomas. Now it is my turn to help those on their way up. I want to help in the same way I was helped at Highbury. I am still only 26 but I've won titles and played for England – I like to think I know a bit about the game. And I want to be big enough to take some real responsibility.'

This was exactly the role Horton had hoped Rocastle would take on. 'He was a fantastic person,' he said. 'The lads loved him, and the staff loved him, because he was so polite and nice. He was a genuine pleasure to work with. He was one of those lads that was a great trainer, had great ability and the fans loved him as well. I couldn't have asked for a better person, or a better player.'

These thoughts were echoed by everyone I spoke to at the club. 'He was one of the nicest men in the game,' Salmon recalls. 'Quiet, mild-mannered and gentle. I can see him now getting ready for training with a smile on his face. He was always smiling. We were struggling at the time but he gave us a lift. He was like a breath of fresh air.'

At just 22 years of age, midfielder Fitzroy Simpson had grown disenchanted because of his inability to become a first-team regular. He freely admits that, at this time, he was finding it hard to channel his frustration, yet Rocastle was always there for him. 'Playing with him, and being around him, I used to take a lot of advice from Rocky,' he said. 'He really encouraged me when I was

An 'outstanding' performance from Rocastle in the Under-21 European Championship qualifier helped England to a record 5-1 away win against Yugoslavia. *(Getty Images)*

With the likes of Barnes, Waddle and Robson in the side, Rocastle felt almost overawed in the decisive World Cup qualifier in Poland in October 1989. Happily, England got through despite a low-key performance. *(Getty Images)*

Back to Poland, this time under Graham Taylor, when England scraped through another vital qualifier to reach Euro 92, helped by a Rocastle assist for the crucial goal. *(PA/Empics)*

When David Dein had first seen Rocastle, he'd described him as the 'nearest thing to a Brazilian footballer', but sadly this May 1992 game against Brazil at Wembley, just a few days after his 25th birthday, would be his last England cap. *(Mirrorpix)*

More trouble with United. Rocastle was at the centre of things in the Battle of Old Trafford in October 1990, which resulted in the Gunners being docked two points, threatening their title challenge. *(PA/Empics)*

Despite which, the Gunners went on to secure the trophy once more, and Rocastle was able to show it off to his daughter. *(Getty Images)*

Rocastle was thrilled to line up with his friend Ian Wright in September 1991, little realising that it would be his last season with Arsenal. *(PA/Empics)*

A perfect debut for Leeds United in August 1992, as Man of the Match Rocastle scores the winner against VfB Stuttgart at Elland Road. *(Getty Images)*

But the form of Gordon Strachan and injury problems left Rocastle struggling. Here, he is beaten to the ball by former team-mate Paul Merson. *(PA)*

Fitzroy Simpson runs to join in the celebrations after Rocastle's goal against Swindon Town in February 1994. The young City player described the Londoner as 'always an inspiration'. *(PA/Empics)*

A sublime piece of skill from Rocastle helped turn the game against Ipswich Town as the Francis Lee era appeared to offer a new dawn for City. *(PA/Empics)*

Rocastle joined Chelsea in the summer of 1994, his knowhow and guile well suited to European competition. *(PA/Empics)*

For much of the time that he was at Chelsea, Rocastle was confined to the Reserves. In this case, however, he was surrounded by talent as he tackles Tony Adams, while a 17-year-old John Terry watches on. *(Getty Images)*

31 March 2001: a minute's silence is impeccably observed at Highbury to mourn the loss of Rocastle at the tragically early age of 33. *(PA/Empics)*

Rocastle's son Ryan leads out the Arsenal team ahead of the 2001 FA Cup final.
(PA/Empics)

David Rocastle – champion!

down, or in and out of the team, on the bench and so forth. He was always an inspiration, someone to talk to. He always had time and freely gave me advice. I respect him eternally for it.'

A regular visitor to Rocastle's hotel, Simpson was desperate just to talk football with him. His favourite topic of discussion would usually be Arsenal, George Graham and his former team-mates, a subject Simpson was keen to press him on, especially as he wanted to model his game on Paul Davis.

Coach David Moss recalls that Rocastle's mere presence gave everyone a much-needed lift: 'With all the rubbish going on from day to day, and then dealing with demonstrations and all the rest of it on a Saturday, there had been a real feeling of negativity about the place. But he just came in with that big smile, and easy-going nature, and you couldn't help but to take to him.'

Earning respect for his stature and personality, Rocastle's primary objective was nevertheless to help City on the pitch. In their last 12 matches they had recorded just one win. The relegation trapdoor was wide and yawning. Things needed to change swiftly, starting with Rocastle's debut against Southampton at Maine Road.

Immediately making himself a fan favourite in the opening minutes, Rocastle cleaned out Southampton fullback Micky Adams with a ferocious tackle, before spraying the ball wide to Mike Sheron. Although he was bought with his finesse and technical virtuosity in mind, the Maine Road crowd were certainly happy also to see some guts and fight.

The game might have ended in a 1-1 draw, but *The Times* reported that Rocastle had enjoyed a 'quietly satisfactory game, rather than a heroic one, although Leeds supporters will be interested to hear that he lasted the full 90 minutes'.

However, if his debut represented a solid though not spectacular start, then the subsequent 2-0 loss to Newcastle really let him know what he had let himself in for. The *Independent* said of this, 'David

Rocastle, you suspect, is already looking back to his "hell" at Leeds as purgatory to prepare him for the real thing in a sky blue shirt.'

And if he hadn't already had a sufficient taste of what life at Manchester City was all about, the following game against Ipswich would have left him in no doubt. After 39 minutes, City were leading 2-0 and had been majestic. The rain was torrential at times, and had soaked the pitch, but that hadn't hindered Rocastle in the slightest. 'He took the game by the scruff of the neck,' Simpson recalls. 'I remember being sat on the bench, watching, and I was like "wow". Most people were wearing long studs and slipping and sliding but he just seemed to glide across the pitch. It was as if he was wearing slippers. He made the game look so easy.'

But as the game approached half-time, and City were coasting to just their second win in 15 matches, referee David Elleray decided that the waterlogged pitch had become unsafe. Blowing his whistle, he pointed towards the dressing rooms, calling off the game. The scenes that followed were unsavoury, but understandable. Rocastle and Tony Coton jostled and chased Elleray, while 200 fans invaded the pitch and staged a demonstration, leading to Brian Horton appealing for them to leave or have the club face a potential points deduction. Even when City and Rocastle were playing well, they still couldn't get a win.

With frustration mounting, they took it all out on Leicester, running away 4-1 winners in the FA Cup. The victory was certainly good for morale, but it was also notable for the fact that Rocastle's knee came under a severe test. In a game totally dominated by Rocastle, Leicester's David Speedie appeared to lose control. First elbowing defender Richard Edghill, he was also involved in a confrontation with Alan Kernaghan before chopping Rocastle down at the knee. Never one to show that he was hurt, Rocastle jumped straight back up. However, his limp afterwards told its own story.

It certainly seems from watching contemporary footage of

Rocastle that his knee wasn't hindering his movement, and all the staff at Manchester City recall that it never posed a real problem.

'I don't remember ever needing to treat him,' Salmon told me. 'He may have had a knock here and there but never anything serious. He trained every day and certainly never required an individual training programme to accommodate his injury.'

Horton also told me that Rocastle just wanted to be out on the pitch. 'David always wanted to play. He never asked for the morning off or said he was struggling. No matter what, he was always out there.'

'I was initially a little concerned about his knee,' David Moss recalled. 'I think that you could see that he'd lost a little bit of zip. But he tailored his game to cope with that as he gathered experience. His first touch was still perfect, and his football brain, along with his personality, still meant he was a very good player.'

Seemingly unhindered by injury, even if he had lost some pace and mobility, Rocastle was soon match fit and playing consistently for the first time in three years. And there was no better time to show that he could still cut it at the top level than for the visit of Arsenal to Maine Road.

The ensuing game was by no means a classic, as Arsenal were intent on grinding out a dreary 0-0 draw. Still, Rocastle earned applause from all sides of the ground for his contribution. The *Independent* reported that he had 'contributed an important influence over the game, both in his willingness to check back as Arsenal counteracted, and, more importantly, moving forward with an eye on space and openings'. The flourishing midfield partnership between Rocastle and Garry Flitcroft was also singled out for praise: 'Both players retained possession confidently, leaving Arsenal to spend the last quarter of an hour doggedly closing doors and turning off the lights of a match that had begun brightly.'

However, while the *Independent* stated that Rocastle had taken 'the loudest cheers of the standing ovation', it nevertheless sounded a note of warning on his supposed renaissance: 'Whether his clanking knees will last much longer is another matter.'

At long last, City looked to have turned a corner, and Rocastle was earning credit from all quarters for his influence. But as always it was one step forwards, two steps back. A 2-1 defeat at Anfield was nothing to be ashamed of, but the 1-0 collapse to third division Cardiff City in the FA Cup was a severe blow to morale.

How the team reacted to such a giant-killing would prove to be a real test of their mental resolve. The defining point of the season had been reached, and if they didn't concentrate their minds fast then it could be too late by the time they had recovered. Thankfully, their next game was the rescheduled fixture against Ipswich. The players believed that they had been robbed of three points when the original match had been abandoned and Rocastle in particular felt he had a point to prove, having delivered his best performance in a City shirt in that game, only to see it count for nothing.

The game also marked the end of the internecine struggle that had caused so much distraction. Watching on from the stands, new chairman Francis Lee accepted the applause of the 28,000 fans who had turned up to cheer him on. As 10,000 white-and-blue balloons heralded his arrival, the stadium announcer proclaimed that he was the man 'who will put the word "great" into Manchester City once again'.

Within 16 minutes, Ipswich's Ian Marshall, the man with the best mullet in the Premier League, struck to spoil the party. But this setback seemed to inspire City, and just after the half-hour mark Rocastle produced a piece of skill that is still fondly remembered. Out on the right-hand touchline, he enticed two opponents on to him, before dragging the ball back with the sole of his foot. As the two Ipswich players flinched, he swiftly turned and dragged the ball in the opposite direction, spinning 360 degrees in a blur of deception as he set off to the by-line. The crowd rose to its feet as he then delivered an inch-perfect cross for Carl Griffiths to equalise at the back post.

Everyone I interviewed from Manchester City brought up this moment unprompted. 'I don't know how he did it,' Salmon laughed. 'He somehow jimmied around with the ball and suddenly he had left two players for dead. It was remarkable.'

'You couldn't coach that,' Horton told me. 'He just had such natural ability. But with David I didn't have to teach him how to play. There are some players you don't have to tell what to do. You could see that he was enjoying his football again and, if you enjoy your football, you play your best and feel that you can express yourself.'

Fitzroy Simpson felt that this moment of skill didn't just help City to equalise in this game but it was also a vital spark to their season. 'There's no question that it inspired us,' he said. 'We were really facing it at one stage, and it actually wasn't a good place to be around, but that just showed the quality we had in the team. It made us believe.'

On the City bench, David Moss not only appreciated Rocastle's stunning piece of skill but also admired the end product. 'I could see in training he was a quality player with a lot of skill,' he said. 'He always had plenty of tricks but this was a real bit of magic and, best of all, he used it to create a goal out of nothing. It got the fans out of their seats and had them thinking, "Wow, what have we got here?"'

From that moment on, City took full control, with Garry Flitcroft going on to score the winner. It was just their second win in 17 matches yet Horton told the press, 'If the team continues to fight and play like this then we'll be all right.'

However, instead of a bright new era under Francis Lee, City remained frustratingly inconsistent. Scoring goals was always an issue, as was defending them. A humiliating 4-0 defeat to Coventry

City was sandwiched between goalless draws against West Ham and Aston Villa.

With a new man at the helm, the press speculated that he might choose to sack Horton and bring in his own manager. The game against fellow strugglers Swindon Town was therefore considered a must win. Anything less than three points and the cries for Horton to go would surely grow.

The performance against a team already destined for the drop certainly didn't provide Horton with much comfort. City were insipid and benign, and the crowd soon got on their backs, especially after Swindon had taken an early lead. While a Horlock own goal levelled the scores, it was Rocastle who scored the winner in the second half, repaying the faith his manager had shown in him. As usual, he was the man for the big occasion.

The Times may have felt that City's victory was 'undeserved', but it still had praise for Rocastle's performance, stating, 'David Rocastle again made nonsense of his struggles at Leeds with a fine display culminating in the winning goal.' The *Independent*, meanwhile, said that he had delivered a 'virtuoso' display and that the Kippax Stand had 'showed their appreciation with a wealth of applause' for him.

And the man of the moment was keen to tell the press after the game that, despite the challenges facing the team, he was optimistic about the future. 'I know it sounds crazy to say this,' Rocastle said, 'but we will be a real force next season when we get everybody fit.'

The press might have scoffed at such talk but this win kickstarted City's best run of the season. Losing just two of their remaining 11 games they steered themselves to safety with games to spare. Struggling to maintain his high standards in every game, Rocastle was still the difference in many. Setting up vital goals in wins against Villa and Southampton, he was also inspirational in the shock win against Newcastle, which pushed City up into mid-table, banishing any talk of the drop.

Rocastle had been so influential at City that the *Independent* named him in their top 10 signings of the season. Simpson said of this, 'He was phenomenal. His touch. His awareness. His skill. Everything was at the top level. And he commanded respect. He was an absolute gentleman. He made a huge impact.'

Rocastle might have felt that he had proved a point to George Graham and Howard Wilkinson. He might have felt that the following season he could build on his form at City. He might have felt that finally the tide had turned for him. Sadly, he was wrong.

When he returned for pre-season he found himself out of the picture. The likes of Peter Beagrie and Nicky Summerbee had been signed in an attempt to freshen things up and suddenly Rocastle was consigned to the bench. Sensing his frustration, and knowing that he would have a more limited role in the season ahead, Brian Horton decided to accept a £1.25m offer from Chelsea. It gave him the opportunity to bring in a decent transfer fee for a player he now considered to be a reserve, and for Rocastle it meant he could return to be with his family in London. On the subject of the move, Horton said, 'It was hard to see where I could have accommodated him. David was upset about being left out of a couple of pre-season games. When the offer came in I felt it was good business.'

Although slightly perplexed by this turn of events, Rocastle was also happy. 'The move came completely out of the blue,' he told the press. 'I was on my way to training this morning and was told that the club had accepted a good offer from Chelsea. Chelsea are a young side with a lot of good players. Following their success at reaching the FA Cup final last year, they're in Europe. Hopefully I can use my experience to help them and I'm looking forward to some exciting times. I'm raring to get going and I hope this is my final move ...'

CHAPTER 24

BACK TO THE FUTURE

The last few weeks of 1987 had seen Arsenal flatline. While the team was not quite on life support, Graham decided to put some of his players out of their misery.

His first move was to strip Kenny Sansom of the captaincy and pass it over to 21-year-old Tony Adams. Sansom was considered by many to be England's number one fullback, as well as Arsenal's best player, but it seems he never fully bought into the Graham regime. Arguing with the boss in the dressing room was one thing, but then going to the press to complain about his tactics was quite another.

Although he was young, there was no doubt that Adams was captaincy material. Ever since his days in the youth team, he had always been a dominant force in the dressing room, and had been completely undaunted by the step up to the first team. Inspiring, organising and barracking his team-mates, Adams was certainly a popular choice to replace Sansom.

Sansom's time as first-choice left back was also coming to an end, as Graham started to blood Nigel Winterburn, his summer signing from Wimbledon. Sansom may have been a better footballer than Winterburn, but crucially his replacement was on board with the Graham philosophy. When it came to an argument between talent and obedience, there was no contest in Graham's eyes. He knew exactly how he wanted his team to play and he needed men he could trust on the pitch. Far too often he felt that Sansom's foraging runs forward had forced his players to move out of position in order to cover him.

Once again proving his mastery of the transfer market, Graham bought unheralded fullback Lee Dixon from Stoke City, with centre back Steve Bould joining in June. The building blocks of the famous Graham back four of Dixon, Adams, Bould and Winterburn were taking shape for the first time.

While the defence was falling into place, Graham felt that the sluggish midfield also needed addressing. The central trio of Davis, Williams and Richardson were all gifted footballers in their own right, and brought particular strengths to the team, but Graham needed someone in the middle who could provide energy and get forward to support the increasingly isolated Alan Smith. To much surprise, right back Michael Thomas was given the opportunity at the expense of the combative Steve Williams, and he soon flourished in his new role.

Tinkering with his team, Graham also awarded new contracts to those players he trusted. One of those was David Rocastle, who in January 1988 committed himself to another four years at the club. 'I was happy to commit myself to Arsenal,' Rocastle smiled, 'because I'm very optimistic about our future. We're still a young side and we're getting better all the time.'

With Graham tying down a number of his team-mates on long-term contracts, Rocastle was also excited at the prospect of them all growing together. 'It must be good for our chances that we can expect our present squad to be together for the next three or four years,' he proclaimed. 'That's important because playing together builds understanding. And if the manager does make signings, it will be easier for them if they can slot into a side in which everyone knows exactly what's expected of him and the players around him. Because we're a young side, we're still developing as a unit. We can still improve a lot. I don't think we'll be at our peak for another two years at least.'

Despite Graham's changes there wasn't an immediate upturn in results in the league, with Arsenal failing to register a single victory during January. However, the opportunity to progress in the cups seemed once again to bring out the best in them. In the FA Cup, Millwall and Brighton were vanquished to set up a February tie with Manchester United, while in the League Cup a semi-final clash with Everton awaited following the defeat of Sheffield Wednesday.

In a hectic few weeks that threatened to be season-defining, Arsenal made the journey to Goodison Park on 7 February to contest the first leg of the League Cup semi-final. The team was not, however, travelling in high spirits. Not only was their league form poor, but the previous day the first team had been beaten by the youth team in training. The omens were not looking good.

If the team was suffering from a lack of confidence, their nerves were settled as early as the 10th minute when Perry Groves struck a rasping volley past Welsh goalkeeper Neville Southall. Sitting deep and soaking up the relentless pressure, it appeared that Arsenal were going to hang on for a famous victory, until Graeme Sharp was awarded a penalty. The decision was so contentious that Rocastle had to be physically restrained by Michael Thomas from haranguing the referee. Even after Trevor Steven missed the spot kick, Rocastle still could not keep his emotions in check. Sensing that his number 7 had lost his composure, Graham duly substituted him, but Arsenal and Rocastle would go on to leave Merseyside with the win.

Reinvigorated by their win at Everton, the team were in buoyant mood when they left Kenilworth Road after their next match. Rocastle's brilliant winner, which had seen him flick the ball past the onrushing Les Sealey before proceeding to curl it into the net from 20 yards, was proof that confidence was again coursing through his veins.

Suddenly, as they prepared to face Manchester United in the FA Cup, Arsenal had momentum. Just weeks earlier United had confidently beaten them 2-1 at Highbury. Now they were a very different proposition. In front of 53,000 fans, the teams positioned fifth and second in the league delivered a pulsating cup tie, which *The Times* declared 'a classic'.

Arsenal, fast, powerful and determined, were at their best in the first half, dominating the midfield and going in at the break 2-0 up, courtesy of an opener from Alan Smith and a Mike Duxbury own goal. The second half continued in a similar vein. Penning their opponents into their own half, Arsenal looked to have tamed the United beast, until Brian McClair struck a goal against the run of play. Suddenly, United were rampant, and they looked set to equalise after Norman Whiteside won a penalty with just four minutes to go.

Incredibly, McClair, the second top scorer in the league, blazed the kick over the bar. As McClair held his head in his hands, he was pursued by a wild-eyed Nigel Winterburn. While this flashpoint would not have any immediate repercussions, it sowed the seeds for the brawl at Old Trafford, which was still some two years away.

In any event, another missed penalty had seen Arsenal cling on for the win, which put them in high spirits for the second leg of the League Cup semi-final. Just a year earlier Rocastle had famously been the match-winner in the semi-final clash with Spurs. Once again coming to the fore, he delivered one of his finest performances in an Arsenal shirt.

Just days after 53,000 fans saw Arsenal defeat Manchester United, Highbury was again in tumult as another 51,000 supporters filled the stadium, most of them hoping the team in red and white could continue their remarkable cup form. A solitary goal divided the teams going into the game but it should have been added to in another mesmerising first-half display.

The young tyros Rocastle and Thomas rampaged through the champions' midfield at will yet couldn't finish them off. Rocastle was guilty of a particularly glaring miss, as he rounded Southall only to stroke the ball wide of the empty net. Desperate to make amends, he buzzed around the pitch before putting Hayes through, only for him to be tripped by Southall just inches from the goal line. Stepping up to take the spot kick, Hayes duly smashed it over the crossbar.

All square at half-time, it seemed that Everton would surely regroup and make Arsenal pay for their profligacy in front of goal. The tension in the Highbury crowd certainly made it feel that a significant opportunity had gone begging.

However, just minutes after the restart, Thomas grabbed the all-important goal, unleashing a huge Highbury roar. Suddenly, the final was within touching distance, until Adrian Heath pulled a goal back. With Arsenal nerves frayed, it fell to Rocastle to atone for his earlier miss. Collecting the ball from Groves on the edge of the box, he calmly passed it into the far corner of the goal, as if it were nothing more than a training routine. Rocastle had done it again and now surely Wembley beckoned. And if there had been any remaining doubts, Rocastle's defence-splitting pass for Winterburn to cross for Smith settled the game once and for all.

For the second consecutive year Arsenal had a cup final to look forward to, where they would face lowly Luton. With Rocastle in dazzling form, it looked to be Arsenal's for the taking. Indeed, he was now the team's joint top goalscorer with 11, delivering on his pre-season promise to be more of a goal threat. 'I've been a lot happier with my form over the last couple of months,' he said, 'and pleased that I've been scoring regularly. I've already scored more than I did last season. I've always thought that finishing was one of my strengths – but I hadn't been getting into the positions where I could use that ability. This season I've been more positive. I've tried to do more of my work inside the box. I'm much more of an attacking midfield player than a defender, so I've aimed to play 20 or 30 yards further forward, firing in early crosses and shots. I'd have been happy to get into double figures. Now I think I can even reach 15. It's important that midfield players score, because it lifts the pressure off the two strikers.'

Although Rocastle's scoring streak would continue in the quarter-finals of the FA Cup against Nottingham Forest, the prospect of two Wembley cup finals was at an end following a 2-1 defeat.

Expected by most to sweep Luton aside in the League Cup final, the team's form going into the game was patchy. Following the Everton semi-final victory, they won just four out of 11 games. This run included a 4-2 defeat to Southampton, where an unknown debutant by the name of Alan Shearer scored a hat-trick.

Having expected to see Colin Clarke lead the line for Southampton, there was confusion in the Arsenal dressing room when the team sheet had Shearer's name in his place. When Graham asked his team if anyone knew anything about him, it transpired that Paul Merson had played with Shearer for the England Under-19 team. Relying on Merson to give his critique of the 17-year-old, Graham and the team were told that he 'wasn't a natural goalscorer' and that he 'wasn't a box player'.

Ninety minutes later Shearer had become the first player in first division history to score a hat-trick on his full league debut. To make matters worse, all the goals were in the box. As we know now, Shearer would go on to become the Premier League's all-time record goalscorer and England captain. Unsurprisingly, Graham was none too amused in the dressing room after the game. As Merson hid in the showers, trying to escape his boss's wrath, Graham told his team, 'Remind me never to send Merse on a scouting mission.'

Despite this erratic form in the league, the team was very much aware that their whole season rested on victory in the League Cup. Keeping the cup in the Highbury trophy cabinet would represent encouraging if not spectacular progress, and would certainly add momentum to a potential title challenge the following season.

The previous final against Liverpool had seen an unwell Rocastle turn in a subdued performance. On this occasion he was determined to deliver, although he expressed some concerns about the team's recent form, as well as his own. 'Our season has gone quiet after our FA Cup exit,' he admitted. 'I'm sure we will be keyed up for the big occasion, though – and I know I have to play better than I have lately. I've been a bit tired but I can't use that as an excuse. So I'm looking on Wembley as a great opportunity. I'd love to go past tackles and show my strengths. I want to get in shots and crosses. I want to get at their defence. It would give me tremendous satisfaction if I could show my best form on such a grand occasion.'

Rocastle's honesty in his interviews is always striking. These days it is extremely rare to find any player confess that they are feeling tired before a cup final. Such comments would be seized upon and endlessly debated in the 24/7 news loop as well as across social media. No doubt there would be phone-ins criticising him for showing weakness, or for not being more professional, and some would surely campaign for Graham to drop him. Thankfully, while the media at the time exerted a degree of pressure, it was nowhere near the intense and constant scrutiny we get today.

On a perfect spring day in April, Arsenal returned to Wembley fully expecting to retain their trophy. Just a month earlier, Luton had lost 4-1 to Reading in the Simod Cup final and, of course, they would not have the advantage of playing on their artificial pitch. As such, all the clever money was on the Gunners.

However, Luton clearly hadn't read the script, as Brian Stein put the Hatters in front and proceeded to dominate the first half. Graham was not amused at half-time. Tearing into his team, they emerged for the second half looking to prove that they had not just turned up and expected their opponents to roll over.

The emergence of Martin Hayes, who had replaced Groves, gave Arsenal a new dynamic. Suddenly rampant, goals from Hayes and Smith gave them the lead, and it looked as though Arsenal would score with every attack. Rocastle and Thomas were particularly threatening. Like predators toying with their prey, they surged forward at every opportunity, putting the panicking Luton defence on the back foot.

During this 20-minute spell, Arsenal were imperious. Adams appeared to be impregnable at the back, the midfield was easily outmanoeuvring and outwitting their tiring opponents, while the height of Smith, combined with the pace of Hayes, saw Luton constantly back-pedalling, resorting to hoofing the ball out of harm's way, only to unleash another Arsenal onslaught.

When Smith hit the crossbar with a header and Hayes missed the rebound on the line, somehow hitting the post, it seemed to be a moment the Arsenal fans could laugh about in the pub afterwards. Indeed, even when Rocastle won a penalty, only for Winterburn to miss, it still seemed inconceivable that Arsenal could lose the game, such was their dominance.

Yet with eight minutes to go, a Gus Caesar error allowed Danny

Wilson to equalise. Nevertheless, Arsenal had been so superior in the second half that the game still appeared to be theirs to lose. Somehow, though, they contrived to do just that. Failing once again to pick up Stein, he swooped in the final minute to give Luton a famous victory. Just as they had done in the first half, in the last 10 minutes Arsenal were guilty of taking their opponents for granted.

In his autobiography, Tony Adams had this to say: 'Just as Nigel Winterburn was about to step up to take the penalty to give us a two-goal cushion, I remember looking up to the Royal Box to where the trophy was resting and thinking that I would be lifting it in 10 minutes or so.'

Such an admission merely underlines that Adams was at that point a naive 21-year-old, still finding his way in the harsh world of professional football, as were the likes of Rocastle, Thomas, Hayes, Caesar and Groves. This would prove to be a vital lesson for them all in years to come.

It was ironic that the previous year Rocastle had played poorly but Arsenal had caused a major upset in beating Liverpool. On this occasion, he had played well but was now on the wrong end of an upset. It was no consolation, and on both occasions he left Wembley feeling as if the day hadn't gone to plan. 'I've got to see it as an experience and learn from it,' he said afterwards. 'We know we should have won the match when we took the lead 2-1. A more experienced team would have shut the door on Luton Town. We left it slightly open and they took their chance. We're a very young team at Arsenal. The season is long and tough.'

As Arsenal finished the season without a trophy, and in the disappointing position of sixth in the league, Rocastle could still look back on the campaign with some satisfaction. Finishing third in the PFA Young Player of the Year award, behind Paul Gascoigne and Nigel Clough, he also had a fridge full of champagne, thanks to a bet he had made with coach Theo Foley. 'From the start of the season he [Foley] was betting a bottle of bubbly that I wouldn't score in certain games,' Rocastle laughed. 'But I kept getting on the scoresheet!'

However, if the team was to improve the following season they would need to grow up fast. Thankfully, the season to come would be one to remember.

CHAPTER 25

LONDON CALLING

'At the training facilities in Harlington I didn't have an office or a phone. I remember that when I was selling Andy Townsend to Aston Villa for £2m I had to do the negotiations over a payphone in the corridor. Graham Rix was standing next to me with a handful of change to keep topping it up!'

This anecdote, told to me by Glenn Hoddle, illustrates the state Chelsea Football Club was in when he was appointed as player-manager in 1993. Far from the status it enjoys today as one of the richest football clubs in the world, Chelsea were then mired in poverty and mediocrity. Promoted to the first division in 1989, the club had not won a trophy since the European Cup-Winners' Cup in 1971. Indeed, in that time it had become more renowned for its hooligan element than for its style of football.

Hoddle was brought in to change all of that. Regarded as one of England's most elegant footballers, he had enjoyed great success at Monaco where he had played, and learnt, under Arsène Wenger. Taking on board many of Wenger's philosophies, he had reaped rewards at Swindon, leading them to the Premier League, before accepting the challenge of reinvigorating Chelsea.

When I spoke to Hoddle, as well as some of his former staff and players, they all reminisced at just how poor the facilities at the club had been. Training at Imperial College's playing grounds near Heathrow, they often found that they were unable to use the pitches as the university students needed them. There were no baths. No gym. No manager's office. No masseurs. No nutritionists. Not even any proper food. Many other clubs in the Premier League also had similar issues, but Hoddle's time at Monaco had shown him that things could be different.

Wrestling every penny that he could from chairman Ken Bates, Hoddle was convinced that for the English game to progress there needed to be a complete overhaul. 'We didn't have much money,' Hoddle told me. 'So we had to dig in deep as there was a lot of work on the training ground that needed to be done. It was top to bottom stuff, really.'

Nutrition became a particular obsession. Before Hoddle arrived, club captain Dennis Wise would call a designated player before training to ensure that they were bringing biscuits with them so that the players could enjoy them with a cup of tea. After training it was not uncommon to see a queue of Chelsea players in the local McDonald's.

Suddenly, with Hoddle's arrival, there was a chef who prepared pasta, salmon and chicken for lunch. There were individual nutrition programmes, masseurs for pre- and post-training rubdowns, a gymnasium, as well as full-time medical staff. On the pitch, things changed just as dramatically.

'Technically, the players hadn't worked with the ball enough,' Hoddle remembered. 'So I tried to do a lot more drills focused on ball work.'

Michael Duberry, a young central defender of promise, was one of those who eagerly took to Hoddle's new methods. 'It was very technical,' he said. 'Even the warm-up would be a little bit of five-yard volleys to get your technique right.'

It also helped that Hoddle was not only the manager, but still a highly regarded footballer. 'He would explain the session and do a demonstration,' Duberry told me. 'He would say, "You get the ball, you chest it, bring it down, ping it out wide." Then, boom, he would hit an inch-perfect 50-yard pass. And you would think, "Oh my God." He raised the bar.'

Rocastle might not have realised it, but he was about to play for a manager who was totally changing the face of English football for years to come. Many have credited Arsène Wenger's arrival at Arsenal with revolutionising the game in this country, but a lot of his methods had already been in operation at Chelsea thanks to Hoddle. It wasn't an easy matter to change the culture, certainly not overnight. Most British players were ignorant about their diet, and were used to the focus being on fitness rather than technique. As such, Hoddle and his ilk met a good deal of opposition.

Other young British managers in the game had already found their careers affected by trying to do too much too soon. By the mid-1990s, the likes of Graeme Souness at Liverpool and Ray Wilkins at QPR had also tried to change the culture of the game by preaching what they had learnt during their time in Italy. Encountering considerable resistance, which translated into mixed results, they ultimately faced the sack.

With Hoddle trying to avoid that fate at Chelsea, it might seem strange that he would choose to spend big money on a player who had well-publicised injury issues, and who was also being sold by a club that had just escaped relegation. However, Hoddle saw things differently.

'I needed to improve the squad,' Hoddle revealed. 'I needed to get some experience in there and I needed some good players who could play the way that I wanted to play. I remembered Rocky at Arsenal, in his heyday, a wonderful player. He had such good ability on the ball, great technique, a smooth runner, and he could cope with it under a bit of pressure. I knew he had a slight knee problem, but I felt that with his experience and ability he was good value.'

The days of Rocastle operating as a flying winger were now long behind him but Hoddle had earmarked him to be his ball-playing central midfielder. 'I knew he could control a game,' he said. 'But I wanted him to move the ball a little quicker than he had been, probably because he was still thinking a little bit as a winger. I remember him getting caught on the ball a bit and I told him, "Look, it's a quicker game than that, you've got probably one- or two-touch before you give it. I know you can see things so just let the ball do the work."'

There was another reason why Hoddle wanted Rocastle. As FA Cup runners-up the previous season, Chelsea were in the European Cup-Winners' Cup. Hoddle not only needed to boost his squad to cope with the increased number of fixtures, but he also felt Rocastle's game was perfect for European football.

As teams in Europe tended to keep their shape rather than press the midfield, Rocastle would be afforded more time than he might in the hurly-burly of the Premier League. Moreover, after his experiences at Arsenal and Leeds, he was also one of the few available English players who had played European football, following the lifting of the ban on English teams. Furthermore, teams in European competition were restricted to playing just three 'foreign' players. This was a challenge for English teams as that rule was supplemented by allowing just two Welsh, Northern Irish and Scottish players as well. Hence Rocastle being an Englishman would prove to be vital.

The knee problem was, of course, still a concern but Hoddle believed he was just the man to manage it: 'When I came back from Monaco, I had an infection in my knee that ate away into the cartilage. So I had a similar issue to David. I may have been at the end of my career but I was still playing. I had two seasons at Swindon where my knee was always swollen, but if you treated it right, and you protected it at the right time, then I could play. I knew I could do the same with Rocky. I knew where he was coming from as he had a manager that was going through some of the same things. I knew when to protect him, that sometimes he'd have to sit out training to protect his knee, and I helped him through certain weeks if it was sore.'

Terry Byrne, who was assistant physio at Chelsea, also told me about the situation regarding Rocastle's knee. 'It was clearly in the late stages of arthritis,' he said, 'which is extremely restrictive, particularly for a footballer, who has to run for a living. I remember he ran with a slight limp but he never let that hold him back. He gave everything that he had.'

To get him ready for games, Byrne and physio Mike Banks spent a lot of time in the gym, building up Rocastle's quads to strengthen his knee, and also doing a lot of electrotherapy, and manipulation, to try to alleviate the pain.

It was clear to many of the players that Rocastle's knee would need careful management. 'When he came to Chelsea, his knee, even the shape of it, you could see he had a problem,' Gavin Peacock told me. 'He said to me, "Gavin, you don't realise the pain I go through to get through training every day." He was a brave man, but he wanted to continue training so that he could be with the team on the Saturday. He didn't want to have special treatment but he'd be taking painkillers just to get through training. And Rocky really went through the pain barrier to earn his money.'

While Rocastle's ravaged knee continued to cause him considerable difficulty, Michael Duberry was still impressed. 'He might not have been the player he was back at Arsenal,' he said, 'but he could still drop some skills. Technically, he was a very good player. He played well but at the same time you could see him suffer from his knee. It wasn't 100 per cent.'

Rocastle's football ability spoke for itself. Everyone could still see that. And behind the scenes, he was an extremely popular member of the dressing room, who always had time for everyone, whether it was players, staff, the kit man or fans. The compliments from everyone I spoke to about his character were all essentially the same – 'fantastic', 'humble', 'generous', 'kind', 'hard-working'.

'I still remember my very first experience with him,' Byrne told me. 'We signed him from Manchester City, and he was to join the team hotel for a game. I was asked to go and drop a kit off to his room. I knocked on his door and he answered with just his under-pants on. I handed him his kit and I told him my name was Terry. He just laughed and said, "I'm sorry, I just woke up," with a great beaming smile. He is one of the few people I know who had this natural, unique skill of making everybody – backroom staff, play-ers, coaching staff – believe they were all his friend. He was a loveable character.'

'The minute he came in, everyone respected him,' Gavin Pea-cock said. 'You knew you weren't going to have an ounce of a problem. He got on with everyone. Such an honest, lovely guy. He may have been an older player, who had been around a bit, but I remember he always had time for the youngsters.'

At the time, Michael Duberry was just 19 and had only made his first-team debut the previous season. As a young black footballer from London, he told me that he had idolised Rocastle growing up and was therefore thrilled to play with, and learn from, him.

'I was in awe of him when he arrived,' Duberry laughed. 'I remember thinking he wasn't as big as I thought he would be because in my mind he was a giant. Remember, I was two years out of school and suddenly here I was mingling with one of my heroes.

When I met him, I think I laughed and just said, "You're Dave Rocastle." As a young black footballer I had looked at him as a kid and thought, "Yeah, this is possible. A black kid from London can be a professional footballer and be a success." He was synonymous with Arsenal and England and a real inspiration to me. Everyone knew the Rocky stepover. I'd practise that for hours. Foot over the ball, drop the shoulder and then boom! I would pretend to be him in my school playground. And now he has time for me, now he speaks to me, now he can have a joke with me, now he's got advice for me. I found him funny. I found his mannerisms funny. I thought he was cool.'

With players like Duberry, Eddie Newton and Jody Morris hanging on his every word, Rocastle found he always had a captive audience, yet he never chose to lecture. If someone asked for advice he would give it without going over the top. 'There was no specific *Braveheart* speech,' Duberry said. 'It was all gradual. Little bits and pieces. Just sitting and talking. If I had an issue he would go back to his experience growing up at Arsenal. We always liked that. I'd be like, "What was so-and-so like?" or "What was that game like?" There are always those horrible old pros who don't help you or don't speak to you, but Rocky was one of those pros who made me say, "When I become a senior pro, that is who I am going to be like."'

And while Rocastle was always friendly, he was certainly no pushover. 'Sometimes if you got a little too familiar, like any young kids will do, he would say, "Steady now,"' Duberry recalled. 'As long as you were respectful around him he was great. If you were disrespectful, he'd tell you. No one crossed the line with him. He didn't have to flex his muscles. He just had everyone's respect.'

Making his Chelsea debut against Norwich at Stamford Bridge on the opening day of the 1994/95 season, the starting line-up shows just how times have changed. With only a smattering of foreign players, and no world-class stars, this was still very much an honest, workmanlike team. Kharine, Clarke, Kjeldbjerg, Johnsen, Sinclair, Furlong, Peacock, Wise, Spackman, Shipperley and Rocastle certainly weren't going to gate-crash the top four, but there was still enough talent in the squad for them to give any team trouble on their day.

Norwich would certainly testify that Rocastle could still cause trouble at this level. *The Times* was effusive in its praise for his performance and his role in orchestrating the 2-0 win. It stated that 'Rocastle was conspicuously the most complete player on the pitch'. And added that 'at £1.25m from Manchester City Rocastle must be a bargain'. The *Express*, meanwhile, proclaimed that he had brought both 'delicacy and strength' to the midfield.

Sadly, Rocastle's body was no longer cut out for the weekly grind of the Premier League. Hoddle knew that he had to be carefully managed and that he wouldn't last the pace if he played every week. When he did play in the league, he was by and large a success. Returning to Elland Road, he showed Wilkinson what he was missing as he helped Chelsea to a 3-2 win. He was equally impressive in a 3-0 victory over Manchester City, while the *Independent* claimed that he had enjoyed a 'flawless game' against Leicester.

Chelsea ultimately finished the season in 11th place. It came as no surprise to anyone to see them marooned in mid-table. However, while this was a team built for the middle ranks of the Premier League, Hoddle also knew that on their day they could beat anyone. As such, Chelsea and Rocastle were made for cup competitions.

One of the main reasons Hoddle had brought Rocastle to the club was for European competition and it was here that he really excelled. In their first game, against Czech side Viktoria Žižkov, he was imperious, scoring a brilliant chip from 25 yards out, in an impressive 4-2 victory at Stamford Bridge. In the away leg, while

Hoddle was loath to play with a solitary striker he also knew from his experience of continental football that he needed to pack the midfield. Such tactics resulted in a 0-0 draw and saw Chelsea progress to the next round.

Lauding Rocastle, the *Independent* declared that he had displayed 'skills from yesteryear' in the subsequent goalless draw against FK Austria at Stamford Bridge. Yet most of the press used the headline 'Goodbye Vienna' to describe Chelsea's chances in the away leg. Indeed, in a frantic first half in Vienna, *The Times* reported that Chelsea had been 'pounded' by their Austrian opponents and only 'loose finishing' and 'luck' had kept them in the game. However, a John Spencer breakaway goal, just before half-time, had given Chelsea an all-important away goal. Protecting their vital lead in the second half, Rocastle virtually played in front of the back four, meticulously keeping possession and flying into tackles when required. FK Austria might have pulled a goal back and given Chelsea some nervy moments in the closing stages, but the Blues hung on for a famous victory on the away-goals rule.

Through to the quarter-finals, Rocastle was named as a substitute for the clash away to Brugge. A 1-0 defeat was by no means anything to be ashamed of, but the spectre of the away goal at Stamford Bridge meant that Chelsea were now in a very precarious position.

At the Bridge, Chelsea knew they would have to deliver a performance full of courage and passion if they were to progress, and they did just that. Trailing by the one goal from the first leg, it took Chelsea just 16 minutes to draw level, as Mark Stein finished off a Paul Furlong header across goal. Devouring every blade of grass, Rocastle probed and prodded, either hitting long balls to the towering Furlong or playing in the rampant Stein.

Chelsea's big moment finally came in the 38th minute. Stein was this time the provider as he stole the ball off a defender and whipped in a cross for Furlong to slam the ball home. Every player dug in deep to defend their precious, unexpected lead, with the *Mirror* hailing Rocastle, who 'gave everything'.

Far from dazzle in meaningless contests, Rocastle had proven time and again that he could deliver with relevance. His performance certainly hadn't been one of breathtaking ingenuity. Instead, it had highlighted a new-found maturity to his game. Taking just one or two touches, he had been instrumental in using the ball diligently and effectively, all the while showing a glint of steel when required. At the final whistle, he had stood tall and proud. His shirt soaked in sweat, he breathed heavily through his parched lips, which were flecked with saliva. There was nothing left to give. But what he had given had been enough.

'If somebody had told me at the start of the season that we would get this far in the competition with all the injury problems we've had to contend with, I wouldn't have believed them,' he told the press after the famous victory. 'We've only got a handful of players with any previous European experience – and most of our key men have missed at least some part of the campaign. To get this far has been a magnificent achievement and even if we don't reach the final we can't be too disappointed.'

Against all odds Chelsea were through to the European Cup-Winners' Cup semi-finals. Incredibly, so were Arsenal, and while they were drawn apart in the semis Rocastle was no doubt eagerly anticipating a European final against his old club. 'I never had any doubts Arsenal would win in Auxerre,' he said. 'I know the boys, I knew the situation they were in and I knew they'd come through. When you play European football, it's all about being disciplined and rock solid at the back. Arsenal are brilliant at that, while we are learning all the time. In an ideal world we'll be playing Arsenal in the final. There's still a lot of work for us both to do yet, but with a bit of British desire and determination I think it could happen.'

Facing Spanish team Real Zaragoza at their intimidating La Romareda Stadium was always going to be a tough ask, but on the night Chelsea were taught a harsh lesson. With Hoddle having told his defence to push up in order to squeeze the play, the Spaniards were still able to dominate the midfield and break through almost at will. Suddenly, for the first time in the competition, Chelsea looked out of their depth. Chasing shadows at times, Rocastle was substituted in the 64th minute. His dream of facing his former club in the final was in tatters as Chelsea lost the game 3-0. While the home leg was still to come, Chelsea had scored three goals in a game just once in their previous 38 matches.

However, in what was the team's finest performance of the season, Chelsea almost did the impossible back at Stamford Bridge. Leading 1-0 at half-time thanks to Paul Furlong, they proceeded to score two more goals in the second half. Yet Zaragoza's goal in the 55th minute effectively finished the tie once and for all. The European adventure was over, but what an effort it had been.

Rocastle was disappointed but he nevertheless felt that over the season he had once again proven that he still had so much more to offer. He was just short of his 28th birthday, with surely many years at the top level to come. Sadly, he was not to know that this game effectively signalled the end of his top-flight career. From here it was all downhill . . .

CHAPTER 26

SMALL SEEDS

'The league championship was won on the playing fields of London Colney,' George Graham has stated. Having finally cleared out most of the players from the old regime, by the summer of 1988 Graham at last had his own squad to hone and craft.

John Lukic may have remained in goal, and David O'Leary was still a reliable presence at the back, but the team now very much consisted of players Graham had brought through from the youth team or cut-price purchases. The back four contained the familiar rearguard of Winterburn, Adams, Bould and Dixon, while the midfield was predominantly made up of Rocastle, Thomas, Davis and Marwood, with Groves and Richardson accomplished deputies. Up front, Alan Smith ably led the line, alongside the emerging Paul Merson, Martin Hayes and Niall Quinn.

'It wasn't a team of household names,' Brian Marwood, who had signed at the back end of the previous season, told me. 'There wasn't one star player at that time who grabbed the attention. It was either players trying hard to prove themselves in the first division, or young players breaking through. It was a great mixture.'

Graham had assembled a perfect combination of defensive stability along with attacking flair. There was the option to go long to Smith if required, while the likes of Rocastle, Thomas and Merson could carry the ball at pace and provide defence-splitting passes. Graham told his wingers time and time again that if they got to the by-line then they were to clip the ball to the back post. If they couldn't, then they were to hit the front post. This meant that Smith always had a good idea of what area to attack rather than relying on instinct alone.

If that line of attack failed then there was the new armoury of Brian Marwood's set pieces. Typically, a Marwood corner would be flicked on at the near post by Steve Bould for the rampaging Tony Adams to run on to in the middle of the goal. It was simple stuff, and very predictable, but it is astonishing just how many goals Arsenal scored during the forthcoming season from this route.

When reminiscing about the threat Arsenal possessed on both flanks, Marwood told me, 'Me and Rocky were very different players. My game was about one-twos and getting crosses in, while Rocky was a lot more intricate and had more pace. I think that together we gave teams a lot to think about.'

To Graham this was all a bonus to add to the mix. First and foremost, he wanted to make the back four an impregnable unit. As he himself said, 'It's pointless going forward if you are going to keep leaking goals at the other end.' So once again, throughout the summer months, he spent hours working with his new-look back four behind closed doors.

Fullbacks Winterburn and Dixon were told to steer the opposing wingers inside, bringing them into the congested centre for the likes of Tony Adams to pick off. This was also a tactic demanded of the wingers. Graham wanted to force the opposition to play sideways and not have the opportunity to get crosses into the box. Highbury was also the smallest pitch in the league and was therefore ideal for Graham's strategy of squeezing teams.

The famous Arsenal offside trap was practised day in and day out, with the fullbacks told to take their positions from the centre backs. If Graham ever saw Dixon or Winterburn behind Adams' line, he would go berserk. As the opposition attacked, Adams would wait for the perfect moment before bringing his defensive line forward in a straight line, arm raised, signalling for offside. If the linesman subsequently raised his flag, Adams would applaud him, shouting, 'Well done, lino!' Again, this was a psychological ploy designed to keep Arsenal in the officials' good graces.

'That back four was the best in the world,' Colin Pates purred. 'In training there would be drills with seven attackers against the four defenders and no one could ever score.'

Keeping his preparations a closely guarded secret, Graham utilised his trusted 'spy', Steve Rowley, to observe the opposition. As Rowley compiled detailed dossiers on opponents' strengths and weaknesses, Graham was armed with all there was to know about them, while they knew next to nothing about Arsenal. Nothing was being left to chance. Rarely had a first division team been better prepared.

As for Rocastle, he had his own ambitions for the season ahead. 'I've spent pre-season wondering how I can improve my consistency for Arsenal,' he told Kevin Connolly. 'The most important part of my career is to be successful with Arsenal. Any honours that follow are a bonus. I was a bit in and out last season. I can't keep saying I'm a young player and my best is yet to come. I need to impose myself more; attack defenders, get into the box and score goals.'

Fired up for the new campaign, Rocastle also felt that the young Arsenal team was ready to take a step up. 'Our supporters have heard all about our potential,' he continued. 'Now they expect us to maintain our form throughout the season. We're still a young side that's not at its peak. However, the experience that young players like myself, Michael and Tony have gained should help us cope much better with the demands of a long season than we did last time. Consistency has been our big problem, really. Last season we often played well in spells, without controlling the game for 90 minutes. Sometimes our in-form periods were enough to win the game. On other occasions, though – like the Littlewoods Cup final – they weren't.'

But for all the talk of the team's great potential, Rocastle wasn't yet predicting a title challenge. 'There is a lot of room for improvement,' he admitted, 'and I don't think we shall be at our peak for another couple of years.'

This was a view shared by most pundits. It appeared fanciful that the team that had finished sixth the previous season, and had only added Steve Bould to its ranks, could have title aspirations. After all, Liverpool had run away with the league, winning it by a margin of nine points ahead of Manchester United. And if the Merseysiders had boasted a strong attacking line-up before, they had now re-signed the prolific Ian Rush for £2.8m from Juventus, breaking the British transfer record in the process.

Also spending big money, and bolstering their squad with the return of a former favourite, was Manchester United, who brought Mark Hughes back to Old Trafford for £1.8m. Everton, who had won the title in 1987, had also been busy, spending a club record £2m on West Ham striker Tony Cottee. As such, it seemed that Arsenal's quiet summer in the transfer market meant that they were destined once more to be also-rans. There was certainly no fanfare from the Highbury faithful, nothing to indicate that they believed the 1988/89 season could finally see the return of the league title for the first time since 1971.

While expectations were low, some fans were heartened by the team's pre-season results. Beating Yeovil 5-0 might have been expected, and finishing a tour of Sweden unbeaten was encouraging yet hardly set pulses racing, but it was Arsenal's performance in the Makita tournament that really turned heads. A 4-0 demolition of Tottenham was followed by a comfortable 3-0 win against German giants Bayern Munich. Something was clearly happening, and this feeling was cemented by Arsenal rounding off their pre-season fixtures with thumping victories against Birmingham and Leicester. Eight pre-season games had been negotiated, with no losses. In the process, 30 goals had been scored with just three conceded.

The figures were impressive and clearly sent out a statement of intent. However, in previous seasons Arsenal had enjoyed plenty of winning streaks. Consistency had been the issue. And with FA Cup winners Wimbledon at Plough Lane to kick off the season, they could not have asked for a more testing examination.

The stadium was tight and hostile; the team full of rough-and-ready players; the pitch small and weathered. And in the early stages Arsenal appeared nervous, with passes going astray and players pulled out of position.

With the Gunners struggling for fluency, it was no surprise when a soaring John Fashanu header gave Wimbledon the lead. However, a fumbled Marwood cross soon restored parity and Arsenal started to grow in confidence. Smith and Merson were in sparkling form, slowly but surely picking at the threads of the Wimbledon defence until it unravelled. Unable to contain the little and large duo, Merson scored one while Smith plundered a hat-trick to give Arsenal a resounding 5-1 away win. Smith's third strike in particular was an archetypal Graham goal.

With the ball in Lukic's hands, he quickly threw it out to Rocastle on the right wing. Bursting forward, Rocastle accelerated into the Wimbledon half before being held up in the final third. He passed inside to Davis and the ball then found its way to Smith, who stroked it past Dave Beasant in the Wimbledon goal. The move, from Lukic's hands to the back of the Wimbledon net, had taken less than 20 seconds.

It was the perfect start to the season yet it was also a brief glimpse of the problems Arsenal's style of play might present. Soaking up pressure and hitting teams on the break was all very well away from home, but at Highbury it would be a different matter. With the crowd roaring Arsenal on to attack, it would take discipline for the players to follow Graham's orders. And this style of play also relied on something else – a solid defence.

Graham's defence may have had all the key players in place, each knowing their jobs back to front, but there was something he hadn't bargained for: Adams' fragile mental state. Having returned that summer from a chastening experience at the European Championship, where the world's best striker, Marco van Basten, had demolished his confidence with a hat-trick, the mental scars still looked a long way from being healed. Against Wimbledon it had been clear that he was still struggling, and Graham feared that pairing him with a new partner in Steve Bould might have been too much too soon.

For the following game against Aston Villa, Graham brought David O'Leary back into the team to help give Adams some guidance and stability. Although Adams was the captain, he was still relatively young, and Graham no doubt felt that O'Leary's presence would allow him to focus on his own game, rather than to help a new signing along.

At home to newly promoted Villa, it was thought that Arsenal's form, and Graham's defensive tweak, would see them record two consecutive victories. But Highbury was stunned into silence as Villa shot into a two-goal lead. Marwood and Smith may have levelled the scores in the second half but an Andy Gray thunder-bolt meant that Villa still left Highbury with the three points.

This topsy-turvy form seemingly set the tone for the weeks ahead. A 3-2 victory against Spurs at White Hart Lane, which had been billed as 'Rocky v Gazza' by some elements of the press, was then followed by a 2-2 draw against Southampton at Highbury. Arsenal certainly had no problem with scoring goals. Smith, in particular, was on a red-hot streak of form, but keeping them out was another matter.

Of further concern was that Paul Davis had been caught on camera swinging a punch at Southampton's Glenn Cockerill, which resulted in a broken jaw. Davis was perceived to be a quiet, gentle personality, but this out-of-character assault earned him a nine-match ban, and saw Arsenal deprived of one of the few central players in the squad who could prise open a defence.

A morale-boosting 2-1 victory against league champions Liv-erpool in the semi-final of the Mercantile Credit Cup may have lifted spirits, but a 2-1 defeat at Hillsborough a week later, and yet more defensive calamities, had the travelling hordes of fans enraged. While some in the stands openly questioned Graham, it was the performance of Adams that led to the most outrage. Many were of the opinion that it was time for the captain to be dropped, and they didn't hesitate in letting Graham know their opinion.

Some fans had also grown frustrated with Rocastle's inability to break forward. Renowned for his pace and trickery, it seemed that he now spent most of his time in his own half. When asked about this, Rocastle suggested two reasons for his reluctance to get for-ward. 'We've come up against sweeper systems this season, and it's easier for the fullbacks to get forward instead of me because they're less tightly marked than I am,' he revealed. 'So Lee Dixon has often gone running on ahead of me – and I've finished up marking the left back who's supposed to be marking me. It sounds strange. But if that's how we have to play to unhinge our opponents' system then I'll do it.'

Another reason for his quiet spell was the fact that the ball had not been coming to him. 'We've been gaining so much joy on the left, through Brian [Marwood] – and through Nigel Winterburn pushing up – that the ball hasn't been coming down the right nearly as often as it did last season,' he said. 'We can't have both flank players charging forward at once. So sometimes I've adopted a less prominent role than usual.'

It was typical Rocastle. The fans might have been getting upset but he knew that what he was doing was for the good of the team.

By the end of September, Arsenal were six points off the surprise leaders, Norwich, while Liverpool, most people's favourites, were still unbeaten. If they were going to stand any chance of catching up, then Graham knew that he needed to rectify his rocking defence.

The trip to West Ham saw him finally make a change, although not one most Arsenal fans were expecting. Adams surprisingly kept his place while O'Leary made way for Bould. Thankfully, it seemed to do the trick. Conceding just the solitary goal, Adams looked more composed, and authoritative, than he had done all season. This renewed confidence suddenly gave the midfield licence to go forward and they did so with relish. Rocastle was a constant factor, turning defence into attack in an instant, while Marwood's supply from the left was plentiful. With Smith adding another two goals to his ever-increasing tally, and Rocastle and Thomas completing the scoring, this was a performance that suggested Arsenal were capable of something special, if they could just find their consistency.

Suddenly, with a settled back four, Arsenal truly began to hit their stride. Winning the Mercantile Credit Cup might not have been much to shout about, but the performance against a strong Manchester United side in the final at Villa Park was further evidence that this Arsenal team were to be taken seriously. What's more, as well as providing another trophy for the marble halls of Highbury, it came with the bonus of a much-needed cheque for £50,000.

As Arsenal went 11 games without defeat in all competitions, Rocastle really started to emerge as a force to be reckoned with. Always mindful of his defensive responsibilities, but also breaking forward at will, he found the consistency he had long hoped for, while he also scored two of his most iconic goals.

In the form of his life, he went to Anfield for a Littlewoods Cup tie against Liverpool, preparing to come face to face with his England rival John Barnes. In many ways, Rocastle and Barnes were carbon copies. Direct, skilful, with an eye for the spectacular, they were often the one player looked to by their teams to settle a contest. Barnes may have still held the advantage at international level, but Rocastle was keen to show that he could be his equal, if not superior.

Both teams started the game at breakneck speed, with chances spurned at either end, before Barnes opened the scoring with a brilliantly taken solo goal. Rather than be daunted, Rocastle stepped up to the challenge and bettered it soon afterwards.

A long ball from Adams was laid off by Smith to Thomas. In the middle of the pitch, 25 yards from goal, he looked to his right-hand side to see Rocastle charging up alongside him. As Thomas swept the ball out wide, Rocastle feinted his body towards it and then away, losing his marker before it had even reached him. Taking a touch, he found himself on the right-hand corner of the box. The angle was tight, and goalkeeper Mike Hooper looked to have covered his goal. Yet rather than opt for precision Rocastle went for sheer power. Blasting his shot with a vicious certainty, his body lifting off the floor as he did so, the ball screamed past Hooper and nestled in the opposite top corner. Anfield was stunned.

He later said of the wonder goal, 'We were losing 1-0 at the time but we were playing out of our skins. It was the best I'd seen us play. It was harsh we were losing. Then I got the ball on the edge of the box from Michael Thomas and I saw the goal in front of me and I said, "I'm gonna hit it." Mike Hooper was in goal at the time having an outstanding game, saving everything. I thought he'd saved about four good chances already so I may as well just hit it. To my relief it went into the back of the net.'

As I enthused in the prologue to this book, just two weeks after this incredible goal at Anfield he danced through the Middlesbrough defence and scored what to my young mind was the greatest goal of all time. The skill, balance, pace and crashing finish, all executed on a bobbly pitch, encapsulated Rocastle at his very best and was unlike anything I had seen from a British player. For a split second, everything he had worked on at the 'Crem' in Lewisham came to pass in a first division football match. It was truly breathtaking stuff.

However, while Rocastle's form was earning plenty of plaudits, Arsenal suddenly collapsed, as was fast becoming an annual tradition. First up, Liverpool returned to Highbury, where their 2-1 victory knocked the Gunners out of the League Cup. Then, a shock defeat to Derby at the Baseball Ground looked to have dented their burgeoning title challenge, with Rocastle coming in for criticism from *The Times*: 'Where on earth were the instincts that a week ago carried David Rocastle through the entire Middlesbrough defence for such a superb goal?'

All the familiar foibles were suddenly back on display. Hopes had been raised and now they were set to be dashed. The pattern of being out of title contention by Christmas, and then concentrating on a cup run, was becoming sadly predictable. With the next three games seeing the visit of title favourites Liverpool, a trip to league leaders Norwich, followed by Manchester United at Highbury, the season's obituaries were already being written.

CHAPTER 27

OUTCAST

While Glenn Hoddle had set in motion a transformation of the English game the previous summer, there had been one revolution that had passed him by – the foreign one. Although there had been previous experimentations with foreigners, most notably in 1978 when Spurs had signed the Argentinians Ossie Ardiles and Ricky Villa, such signings had mostly been exotic flirtations until the start of the 1990s. But the dawning of the Premier League era, and the television it brought, would prove to be the catalyst for the foreign revolution that would in time sweep across all clubs.

Tottenham led the way once again, improbably signing German superstar Jürgen Klinsmann, as well as the two Romanians, Ilie Dumitrescu and Gică Popescu. A year later, Swede Tomas Brolin would sign for Leeds United, while Italian Andrea Silenzi moved to Nottingham Forest.

During the 1994/95 season Chelsea had been a predominantly British team, signing mid-tier British players. Yet in the summer of 1995 they joined the party and caused a sensation. Pulling off a major coup, Hoddle persuaded former world player of the year, Ruud Gullit, to join the Blues on a free transfer.

'I think people were pinching themselves,' Hoddle told me. 'I think they thought it was April Fools' Day.'

Apart from the many qualities Gullit would bring to the team on the pitch, Hoddle knew that he would also prove vital in helping to change the culture off it. So far, his methods had been embraced enthusiastically, but he was aware that things could really take off when his players saw Gullit, one of the most iconic players in the world, also endorse them.

'His attitude with the players was great,' Hoddle told me. 'He didn't come in, like, "I'm Ruud Gullit, big-time-Charlie." He integrated with the players straightaway and the players loved him. He had an English-type sense of humour. And for the younger players, like Eddie Newton, he was great. They were pinching themselves playing with him. He really helped their game. He helped everyone's game. You could see that on the training ground. Everyone wanted to impress him.'

And it wasn't just with their skills that they wanted to impress. 'Before Ruud came the guys were never too bothered by what they wore in training; it was usually a tracksuit or scruffy jeans,' Gavin Peacock laughed. 'Suddenly, it was Armani and Hugo Boss. There was a total change in mentality. We even drank more red wine instead of pints of beer!'

Chelsea was a club that was rapidly evolving. Gullit's signing was swiftly followed by those of Mark Hughes from Manchester United and Dan Petrescu from Sheffield Wednesday. The likes of Robert Fleck and David Hopkin were moved on.

And while it was all change at Chelsea, it had also been all change for Rocastle's personal life. After eight years with Janet Nelson, which had produced two children, Rocastle finally got married that summer in Ocho Rios, a port town on Jamaica's north coast. The ceremony was only small, but in paradise the two promised to put the past behind them and looked forward to a glorious and happy future.

However, on his return to training, with Chelsea suddenly attracting a higher calibre of player, Rocastle once again found himself in a vulnerable position. The previous season had been a relative success. But with his injury problems, and Chelsea's newfound spending power, he knew he was easily replaceable. Those fears must have escalated when the press started running stories that he had been offered to Southampton as makeweight in a potential £9m deal for Matthew Le Tissier. Ken Bates immediately dismissed such tittle-tattle, while Hoddle informed Rocastle that he was still very much in his plans. However, Rocastle knew that he would have to prove himself once again if he was to remain in the team.

But then disaster struck at the worst possible time. A broken toe in pre-season ruled him out for the first three months. Watching on as Chelsea made an indifferent start to the 1995/96 season, winning just four of their opening 10 games, he worked his way back to fitness and was finally recalled to the team for the trip to Blackburn on 28 October.

If Rocastle had hoped that his return could spark Chelsea into life then he was wrong. An emphatic 3-0 defeat to the defending champions had seen Ruud Gullit trudge off the pitch in despair. At least Gullit could still walk. Rocastle's limp, after an anonymous game, sadly told its own story. He had broken his toe again yet had tried to play through the pain.

He wasn't to know it, but this would be his only appearance for Chelsea that season. Incredibly, at 28 years of age, it was also his last in the Premier League. Time and time again he would return to training only to break down. Such was his frustration that he eagerly took up Hoddle's advice to visit faith healer Eileen

Drewery, who would be the subject of many headlines during Hoddle's time as England manager. Nothing seemed to work. After all the problems with his knee, it was a broken toe that had kept him out for virtually an entire season.

Despite the presence of Gullit, Chelsea finished in 11th position in the league and Hoddle expressed his regret at not being able to call on Rocastle. 'Your heart bled for him,' he said. 'He really tried his hardest, and he'd get fit, but then it would go again. You could see the frustration in him and it was frustrating for me as manager because I wanted to use him. I wanted him to play with the likes of Ruud. I knew they would have been great together. It was just a freak injury.'

Sadly, the 'freak injury' was to have a significant impact on his career. By the summer of 1996, Hoddle had moved on to the England job, where he succeeded Terry Venables. Gullit was to be his replacement as Chelsea manager, and he brought even more change to the club. If Hoddle had kicked off the foreign revolution then under Gullit it went into overdrive. Stars such as Gianluca Vialli, Roberto Di Matteo, Gianfranco Zola and Frank Leboeuf arrived, squeezing out the likes of Gavin Peacock, John Spencer and Mark Stein.

Had Rocastle been in any doubt about his status under Gullit then he got his answer when he returned for pre-season. Not even given a squad number, he was instead sent to train with the kids. There was no explanation. It was that brutal. Rocastle had of course found himself in a difficult situation at Leeds under Howard Wilkinson, but this was different. At least with Wilkinson he was given hope that he could break into the first team. Now he was being tossed on the scrapheap.

'The boss, Ruud Gullit, told me I would not be involved in his plans in any way,' Rocastle told the press. 'And he's been true to his word. But he has never, ever told me why, and it's driving me crazy.

But then nothing has gone really right for me since I left Arsenal in 1992.'

When asked to speculate why Gullit had left him out, Rocastle said, 'Maybe it's because the manager likes to do things the Italian way. It seems he's chosen a squad of 22 for the season. And I'm not one of them. That's the only thing I can come up with because he's never explained it to me. I know I won't ever get a chance here though I know I can still do the business at the top level. It hurts me a lot. I was so excited when Glenn Hoddle signed me for Chelsea. People forget I played almost 30 games that season and helped the club reach the semi-final of the European Cup-Winners' Cup. But I broke my toe and it messed everything up. Since it healed, I've never had the chance to fight my way back in. There have been all sorts of rumours flying about saying I've got serious injury problems. Well, I can assure everyone I haven't missed a training session since last June.'

Some players in his position might have lost their temper and berated Gullit, but Rocastle was experienced in such matters. He knew that it wouldn't get him anywhere. The message was clear. Find a new club. In the circumstances, all he could do was keep himself fit and try not to let it drag him down.

Gavin Peacock, who was one of those also forced out by Gullit, recalls just how professionally Rocastle took his demotion. 'He was a great example to young pros today that if you go through life with a sense of entitlement you'll be the guy who is always angry,' he said. 'The way Rocky behaved was right in the circumstances. He acted honourably. He didn't throw a tantrum. Even now, years on, I really admire him for that.'

Michael Duberry was another who was impressed by how Rocastle took the news. 'Ruud had opinions of players from when he was a team-mate,' he said. 'As soon as he became a manager, that was it, some of those he didn't rate were out. But it was about football.

Rocky understood it. He just got on with things and did what he needed to do. He wasn't a bad egg. He would always come in smiling. Always respectful. But it was sad. He was a renowned player. A title winner. An international. I thought he deserved a little more respect.'

Despite the influx of overseas players at Chelsea, Rocastle was far from resentful. Indeed, he welcomed the likes of Zola with open arms. When I spoke to Terry Byrne, he told me that the foreigners and the Brits happily mixed. 'Dennis Wise was the captain and the heart of the team,' he said. He would take all of the players out once a week on a Thursday night for dinner, and make sure there was no divided camp. He unified the foreign players with the English players' mentality.'

As rumours of moves to Celtic, QPR and Wolves filled the press, Rocastle was restricted to playing for the reserves at an empty Stamford Bridge, alongside budding apprentices like John Terry. Terry reminded Rocastle of Tony Adams. Not only the way he played the game but also how it was clear from a young age that he was a natural leader. He certainly had no qualms about telling a senior pro if he wasn't performing. Rocastle liked that. Indeed, his brother Sean told me that he admired Terry so much that he would give the youngster match tickets whenever he needed them.

With players left to rot in the reserves, Gullit's man-management techniques were coming under scrutiny. As early as 9 October, the *Sunday Mirror* carried a back-page story claiming, 'Ruud Gullit is facing a £15m walkout from disillusioned Chelsea stars unhappy with his managerial methods. Up to 10 of the squad that Dutchman Gullit inherited from Glenn Hoddle are considering their futures.'

When questioned on this, Gullit hit out: 'I don't want them moaning. That upsets the fans and they turn against the player. If the players want to play in the first team they should go out and show it.'

Duberry was candid on the players' dissatisfaction with Gullit. 'Obviously there was a bit of a rebellion,' he said. 'I was just a young pro, so I wasn't really involved, but you could tell some of the players weren't happy with him. In England, if you get dropped the manager explains to you why you got dropped. But Ruud had his ways he'd picked up in Italy under the likes of Capello. He felt he didn't have to explain why he had done something. It rubbed some people up the wrong way.'

With Gullit unwilling to change his ways, and Ken Bates giving him a vote of confidence, Rocastle turned to his old friend, Michael Thomas, for solace. After all, he'd also had a difficult time since leaving Arsenal. 'It's a big help talking to Michael,' he confided. 'He went through a long, long time on the sidelines at Anfield before he really made an impact there so he understands my feelings. It must be something about leaving Arsenal. Things haven't really worked out for Anders Limpar since he left, either, have they? But I know what I'm capable of and have a lot to offer this game. I just want someone to give me a chance.'

Rocastle was still only 29 years old. He'd never been regarded as a troublemaker. Yet despite all of this, Gullit completely shunned him. Perhaps even more surprising was that not one club in the Premier League expressed any real interest in taking him.

One of the many issues Rocastle faced was that people were unable to adapt to his 'new' position. 'Maybe the problem is that people still see me as a winger,' he confided. 'But even I'll admit I'm too old to be chasing up and down the flank all afternoon. Players who are much younger than me, like Nick Barmby, can't manage that any more and have come inside.'

Thankfully, a club finally made their move. What's more, they had earmarked Rocastle for his preferred central role. The one drawback was that the club was not in the Premier League. In any event, Rocastle happily packed his bags for East Anglia, and prepared to spend a month playing for Norwich City in the first division.

CHAPTER 28

TRIUMPH AND DISASTER

4 December 1988. Arsenal v Liverpool. Rocastle v Barnes. Just three points between the teams. Everything still to play for.

In the previous League Cup encounter, Liverpool may have emerged victors but wonder goals by Barnes and Rocastle had emphatically shown the quality of the two players.

However, as Liverpool travelled to Highbury there was already a sense that for Arsenal a crucial juncture had been reached. Far too often Arsenal's unbeaten runs had been followed by a complete collapse, and after the defeat to Derby, as well as crashing out of the League Cup, some were already predicting more of the same.

Once more, despite an array of attacking talent, both teams seemed to look for Barnes and Rocastle to settle the game. And it was Barnes who was the first to come to life. Gliding past four challenges, he calmly finished past Lukic to give Liverpool the lead. Not to be outdone, Rocastle soon conjured up an appropriate response. Out on the right touchline, he curled a brilliant cross between the Liverpool defence and goalkeeper for Alan Smith to finish at the second attempt.

Barnes and Rocastle were all square, as was the game, which finished 1-1. A draw was far from a disaster, especially as it kept Liverpool at bay before Arsenal met league leaders Norwich at Carrow Road the following week. With Norwich just two points ahead of Arsenal, the game was another that neither dared to lose. As such, it was unsurprising that it ended 0-0, with Brian Marwood missing a retaken penalty. Arsenal may have been without a win in four but crucially they were still in the title chase.

In an unrelenting schedule, Manchester United were up next and, while many had them down as title contenders, they had disappointed so far. Fragile and unconvincing at times, the Gunners showed real guts to emerge as 2-1 winners. Three tough games against three tough teams had been negotiated without defeat. More importantly, Arsenal had also shown that even when not playing well they could grind out a result. Things were looking up, especially for Rocastle, who came in for praise from reporter Brian Glanville for his 'energy and enterprise'.

Suddenly, Arsenal were back at full throttle. Over Christmas they won four straight games, going top of the league in the process, with the pick of the performances being a 3-0 win at Villa Park. The *Independent* reported that, 'Villa's players were hardly given a moment to think. Every time one took possession, he was surrounded by a pack of terriers.' The highlight of the game was yet another stunning effort by Rocastle. As the ball fell to him 30 yards from goal, he cushioned it with his thigh before hitting a looping volley over the back-peddling Nigel Spink and a host of defenders on the line.

Their surge to the summit continued unabated when, in front of a bumper New Year crowd of 45,000, Spurs were summarily brushed aside 2-0, with goals from Merson and Thomas. Now leading the pack, the pundits were sitting up and taking notice of their title challenge. Philip Coggan, of the *Financial Times*, declared, 'If Arsenal can avoid one of the crippling bouts of injuries that occasionally derail championship challengers, they should have the best chance of being the first non-Merseyside club to win the championship since Aston Villa in 1981.'

While some fans felt that being tagged as title favourites was premature, especially after they had been knocked out of the FA Cup by West Ham, others believed the cup exit was a blessing in disguise. In recent years, good cup runs had seen their league form suffer. Now they had no choice but to concentrate on the league, while their rivals would have to juggle fixtures on two fronts.

If Arsenal had not already persuaded the doubters of their title credentials then their performance at Goodison Park made the naysayers think again. Once again Rocastle captured the headlines with a mesmerising display. In five second-half minutes he destroyed Everton, firstly crossing for Merson to score and then storming past Kevin Sheedy and delivering yet another killer cross, this time headed in at the near post by Smith. Richardson soon made it three before a late consolation goal by Dave Watson saw the game finish 3-1. Arsenal's display, and Rocastle's in particular, had been so dominant that the Everton crowd sportingly clapped them off the pitch. Brian Glanville was just as effusive. His headline read, 'Rocastle's Skill Sweeps Aside Suspect Everton', while he wrote that he was a 'greatly gifted player'.

The result put Arsenal five points clear of Norwich, with just 18 games to go, 11 of which would be at Highbury. However, Arsenal had won just five home matches all season so any talk of the title was still regarded as premature.

Indeed, Arsenal soon found how tough it was to win games at home, especially against teams who were scrapping for their lives. In their next game at Highbury, they had to make do with a 1-1 draw, after struggling Sheffield Wednesday put all of their men behind the ball and steadfastly refused to venture over the halfway line. Playing on the break away from home was all well and good, but in situations like these Arsenal found it hard to break teams down, having to rely on outrageous moments of brilliance, such as Merson's stunning volley, rather than any specific game plan.

Relegation-threatened West Ham were the next visitors to Highbury, and while they tried to adopt Wednesday's negative tactics they hadn't counted on their goalkeeper, Allen McKnight, letting two innocuous efforts from Smith and Groves slip through his hands. Again, Arsenal had not been at their best but the 2-1 win was more than sufficient. If the game had been bland, most fans at least left the stadium talking about another moment of Rocastle skill.

One on one with the fullback, Julian Dicks, he jinked his body towards the touchline, taking his opposite number with him, before dragging the ball back with his right foot and leaving his opponent for dead. Yet just as he had pulled away, another defender was immediately in front of him. Instantly dragging the ball in the opposite direction with his left foot, Rocastle suddenly broke clear, leaving the two defenders bumbling around like drunks in the West End.

However, it would not be Rocastle's skill fans would be talking about following a 2-1 win at the Den. Referee David Elleray had worn a microphone throughout the game, with an ITV documentary screening the results soon after. For Arsenal, it did not make pretty viewing. Captain Tony Adams was recorded telling Elleray he was a 'cheat', while Rocastle had to be contained after he'd been cautioned and called the referee 'crap'.

Out of context, their behaviour looked poor, even though it was hardly surprising to hear footballers scream and shout at a referee. In Rocastle's defence, there were mitigating factors. He had spent most of the game being racially abused by the Millwall crowd, as well as being kicked all over the pitch by some overzealous challenges. So when he was booked for a foul, and his opponents got off scot-free, it was perhaps understandable that he reacted in such a volatile manner.

Still, Arsenal had passed yet another test, winning 2-1, and were now three points clear at the top of the league, with just one defeat in their last 18 league games. In formidable form, they then faced a unique challenge in their next game – the French national team at Highbury.

Preparing to face Scotland in a World Cup qualifier, France manager Michel Platini told the press, 'Arsenal are very British and will be no less difficult to play than Scotland. The original plan was to face Tottenham, but after watching the recent friendly with Monaco Spurs' play is too similar to continental teams. I wanted my players to have a confrontation with the British style before Scotland, and Arsenal will provide it. We hope to be more on the offensive than defensive if Arsenal will allow us.' It is quite incredible now to read that Arsenal so embodied a British style of play that the French national team had handpicked them for a friendly.

With English clubs banned from European competition, this was an unmissable chance for Arsenal's players to test themselves against some of the best on the continent. The fans were also eagerly anticipating the game, and while most might have expected Graham to play a reserve team, with the league very much his priority, he instead opted to unleash his stars.

Rocastle for one was glad to be involved against some of the world's best. 'The more times we face top-class continental opposition, the better it will be for our international prospects,' he said. 'Because of the ban on English teams playing in Europe, we rarely get the chance to meet continental clubs. So when it comes to international competitions, we're going in blind. Many of our young players have never played in the European club tournaments. I hope UEFA will acknowledge the steps our clubs have taken to combat the hooligans and allow us back next season. Such a move would offer our players some valuable experience, and excite the fans because they could watch the teams they don't usually see. But if the Euro ban continues we could lose touch with developments on the continent, because we'll only meet their best players in international matches.'

If France wanted a taste of British football then at Highbury they certainly got it. By February the Highbury pitch had been well and truly battered over the winter months. It was certainly not a surface that would allow some of the best players in the world to exhibit their full repertoire. Graham also set his team up in a traditionally British 4-4-2 formation, with the archetypal front man, Alan Smith, leading the line.

Michel Platini, sporting a beige trench coat with the collar pulled up to his chin to battle the chill, watched from the sidelines with a look of Gallic disdain. As his French players struggled to control the ball on the bobbly pitch, Arsenal adapted to the conditions by playing long balls up to Smith to knock down. Rocastle, one of Arsenal's more accomplished technical players, was one of those who struggled to get into the game, as he repeatedly had to watch the ball rocket over his head. He also found himself caught in no man's land, unsure whether to gamble on a Smith knockdown or to keep his position.

However, despite the poor quality of the football, 25,000 Arsenal fans roared their team on as if it were a championship decider. No one was thinking about the possibility of injuries, or of burnout, not even Graham. The lack of European football over the last two years meant that this would be the team's only real chance to prove themselves against top continental opposition and they intended to show that they could hold their own.

A curling shot into the top corner by forgotten man Martin Hayes was greeted by a roar usually reserved for cup finals. Smith's strike furthered the lead, and increased the decibels, as Arsenal finished the game 2-0 victors.

If Rocastle had felt frustrated at his performance then he at least had Platini's stamp of approval, as after the game he told the press, 'Marwood and Rocastle are very fine technicians.'

Heartened by their win against one of Europe's finest national teams, Arsenal retrained their sights on the league, with Graham perhaps regretting having started so many of his stars in the game. Appearing tired and sluggish, they drew at QPR and then suffered a crushing 1-0 defeat to Coventry. Just as the season was gearing towards its climax, Arsenal had faltered.

While a 2-0 win against Luton seemed to have steadied things, the subsequent 0-0 draw with Millwall at Highbury suggested that their home form remained an issue. Any look at the league table would, however, have consoled even the most skittish of supporters. By the end of February, Arsenal were five points clear of Norwich in second, who nevertheless had a game in hand, while they were a whopping 16 points ahead of third-place Liverpool. Liverpool might have had three games in hand themselves, but as they continued to juggle their fixtures in the FA Cup it was clear they would struggle to overhaul Arsenal's lead.

But then, as Rocastle joined up with the England squad to face Albania, his knee locked during a training session. Forced to hobble off the pitch and ice it on the sidelines, there was real concern that if it didn't settle down he could miss the rest of the season. Thankfully, rest and treatment seemed to loosen up the joint and allowed him to run freely enough, albeit in discomfort. Just two months away from potentially winning a league title, there was no way that Rocastle wanted to miss out.

With or without Rocastle, Arsenal's home form continued to

hinder them. After losing 3-1 to Forest and drawing with Charlton, the now-defunct *Today* newspaper summed up most fans' feelings: 'The cracks are showing and growing alarmingly at Highbury. Arsenal look increasingly determined to blow the first division championship that was there for the taking just a month ago. Defeat by Nottingham Forest means the misfiring Gunners have dropped 10 points out of the last 15 and, like it or not, the title is now more in Norwich's hands than their own. All this is nothing new to George Graham and his team. Two seasons ago they topped the first division from mid-November until the end of January, only to slump to a run of 10 games without a win to finish fourth. Then last season they won only one game in 11 after going top of the table at the end of October, and finished sixth.'

With pressure mounting, Graham suddenly made an uncharacteristic move. After years of prudence and sensible signings, he tried to acquire Celtic's playboy striker, Frank McAvennie. Renowned for his love of the fast life, which would later see him admit to taking drugs, it seemed a strange move by Graham, considering his aversion to the likes of Charlie Nicholas. Incredibly, McAvennie actually turned down the chance to join title-chasing Arsenal, instead preferring to rejoin relegation-threatened West Ham. It might have been a blessing in disguise, as even McAvennie could not keep the Hammers from the trapdoor.

Without McAvennie in their ranks, the off-target Gunners made the trip to the Dell. A daunting place to visit at the best of times, it was even more so on this occasion. Their team fighting relegation, the Southampton crowd was hostile from the first minute, focussing much of their ire on Paul Davis, who was back in the side following his suspension for punching Glenn Cockerill.

Settling any nerves, Groves struck the opening goal before Rocastle, enraged by a section of fans racially taunting him, grabbed the game by the throat. On the break, Merson passed the ball out wide to Rocastle on the right-hand side of the box. Leaning his body to the right, as if he was heading towards the touchline, he suddenly cut back to the left, moving inside and beating a defender with no more than the shape of his body. As another defender attempted to jockey him, he perfected the same trick once again, a flash to the right then pushing off to the left. Again, the defender was left flat-footed as Rocastle found himself in the middle of the penalty area, just 12 yards from goal. The Southampton defence might have been satisfied that it had at least kept him on his unfancied left foot but it mattered not. Striking through the ball, his yellow Nike swoosh on his boots flashing through the air, it was soon past the keeper, past the defender on the line and nestling in the net.

Remembering the goal, and the abuse he had received, Rocastle later said, 'I was getting a bit of stick from a section of the crowd. I scored and went over to them and blew them some kisses. The people who had been calling me names suddenly started to laugh and clap me.'

It had all looked incredibly easy but, watching the goal in slow motion, it is quite incredible just how Rocastle could beat a man with a feint of his body. While Cockerill pulled a goal back for Southampton, Rocastle would help to restore the two-goal cushion, this time turning provider for Merson, sweeping in a cross for him to rifle past Tim Flowers in the Saints goal.

It was a very welcome return to form, particularly as Liverpool were just two points behind, having won all of their games in hand. But there was to be no rest from the unrelenting schedule, as next up was a trip to Old Trafford.

During Graham's time at Highbury, he had stuck to a rigid 4-4-2 formation. However, he now switched to 5-3-2, playing Bould and Adams at centre back, with O'Leary sweeping, in the hope that this would shore up the centre of defence, while also giving Winterburn and Dixon more licence to roam forward. It was a brave move, but in time it would prove to be an inspired one.

Over 8,000 Arsenal fans travelled up the M6 for the game, knowing that with margins so tight at the top of the table, three points were essential. But while Graham had changed his tactics, Ferguson had countered accordingly. Withdrawing McClair from his usual striker's berth supporting Hughes, he now dropped deeper, away from the three centre backs, which allowed United to overpower Arsenal in midfield.

Despite all the talk of formations, it would prove to be a tried-and-tested set piece that would give Arsenal the lead, as a Marwood corner was flicked on at the near post for Adams to head past Jim Leighton. Sadly, Graham's change of formation didn't help with United's equaliser either. This time Adams was the villain, slicing a cross over Lukic and into the back of the net. At this, Old Trafford immediately erupted into hysterical 'Heehaws', as the United fans tried to portray Arsenal's brave and muddied captain as a donkey.

Incredibly, the *Mirror* also chose to get in on the action as the next day their back page featured donkey ears superimposed on Adams' head. It was a poor way to treat a young footballer with outstanding potential, who was still trying to overcome what had been a traumatic experience in Euro '88. As always, while Adams might have been hurt by the criticism, he refused to hide, and would prove to be a colossus as the season reached its climax.

With just seven games remaining, five of which would be at Highbury, Arsenal found themselves in second place on 8 April, owing to Liverpool's defeat of Sheffield Wednesday earlier in the day. The title race was now red hot, and only a win against Everton would see Arsenal return to the summit.

Again, Graham tinkered with his tactics. This time he pushed Rocastle and Marwood further up the field to support Quinn, who was brought in to deputise for the injured Alan Smith. With Richardson and Thomas holding in midfield, Winterburn and Dixon were told to play as wing backs, rampaging up and down the flanks. This strategy reaped immediate dividends as Dixon opened the scoring after just three minutes, with the forgotten Quinn adding a second.

Arsenal were back at the top of the table and, with Graham proving his tactical versatility, the subsequent visit of struggling Newcastle looked to offer a brief respite. Indeed, the uninspiring but welcome 1-0 win, courtesy of a late Brian Marwood goal, saw them stretch their lead over Liverpool, who were engaged in an FA Cup semi-final contest at Hillsborough against Nottingham Forest.

However, as the Arsenal players toasted their victory in the bath after the game, news filtered through of a terrible disaster at Hillsborough. With attention now firmly focused on the tragic deaths of so many fans and the state of the English game itself, suddenly the title race no longer seemed so important.

CHAPTER 29

THE CANARY

It was almost unheard of for a high-profile player such as David Rocastle, still in his twenties, to move to a (then) first division club, even on loan. However, putting past glories to one side, Rocastle just wanted to play football again. It was as simple as that. As such he didn't hesitate to agree to move to Norwich, which had the added bonus that his brother Steve now lived in the city, following a spell at the club himself.

While most in football scratched their heads and wondered why a Premier League team hadn't shown any interest, Norwich fans were understandably delirious at the coup. However, Rocastle immediately tried to manage their expectations. 'They are probably waiting for me to beat two or three players and whip in a cross like I used to at Arsenal,' he said. 'But my game has changed completely now. Then I was an out-and-out winger, now I am a central midfielder. The old spectacular style has gone – now I play a much simpler passing game. When you play central midfield you have to change your whole game. You have to keep it tight and simple. So I hope they don't expect too much from me.'

Despite Rocastle trying to put things in perspective, manager Mike Walker knew exactly what he was getting: 'Everyone remembers David when he was at his peak during the time George Graham was at Arsenal,' Walker said. 'He won a championship medal and a place in the England side. Since then he's been very unlucky with injuries but now he's fully fit and I believe he's still a top-quality player. He played for Chelsea's reserves against us a couple of weeks ago and did well. I've been keeping an eye on him for a while and that clinched it.'

Away from the bright lights of London, as well as his family, Rocastle settled into the quieter pace of life in rural East Anglia and at least looked forward to his first senior appearance in over 17 months. However, with just an initial month to prove himself, Rocastle found immediate frustration as a string of games were called off due to bad weather.

It wouldn't be until 18 January 1997 that he finally made his debut, as he was named in the team to face Grimsby. In the build-up to the game he emphasised just how much he was looking forward to getting his boots on again. 'The manager has been brilliant all week and before the game he just told me: "You've got nothing to prove to me." Now I'm just hoping to use my experience to help the team and hopefully win myself a permanent move here. Norwich are definitely good enough to go up and the whole set-up here is fantastic. When I won two championship medals at Highbury, there were home-grown players like myself, Paul Davis and Tony Adams. They were mixed with some hard-nosed experience and now that is happening at Carrow Road. Darren Eadie, Keith O'Neill, Shaun Carey and Daryl Sutch have come through the ranks, with old campaigners like Ian Crook, John Polston and Rob Newman backing them up.'

With Rocastle added to the mix, Norwich certainly looked a formidable force on paper. But while Rocastle's technique and vision were still well beyond most, his legs were not. Now more suited to the continental game, he would find the hustle and bustle of central midfield far more frantic than he had been used to. Another issue he faced was that in the first division he was a big name and therefore a marked man. Every time he took a touch he found himself surrounded. With his knee no longer giving him the mobility to simply glide away, all too often the cloggers saw it as a point of honour to hack him down. Thankfully, he still had two attributes that elevated his game: the ability to move the ball on quickly, and to put in a tackle, a necessary weapon in the minefield of first division football.

Beating Grimsby 2-1, Rocastle spoke candidly after the match about how he had found the experience. 'This is the first time I have ever played at this level and it was much more scrappy than I am used to,' he said. 'I would like to have played more football, but we had a lot of players missing and the manager, Mike Walker, told us to keep possession and keep it tight. So we had to dig in to get the result. In the end it was a great win for us and from a personal point of view I was just glad to get through the game. But it's been great for me just to get away from Chelsea.'

Settling back into the groove as a first-team footballer, and enjoying having a team built around his skills, Rocastle was in inspirational form during the 2-1 win at Stoke. Seeming to have more time on the ball than anyone else, he kept possession with economical precision, while he also looked to sweep the ball wide to O'Neill and Eadie at every opportunity. Up in the stands, Newcastle manager Kenny Dalglish and Coventry manager Gordon Strachan had been watching the progress of the young Eadie, but instead spoke gushingly of the performance of Rocastle, who had proven that he still had something to offer at a higher level.

Rocastle's impact had been such that immediately after the game Mike Walker contacted Ruud Gullit and extended Rocastle's loan for another month. Reports also surfaced in the *Sunday Mirror* linking Rocastle with a £1m move to Serie A giants Fiorentina, who had apparently been tracking his progress.

From being a Chelsea outcast, Rocastle was suddenly hot property again. The subsequent 3-2 win against high-flying Sheffield United at Bramall Lane only served to emphasise this, as he once again showed himself to be a class above. The match report in *The Times* stated that, 'The visiting side may have an ineffective defence, but they also have David Rocastle on loan from Chelsea, and it was his experience and sheer quality in midfield that allowed them to claw back the initiative. Rocastle controls the tempo of a match, and it is surprising he cannot find a game in the Premiership.'

Feeling happy with his form on the pitch, Rocastle was also enjoying life off it. While he was staying in the Holiday Inn, battling in vain against the likes of Robert Fleck charging drinks and food to his room, he also enjoyed spending quality time with his brother. However, Rocastle's visits would usually be accompanied by a bag of clothes, which he would ask Steve to iron for him. The two may have been grown-ups, and Rocastle a professional footballer, but the dynamics of their relationship never changed, with Steve never able to say no to his brother's requests.

But then, just as Rocastle was building up a head of steam, the spectre of his knee injury returned. Forced to sit out the next few games, all talk of a potential transfer died away, as the grim reality of his situation came to the fore.

Back in the team on 22 February to face Charlton, Rocastle and Norwich displayed all-too-familiar frailties. Despite Charlton being down to 10 men as early as the 28th minute, and Norwich leading 4-2 with five minutes to go, their notoriously porous defence somehow conspired to turn three points into one. With individual mistakes counting against them, Rocastle had also failed to assert his authority on the game. Finding himself swamped every time he got on the ball, the supply line to him was cut off. By now the word was out. Stop Rocastle playing and you could stop Norwich.

His constantly swollen knee clearly didn't help matters. Rocastle's desperation to get back out on the field earlier than advised had been so great that he once again found himself confined to the physio's room for the next two weeks. The swelling was taking longer to go down. The pain was more intense. His hobble more pronounced. It was only his sheer love of the game that kept him going.

Finally, on 8 March, he was fit again for the visit of Port Vale. Setting up the equalising goal from a corner, he still found his influence from open play limited. The *Daily Mirror*'s award of a 6/10 for his performance was indicative of how the early promise of his loan spell had fizzled out.

Mike Walker soon had a decision to make. With Rocastle's loan at an end, Chelsea demanded £400,000 for his move to be made permanent or, if they wanted to extend his loan, Norwich would have to pay his salary until the end of the season. While Walker admired Rocastle, he knew that he couldn't justify such an outlay on a player who was constantly fighting a chronic injury that would only get worse. There was no doubt that he still possessed the talent to influence games, but the big question was – how often could he do it with his body failing him?

To Rocastle's dismay, he returned to Chelsea for more meaningless slogs in the reserves, and more training with the kids. It was a soul-destroying routine and one that found him at his lowest ebb, with Gullit refusing even to look at him. Yet in the reserves, and in training, Rocastle was still proving that he had something to offer. 'You'd look at him sometimes and think he should be in the first team,' Michael Duberry told me. 'We used to say to him, "Rocky, man, how come you're not in the first team?" He would say, "That's football. It happens sometimes. You can be a good player and you still don't always play. You've just got to get on with it and make sure you work hard." Around the training ground, and on the pitch, he was still good. I thought he should have been playing but it was also hard to argue because the team was doing well.'

With the class and bite of Di Matteo and Wise in central midfield, backed up by the legs of young guns Jody Morris and Eddie Newton, Chelsea had more than enough talent in the only position Rocastle could now realistically play. Finishing in a much-improved sixth place in the league, Chelsea had also reached the FA Cup final, where they faced relegated Middlesbrough.

In the lead-up to the game, Rocastle expressed his frustration at his situation. 'I'm fit and I know I could play in this team,' he said. 'I have one year left on my contract, and my career is simply rotting away. It wouldn't be so bad if Ruud had seen me in training and then come to a conclusion. I've been labelled a troublemaker and a difficult player but I vehemently deny all this. You can ask all of the managers I've played for, and I defy any of them to claim that. It's hard when you are forced to train with the kids while the other players are preparing for a cup final.'

While it came as no surprise to him not to be included in the squad for the game, Rocastle discovered that he wasn't even provided with a match-day suit. Nevertheless, rather than avoid the game, he went along so that his five-year-old son, Ryan, could experience his first FA Cup final. Sitting in the stands, trying to feign excitement as his son took in the sights, Rocastle watched on as his team-mates cruised to a 2-0 win and cavorted on the pitch with the cup.

Gullit had triumphed in his first season as Chelsea boss. All avenues back to the first team were subsequently closed. With a year left on his contract, Rocastle knew he had the summer to find another club or face yet another season languishing in the wilderness.

CHAPTER 30

HILLSBOROUGH

The events at Hillsborough still send a chill down my spine. I was just eight years old, and still enthralled by what many had called 'the beautiful game'. Suddenly, in an instant, that innocence was wiped away.

As my father watched the television in stunned silence, he was unable to answer my question: 'Dad, why isn't the TV showing the game?' However, as the cameras cut to the tragic scenes on the pitch, with injured fans being carried on advertising hoardings, it soon became clear that something was seriously amiss.

Following a build-up of Liverpool fans outside the Leppings Lane end, the police had ordered the gates to the central pens to be opened. Suddenly, the thousands of fans from outside poured in, crushing the fans at the front, who were unable to escape due to the perimeter fencing. In the worst sporting disaster in Britain's history, 96 Liverpool fans perished in the most horrific circumstances.

If my father had chosen to shelter me from the news, that

became all but impossible in the days that followed. Soon my young ears were ringing with words like 'hooliganism', 'decrepit stadiums' and then 'police cover-up'. In a single afternoon, all of the game's ills had finally erupted. This time there would be no patching up Frankenstein's monster. From top to bottom, the English game needed to be torn apart and started afresh.

The following week the front cover of the *Economist* carried the headline 'The Game That Died'. The subsequent article cut to the core of the many issues afflicting English football.

On football stadia: 'Britain's football grounds now resemble maximum security prisons, but only the feebleness of the regulations has allowed the clubs to go on pretending that crowd safety is compatible with prison architecture.'

On the football authorities: 'For complacency and incompetence, there's nothing like a cartel; and of Britain's surviving cartels, the Football League is one of the smuggest and slackest.'

On football club chairmen: 'Like old-fashioned newspaper magnates, they are willing to pay for prestige – which they see in terms of owning star players, rather than comfortable modern stadiums.'

And on their remedy to cure the game: 'Having fewer clubs, operating out of smarter stadiums, ought to revive the interest of those who have been driven away from football during the past 10 years.'

Arsenal were fortunate that in David Dein they boasted one of the game's brightest thinkers. As already seen, Dein would be a driving force behind the creation of the Premier League, while he had already pushed through the remodelling of the Clock End, adding corporate boxes to attract a different kind of fan. Yet many blinkered, or reckless, chairmen still clung to the past, packing tens of thousands of fans into decaying stadiums.

But on the afternoon of 15 April 1989 fans and players of Arsenal were still coming to terms not only with what was to be done about the game, but also with what would happen to the season itself, with many suggesting that it should be scrapped.

If some of the players considered continuing the league campaign an exercise in futility, there were others who still thought it was business as usual. In his frank autobiography, Tony Adams stated, 'I'm sure I watched the news pictures of fenced-in fans dying on the terraces that day, but I'm astonished to say that they hardly affected me because, I'm sad to admit, that was the man I was at that time. I wouldn't have allowed it to affect me, wouldn't have cried, because I knew we still had to go to Anfield for what would be a huge match.'

Despite Adams' cold detachment, Arsenal's scheduled trip to Anfield on 23 April had to be postponed as the players, management, fans and city of Liverpool somehow tried to come to terms with the magnitude of the disaster. It was a wonder that any of those players managed to regroup and focus on football, but no doubt the thought that they were doing it for the memories of their fallen fans helped see them through.

With Liverpool bravely vowing to continue with the season, the match against Arsenal was subsequently rescheduled for Friday, 26 May. It would be the last league game of the season and the first time that the season would finish after the FA Cup final. Although the encounter promised a potentially stunning conclusion to the title race, many believed that it would all be over by then in any event, so imperious had Liverpool's form been since January.

On the Monday morning following Hillsborough, George Graham addressed his team at London Colney. Expressing his sympathy for those involved in the disaster, he then told his players that all they could do was focus on football. There was still a title up for grabs and they were still top of the league. If they could just hold their nerve in the remaining five games then they would be champions for the first time since 1971. Now was not the time for distractions, no matter how shocking.

Arsenal had been due to play Liverpool the following weekend, but the game was of course postponed. As a result, their next fixture wasn't until 1 May, when they would face Norwich City, who having led the league for much of the season had now fallen out of contention. Continuing to persist with his new sweeper formation, Graham's only change to the team was the enforced absence of Marwood, who had cruelly been ruled out for the rest of the season with an Achilles injury.

As the North Bank sang 'You'll Never Walk Alone', in tribute to the fallen Liverpool fans, Marwood's absence was glossed over, and Alan Smith returned to the team. Delivering their most devastating performance of the season, Arsenal romped home 5-0 winners. Rocastle was once again superb. Setting up Thomas for Arsenal's third, he then proceeded to score the fifth. Flicking the ball to the right of the defender, he sprinted past him on his left-hand side, before rifling the ball low and hard past Bryan Gunn. With Smith adding another two goals to his impressive tally, Arsenal looked to be back to their very best.

Better yet, the subsequent 1-0 win at Middlesbrough saw them record their fourth straight win, as well as their fourth straight clean sheet. Liverpool were fast making ground, eight points behind with two games in hand, but the title was very much in Arsenal's hands. And with two home games to come, against lowly Derby County and Wimbledon, consecutive wins could potentially see them tie up the title before the prospect of the trip to Anfield if Liverpool failed to win all their matches.

Anticipation was building, as Arsenal prepared to face Derby at Highbury in confident mood. The 5-0 demolition of Norwich had seen them return to top form just at the right time, while their opponents had nothing to play for. The stars seemed to be aligning for Arsenal to see off the season in style.

Despite starting sluggishly, optimism soon spread around the ground like wildfire, as those with radios began a chain of Chinese whispers that Wimbledon had gone a goal up against Liverpool. Things were looking good, even if the team's performance was anything but. Facing an unrelenting wave of pressure from an energetic Derby team, Arsenal also found themselves a goal down shortly after, as Dean Saunders swept a volley into the top corner. This was not what the fans had been expecting.

In response, Graham hurriedly switched Rocastle to the left wing in an attempt to get him more involved in the game, urging him to cut inside and shoot at every opportunity.

But then word suddenly swept the stands that Liverpool had equalised. Anxiety now spread through the crowd, and this was translated onto the pitch, as Arsenal's desperation saw them dismiss their game plan and instead hit hopeful long balls up to Smith, which were easily repelled by Mark Wright.

Ever dangerous on the counterattack, and with Adams looking vulnerable, Saunders preyed on the centre back. One on one, Saunders turned Adams inside out, forcing him to stumble, before flicking the ball through his legs. Finally losing all composure, Adams hauled him down and conceded a penalty. Seconds later it was 2-0, and Arsenal's only response was to put their hands on their hips and look to the heavens.

A late Smith consolation goal halved the deficit but it was not enough. Arsenal had lost. Liverpool had won. The title was now out of their hands.

'The mood in the dressing room was quite sour,' Rocastle later said. 'The lads thought, "What's going on here?" We've got to get it right for Wednesday against Wimbledon. No one believed we would drop points against Wimbledon because we were so determined.'

The day before Arsenal faced the so-called 'Crazy Gang', Liverpool had ramped up the pressure, winning their game in hand against QPR to go one point clear at the top. All the more painful for Arsenal fans was having to hear their rivals chant, 'Champions! Champions!'

With the match at Anfield on the horizon, Arsenal had a final opportunity to regain their tenuous grip on the title by defeating Wimbledon, who were mid-table. If they had thought Wimbledon might be looking forward to their holidays, then the players were shocked to find them fired up before kick-off. Never a team to roll over, Vinnie Jones and co. had arrived intent on spoiling the party.

But before the game, Rocastle received further recognition of his impressive form when England manager Bobby Robson handed him the Barclays Young Eagle of the Year award. His form had been eye-catching for most of the season but particularly so in the previous month, when Graham's shift to a sweeper system had seen Rocastle operating further up the field. 'I like playing as a striker,' Rocastle said of his positional change. 'It gives me more of a chance to do what I enjoy, taking players on, getting in shots and crosses. Now I do my work in the opposition half, rather than tracking back and helping Lee Dixon. I relish the opportunity to run at defenders. Sometimes when I was having to make long runs back and forth I felt a bit tired. So this switch is working well for me. It's working well for the team too.'

However, after the disappointment against Derby, Graham decided to revert to 4-4-2, which meant that Rocastle was once again deployed out wide, with one of his primary duties being to cover his fullback, Lee Dixon. This was a move Graham would soon regret. While a Winterburn howitzer and a Merson volley twice gave Arsenal the lead, it was not enough, as the visitors struck back to draw the game. At the final whistle, the shellshocked players embarked on a subdued walk of honour, to muted applause, with not even the most optimistic of fans now giving their team any chance of winning the title.

'I think the fans thought we had blown it,' Rocastle said. 'The lads were disappointed. We went on a lap of, I can't say honour, but it was a lap of thanks because it was the last game at home and we wanted to thank the fans for being loyal to us throughout the season.'

That night Rocastle and Alan Smith went out for a commiseration meal. Neither admitted defeat in the title race, but they nonetheless agreed that with goal difference now becoming a factor, a big Liverpool win against West Ham, prior to their game at Anfield, could put the championship out of reach.

Any trace of optimism they might have harboured was soon blown away. 'I remember coming in when West Ham were playing Liverpool,' Rocastle said, 'and Liverpool were winning 2-1. I thought something could happen here. But as I was listening it went 3-1, 4-1 and 5-1. I switched it off. I couldn't listen any more. I tried to do the mathematics and I thought we had to beat Liverpool by four goals. I was on a downer.'

Rocastle's calculations were thankfully incorrect. To win the title Arsenal actually had to beat Liverpool at Anfield by two clear goals. Yet with Liverpool in rampant form, and Arsenal floundering, such a result seemed all but impossible. The headline in the *Daily Mirror* summed up how most fans and pundits rated their chances: 'You Don't Have A Prayer, Arsenal'.

CHAPTER 31

MOVIE STAR

In the spring of 1997 David Rocastle became a movie star. Nick Hornby's bestselling book *Fever Pitch*, an autobiographical take on his life following his team, had been adapted into a film, and as such the key protagonists in the famous 1988/89 title triumph were immortalised on the big screen.

Happily striding down the red carpet for the premiere in Leicester Square, Rocastle and Michael Thomas posed for photographs and signed autographs, as stars Colin Firth and Mark Strong also sought them out. 'I remember asking him [Rocastle] if he had enjoyed the film,' Hornby told me. 'He said he did. I only had five minutes with him but I was desperate to ask him as many questions as I could about Anfield. He was great. Just as I had always imagined.'

Watching a film that chronicled their finest hour, it would have stung most to realise that, at just 30 years of age, those glory days were no more. 'I think he was conscious of that at the time,' Hornby said. 'It was sad as he was still so young but it just seemed to be all over for him.'

But Rocastle certainly never felt like that. To most it seemed obvious that his career was slowly going downhill, but his natural positivity meant that he always believed something good was around the corner. However, he knew that wouldn't be at Chelsea. As such, he instructed his agent, Jerome Anderson, to do all that he could to find him a new club. The primary goal was to play first-team football regularly, at a decent level, but finances were also important. Rocastle had just turned 30 and it was clear from the state of his knee that his time at the top was coming to an end.

While he had earned good money compared to the average man in the street, it was by no means going to be enough to retire on. Moreover, his earnings had dipped over the last few years because he had not been receiving appearance and win bonuses, due to being out of the team. With a wife and four children to support, following the birth of his daughter Monique, he needed to ensure that his next contract was a reasonable one as it would probably be his last.

In the past, Rocastle could have had his pick of most clubs in Europe. Now Anderson found that there were virtually no takers. The harsh reality was that, just five years after being the club record signing for the champions of England, any clubs showing an interest demanded that he go on trial first so that they could run their eye over him. However, even the queue of clubs wanting to take Rocastle on trial was small.

One of these was Aberdeen, a mid-table club in the Scottish Premier League. Manager Roy Aitken was certainly intrigued by the cut-price fee of £150,000 for a former England international, especially with the opportunity to try before you buy. 'David will train with us and will probably feature in our pre-season games,' Aitken told the press. 'We recognise he's had one or two injuries but he's a quality midfielder who has played for Arsenal, Leeds United and Manchester City.'

Rocastle, meanwhile, was delighted that a club had at last shown some interest in him. 'I'm so grateful to Roy Aitken for giving me a call,' he said. 'It was only last Wednesday I heard about Aberdeen's interest and I was thrilled. I don't want to waste his time. My first day of pre-season was the most exhausting I've ever had but it will be worth it if I can win a contract.'

Putting his all into trying to win a coveted contract, his treatment at Chelsea under Gullit still continued to rankle. 'I couldn't understand why he didn't give me at least a chance to prove myself to him,' he commented. 'Ruud couldn't have been more unfair.'

But then, just days into his trial, Aitken's heavy pre-season schedule took its first casualty, as Rocastle pulled his thigh. Worse still, while Rocastle was on the treatment table missing out on pre-season games to impress, Aberdeen re-signed Scottish international midfielder Eoin Jess from Coventry City. Soon afterwards, Aitken informed Rocastle that his services would not be required, without him even playing a game.

Back at Stamford Bridge, Rocastle could not so much as join in pre-season training, as he was forced to have further treatment. By the time the season had kicked off, he was still without the prospect of regular football, and also wasn't fully fit because of missing training for much of the summer.

In early September there was a glimmer of a lifeline when Southampton manager Dave Jones offered him a trial. Sadly, the trial was cut short after just two days. When I asked Jones about this, he explained that Rocastle's knee injury had flared up and he therefore had to be sent back.

If any clubs had been minded before to look at Rocastle, they were now few and far between. Facing another season in the reserves, Rocastle was desperate to get away. When he confided this to his next-door neighbour, an offer suddenly materialised, and it would truly test Rocastle's assertion that he would play anywhere.

His neighbour was former England international Mark Hateley, who was now manager of third division Hull City, the club second from bottom of the Football League. To most 30-year-old internationals, who had played in the top flight for the vast majority of their careers, this would not on the face of it have presented an enticing opportunity. Yet when Hateley jokingly suggested it, he was shocked to find Rocastle immediately take him up on the offer.

'Mark was unsure whether I wanted to go to the third division,' Rocastle told a stunned press conference, 'but it gave me the opportunity to play first-team football. The club is second from bottom so no one can accuse me of coming for a holiday. I haven't thought about what I do when the loan period ends. I want to help Hull get as many points as I can and get my fitness levels back. It beats clearing out the guttering every Saturday afternoon.'

So Rocastle packed his bags once more and settled into a hotel in Hull for the next three months, realising that if he didn't earn a contract there then it would very much signal the end of his career.

Gregor Rioch, son of former Arsenal manager Bruce Rioch, was Hull City's club captain when Rocastle signed. When I spoke to Rioch, he reminisced about just what type of club Rocastle was walking into.

'In 1997 there was a takeover of the club by David Lloyd [former tennis professional and fitness club entrepreneur],' Rioch told me. 'He had brought in Mark Hateley, who was a big name, in an attempt to wake the sleeping giant. But for whatever reason it didn't work out and we struggled.'

From top to bottom, Hull was a club in need of a jolt. Lloyd was desperate to relocate from the decrepit Boothferry Park, but he had met with opposition from the council. While the stadium was crumbling, Rioch recalled that it could be a great place to play. 'I loved it,' he said. 'The fans were always passionate and they really embraced you if you worked hard and wore your heart on your sleeve. Even when we weren't doing so well, the passion was always there.'

Although the stadium was far from what Rocastle would have been used to, the training facilities might have been better than at Chelsea, though that wouldn't have been hard. Hull didn't have its own training ground, so would utilise a variety of facilities, the most prominent being Hull University playing fields. It was relatively basic, with a handful of grass pitches and a changing room, but as Rioch said, 'As long as we had some goals we were all right.'

Premier League club luxuries were also few and far between in the bottom division. 'There were plenty of times when you would have to wash your own kit,' Rioch laughed. 'Or if you didn't have it with you, you'd have to go into a basket and sort through old kit to wear. A lot of times the kit was mixed and matched from over the years, so you would need to find a pair of socks that didn't have holes in them and stuff like that.'

Out on the training pitch, Billy Kirkwood would usually take the sessions while Hateley, the player-manager, joined in. Rioch told me that Kirkwood's sessions were always enjoyable and, though the team was struggling, everyone invariably looked forward to them. If anything, Kirkwood's sessions might have been too advanced for a team in the bottom division. Spending hours on shape and technique, using drills he had seen at his previous club, Glasgow Rangers, the players couldn't always carry out on the pitch what they had learnt. However, Rocastle would have been used to such training routines, as they bore a similarity to George Graham's at Arsenal.

Given that it was Mark Hateley's first job in management, and his first experience at a lower level of football, it is perhaps no surprise that the team struggled. However, Rioch has fond memories of his former manager. He emphasised that while results didn't go Hateley's way, he was an excellent people person, who had the respect of the team. Despite this, there was one aspect that he felt might have counted against him. 'He still wanted to be the player-manager,' Rioch said. 'He loved getting his boots on but he had to focus on trying to manage the football club as well. It's not always easy and not many have succeeded doing it.'

While the players were excited to have the opportunity to play with Rocastle, the fans were ecstatic about his arrival. 'There was a lot of excitement and disbelief around the place when the news broke,' Rioch said. 'It was very rare in those days that somebody of that calibre would come and join a club like ours, especially when he had only just turned 30.'

However, there were also some concerns. Some speculated that Rocastle had no real commitment to the club, that he might be joining Hull for a final payday or just using them to get fit. According to Rioch, this could not have been further from the truth. 'From the first day he rolled up his sleeves and just got on with it,' Rioch recalled. 'It was special to see someone from that level be so committed and I think it inspired all of us.'

All that dedication would count for nothing if Rocastle didn't deliver on the pitch. The standard was the lowest he had ever played at and there was no doubting that he would be very much a marked man, as the biggest name in the league by far. Another potential issue was that his team-mates might struggle to be on the same wavelength as him, which would lead to him having to take extra touches and could see him caught in possession. Thankfully, all those worries were put to one side after an exhilarating debut against Scarborough.

With over 6,000 fans cheering him on, double the attendance of the previous game, Rocastle played a part in all three goals during the 3-0 win. Setting up the first, he proceeded to score the second himself before having a hand in the third. As the *News of the World* said in its report the following day, 'David Rocastle made a huge impact on his Hull debut.' Rocastle was equally enthusiastic. 'I was desperate to play,' he said. 'It was a breath of fresh air after 10 months of reserve-team football. I hadn't even worn studs in that time because you can't use them for the reserves in case you ruin the pitch. I loved every minute of it. The pace was frantic, though – quicker than the Premiership!'

His manager was confident that his new signing still had plenty to offer. 'He is in the twilight,' Hateley admitted, 'but he isn't over the hill. I played the best football of my career after I'd reached 31.'

On a high following such an emphatic debut, Rocastle's next game would see him really put to the test, as Hull visited Premiership Newcastle United in the League Cup. This was a game the whole city was excited about, with over 7,000 fans travelling to St James' Park. The Newcastle United side would also feature old adversary John Barnes, who was now playing in central midfield following an Achilles injury during his time at Liverpool. While the injury had restricted Barnes, he was still able to perform at Premier League level. Rocastle, on the other hand, had found that his knee had ruined any possibility of the same. Nevertheless, for one night only, the two would be head to head.

Sadly, the game turned out to be a bitter reminder for Rocastle that he could no longer be a force against such illustrious opposition. Struggling to impose himself, he trudged off the pitch as another name from the past, Ian Rush, celebrated equalling the League Cup goalscoring record of 49, having scored the opener in the 2-0 win. The result was certainly no disgrace, and it at least allowed Hull to focus on their primary objective, Football League survival.

For the next game at Barnet, Rocastle was assigned to room with Gregor Rioch, who relished the chance to be one on one with him. 'I think he must've been fed up with me by the time the kick-off came,' Rioch laughed, 'because when we were supposed to rest, and lay our heads down, I was asking him a thousand questions. He was so polite, such a gentleman. He told me stories about his time at Arsenal, and if I saw he was getting tired I would make him a cup of tea so he could keep going. It's really a vivid and cherished memory of mine, just me and Rocky in the hotel, preparing for the game, and him telling me about the great Arsenal team that he played on with George Graham.'

But Hull's relegation fears worsened. Beaten 2-0 by Barnet, Rocastle had found his influence diminished on a poor, sloping pitch. Although he was unable to contribute with the ball, Rioch said he was still contributing off it: 'I think he was amazed at how tough it was in the third division. But he still worked his socks off. Every single game he gave absolutely everything. He was one of those who, for 90 minutes, dug deep and gave his heart and soul.'

Rocastle was never a loud, brash personality, and Rioch told me that he motivated the players in other ways. 'He would have a quiet word with you,' he said. 'We all respected him because of his experience, and how he conducted himself, so we listened. On the pitch he would sometimes give you a look, like, "Come on!" The entire time he was with us I remember he delivered nothing other than praise and encouragement.'

In Hull's predicament, heart and soul wasn't always enough. There were plenty of players at that level who were honest, hard-working professionals like Rocastle. What Hull really needed was a touch of class. While he had certainly shown that on his debut, he was finding it harder to dominate games, because of the added attention.

There was also another reason for his weakened impact. Following a 0-0 draw with Brighton, his knee once again flared up, keeping him out of action for over a month. In similar circumstances many players might have retreated to Stamford Bridge, where they could enjoy some home comforts, but, ever eager to prove his commitment, Rocastle stayed in Hull. Attending training every day, he also volunteered to help out in the community, visiting hospitals and even turning on the town centre Christmas lights with Gregor Rioch. 'He could have just gone back to London very easily,' Rioch told me, 'but when I asked if he could help out he didn't hesitate. Players don't always feel comfortable doing stuff like that but Rocky felt it was important.'

His return to the team on 15 December, for the visit of Colchester, coincided with a 3-1 win, but it would turn out to be his final appearance for Hull. Not only had his knee injury seen him consigned to the sidelines once again, but Hull and Rocastle had to be honest with one another. His knee was always going to be an issue and they simply couldn't afford to keep him any longer.

Back at Stamford Bridge, not a single team expressed any interest in taking him. 'I would go to Hartlepool straightaway if that's what it took,' he said. 'I can't understand why nobody has come in for me. I know I'm supposed to be on drugs, and that my knees are shot, but that is just an awful lie being spread around. I'd rather somebody say that I was crap than say that.'

The only glimmer of light was a players' rebellion that finally removed Gullit, and put Gianluca Vialli in charge. This might have made the training ground more tolerable but the prospect of a first-team recall, or a new contract, was out of the equation. Instead, he had to sit out the remaining months of his contract, watching on as Vialli led the team to League Cup and European Cup-Winners' Cup glory.

Meanwhile, across London, Arsène Wenger's Arsenal romped to the double. The likes of Seaman, Adams, Bould, Winterburn, Dixon, Keown, Parlour and Wright were still integral parts of the team, many of whom were the same age as, or older than, Rocastle. It must have stung to see that, but for a knee injury, he too could have been playing for Wenger, a self-confessed fan of Rocastle, who had tried to sign him when he was manager of Monaco.

Still, no one can recall Rocastle being bitter about his situation. He was delighted to see his old team, and friends, back at the pinnacle of football. Indeed, despite being on Chelsea's books, Rocastle still attended Highbury regularly. Arsenal was his club. A lot of his friends still played there and he had always remained a fan.

But by the end of the 1997/98 season he had to come to terms with a very hard fact. He was without a club. He would soon turn 31. And he had a chronic knee injury. Was it time to finally admit defeat and retire, or should he sail off into the sunset and have one last adventure?

CHAPTER 32

PREPARATION

'We just enjoyed ourselves. We mucked about.' In the build-up to the biggest game of their lives, you might have expected Graham, a renowned disciplinarian, to have struck the fear of God into his players, but Rocastle recalled it was quite the opposite.

After being given two days off following the disappointment of the draw with Wimbledon, the players had returned to London Colney expecting a week of working on team shape and tactics. To their surprise, they were instead treated to sessions dominated by five-a-sides, shooting practice and early finishes, all in the blazing sunshine. 'The gaffer just said, "Lads, we won't even talk about Liverpool – let's just train and go out there,"' Rocastle remembered.

Although Graham's training routines were relaxed, the players were also amazed that they would not be travelling to Liverpool until the morning of the game itself. 'By the Wednesday everyone was saying to me, "When are you going to Liverpool?"' Rocastle remembered. '"We're not going until Friday," I told them. They couldn't believe it.'

While Graham took the pressure off his players, the media all but dismissed their chances. 'But for injuries [to Liverpool], the climax would doubtless not have been so belated,' *The Times* opined. The rest of the media thought likewise. Not a single publication, or pundit, tipped Arsenal for the win. Even Steve McMahon, the Liverpool midfielder, arrogantly declared, 'We're not worried about Arsenal now.' But such comments merely served to strengthen Arsenal's motivation. 'The papers were saying we had blown it,' Rocastle remembered. 'I think the lads were incensed by that.'

'He told me, "We're gonna do it,"' Jerome Anderson remembered. 'I said, "You're crackers." But he was so sure about it. "Nope, I'm telling you. We're gonna do it."'

Rocastle reasoned that Arsenal had been top of the league for over half the season. They had already drawn at Anfield in their Littlewoods Cup clash earlier in the season and had played well. Moreover, Liverpool were not only still battling with the emotional aftermath of Hillsborough, but in a high-octane FA Cup final they had been forced into extra time by their Merseyside rivals, Everton. While Liverpool had triumphed 3-2, they would surely be feeling emotionally and physically drained. Critics might have scoffed at Arsenal's chances, but if anyone could keep a clean sheet, and score two goals at Anfield, it was Arsenal.

Not only did they boast one of the most prolific goalscorers in the league in Alan Smith, but throughout the season Arsenal had an away average of two goals a game. Indeed, at the back, Adams and Bould had formed a formidable partnership, while in midfield they possessed one of the most dynamic talents in the game in David Rocastle. The only real question that remained was whether Graham would stick with 4-4-2, the preferred formation for much of the season, or would he use the sweeper system, which had been employed in the final few fixtures, Wimbledon notwithstanding?

However, not all of the players shared Rocastle's optimism. 'We've got two [chances],' Perry Groves said. 'Slim and no.'

Groves' thoughts seemed to mirror those of the nation at large. Rocastle's positivity couldn't mask the fact that Arsenal hadn't won at Anfield in 14 years, and that Liverpool had not lost by a two-goal margin to any team on their home turf in three. What's more, Anfield was generally reckoned to be one of the most intimidating stadiums in world football. As such, some bookmakers had them as far out as 7-1 to triumph.

Nevertheless, the joking and smiling Arsenal squad assembled at London Colney at 9am on Friday, 26 May, ready to board the coach to Liverpool. The sun was already shining. And spirits were high. Although Quinn, Davis, Marwood and the young Kevin Campbell were not in the squad, they were still invited to travel, an invitation they all eagerly accepted. Indeed, such was their determination to be at this momentous occasion that Davis even agreed to be seated with the fans, as there would be no room for him on the bench.

Yet while there was a relaxed mood the players were shocked to find some of the directors, and their associates, occupying their usual seats on the coach. Groves recalls that there was initially a standoff, as the directors told the players to sit elsewhere and the players refused to board until they had moved. Players are notoriously superstitious, even down to sitting in the same seats, and it was only when Groves explained that should they lose the game they would blame the directors for interrupting their preparation that the suits made way.

Finally, with the matter resolved, the coach set off on the three-hour trip to Liverpool, hoping it wouldn't become ensnarled in any bank holiday traffic. 'We had loads of biscuits and tea on the way up,' Rocastle recalled of the light-hearted atmosphere. 'We watched some videos and we were all laughing and joking. A few lads were playing cards or getting some sleep.'

After the latest episode of *Only Fools and Horses*, Graham put on a video that showed highlights of the double-winning team he had been part of. Famously winning the 1971 title at White Hart Lane, as well as the cup against Liverpool, the video was designed to show his players that their Anfield job was far from impossible. Despite this, it also produced a few laughs. 'He showed us the '71 final,' Kevin Campbell told me. 'He was telling us he was the one who had actually scored. He'd stop it and say, "Look, I got the touch just there." We were all winding him up, shouting, "No you never, gaffer!"'

Having been quiet and relaxed for most of the journey, Rocastle suddenly leapt up, waving a copy of the *Daily Mirror* in his hand, the one with the headline proclaiming that Arsenal didn't have a prayer. 'Look at this headline!' he shouted, incensed. In response, Paul Merson went down on his hands and knees and said, 'Well, let us pray,' which set everyone off into roars of laughter.

Arriving at the Atlantic Tower Hotel in Liverpool around midday, the players had some lunch before they headed to their rooms for an afternoon nap. Waking at 4.30pm, Rocastle had a quick shower before dressing in his famous Arsenal blazer, with the club crest emblazoned on the pocket. Adjusting his club tie in the mirror, he finally made his way downstairs to meet the team.

In a private room, the players congregated at 5pm on the dot, where they munched on toast with honey, washed down with mugs of tea, before Graham finally told the waiters to leave the room and shut the doors behind them. It was time to get down to business.

Standing in front of his squad for the first time that week, Graham spoke of the magnitude of the match. He told them it was the game of their lives, and they had nothing to lose. Everyone had written them off. He pointed out that, while some Liverpool players would feel the pressure, others would be complacent. Steve McMahon had already shown that.

Turning to tactics, Graham confirmed that they would be playing the sweeper system, with Bould brought back into the team. But on this occasion he didn't give the likes of Rocastle a free licence to get forward, despite the team's need for goals. Instead, he told the midfield trio of Rocastle, Richardson and Thomas to squeeze Liverpool at every opportunity. Not to give them a chance to build up any sort of rhythm.

Then, like a modern-day Nostradamus, Graham told his players how the game was going to go. 'Unbelievably, the manager said that we'll be 0-0 at half-time,' Rocastle recalled. 'And then we'll score two goals in the second half. It was like he had read the script. He said, "Don't be in too much of a hurry. We don't want to give away any early goals. Nil-nil at half-time will do, then we'll score two." The lads were all like, "Of course we will, boss."'

This was the complete opposite of what the pundits had been predicting all week. Given that Arsenal needed to score two goals, they believed that Graham would order his team to attack at every opportunity, with Liverpool expected to have to weather an early storm. Graham knew that patience would be the key. There was no need for such desperation. Settle into the game. Keep a clean sheet. And then worry about scoring goals.

Two hours before kick-off, the players boarded the coach for the 20-minute journey to Anfield, led all the way by a police escort. Sweeping through the terraced streets, making their way slowly towards the stadium, the players looked out at the fans swarming around the ground. Already the tension of a big game could be felt in the air.

Arriving at Anfield, they quickly got changed before they trooped off towards the pitch, passing the intimidating 'This is Anfield' sign on their way. On a still, clear evening, they emerged from the tunnel to find the stadium half-full. Their arrival was immediately greeted by chants from the Liverpool fans of 'Boring,

boring Arsenal!' Suddenly the away end erupted. 'Arsenal champions, Arsenal, Arsenal champions!' came the loud and emphatic response. The players may have been in an intimidating cauldron of noise but they were instantly lifted by their fans. Up in the television studio, the ITV team of Elton Welsby and Bobby Robson watched on. Their verdict? Anything other than a Liverpool victory was hard to see.

After inspecting the pristine pitch – a wonder considering it was the end of the season – the players trudged back to the dressing room for last-minute preparations, only to discover that the game had been delayed for 10 minutes due to fans being stuck in congestion on the M6. As they waited, boots were adjusted, socks pulled up, balls kicked against walls and rub applied, as Graham stood in the middle of the dressing room and prepared to give the most important team talk of his life.

CHAPTER 33

A FOREIGN ADVENTURE

'I think you've got to hold your hands up and know when your time is finished.' In the summer of 1998, Jerome Anderson said these words to his client David Rocastle. It had become increasingly clear that finding Rocastle a club in Britain was going to be difficult, and certainly no one would be likely to pay him anything near the salary he had become accustomed to. However, despite being ravaged by injury, Rocastle had no intention of retiring. He continued to love the game and was open to the idea of playing abroad.

As such, Anderson had a brief to find Rocastle a club in a league that wouldn't demand too much from his knee, but which would also pay him a reasonable wage, knowing that this would almost definitely be his last payday.

Coincidentally, Ken Shellito, manager of Malaysian side Sabah FC, was at this time on the lookout for a high-profile English player. A fullback for Chelsea in the 1960s, Shellito had been close to forcing his way into England manager Alf Ramsey's plans before a knee injury had wrecked his career. Concentrating on coaching, Shellito eventually wound up in Malaysia, going on to become manager of Sabah FC in the late 1990s. When Shellito arrived at Sabah, the club president Datuk Anifah Aman had a request: find a star English player to ignite the team and excite the fans. But this was easier said than done.

'I told the president I would see what I could do,' Shellito told me. 'I made a few calls back home and eventually was put in touch with an agent who said, "Yes, I've got a player that fits the bill. He's coming to the end of his career but he's a hell of a good person." He told me that it was David Rocastle. I was interested straightaway.'

With Anderson and Shellito hammering out the deal, Rocastle and his young family were soon on the plane to Malaysia, a country none of them had ever visited, ready to start a new life.

Situated on the beautiful island of Borneo, Sabah was one of 13 Malaysian states, with an average temperature of 32°C. Boasting an array of national parks and beaches, it certainly promised a luxurious lifestyle for the Rocastles away from the football pitch.

Averaging crowds of 15-20,000, Sabah's size was equivalent to a decent first division outfit, while the standard was perhaps comparable at that time to the Conference. Football had been extremely popular in Malaysia in the 1980s, with 86,000 fans regularly watching the national team, but the game was hit by a series of match-fixing scandals which had seen its support plummet. Although it had recovered somewhat by the late 1990s, there was still some scepticism that the game was truly clean. In order to combat this, ticket prices were kept low, particularly at Sabah, which was not a particularly wealthy area, with many fans working in the surrounding factories.

Meeting Shellito, the two discussed Rocastle's role in the team. It was clear that, even at a slower pace, his knee would restrict him from operating as a box-to-box midfielder, or as a winger, but Shellito had something else in mind. 'I wanted him to be our holding midfielder,' he said. 'I was going to build the team around him so he could pick up the ball from our defence and set us off.'

As had happened with Rocastle before, Shellito discovered that there were added benefits to having him at a club. 'He was brilliant with the kids,' Shellito remembered. 'After training he would usually wait for the academy to arrive and he would join in. They used to ask me, "Is Mr Rocastle coming in today?" They loved him.'

And Rocastle and his family soon came to love Malaysia. Settling into a beautiful house in paradise, Rocastle ensured that they didn't just keep to themselves and follow the traditional expat lifestyle. His son Ryan was enrolled into a Malaysian school, while the family went to areas of the city where foreigners were usually scarce. Eating at local restaurants, with the Malaysian delicacy, banana fritters, becoming a firm favourite, Rocastle immediately ingratiated himself, despite his limited grasp of Malay. He was recognised wherever he went, but the Malaysian fans kept a respectful distance, which meant that for the first time since his days as an apprentice he could go out with his family without being bothered.

Revelling in the slower pace of life, Rocastle appreciated the simple things – the monotony of household chores, taking his children, Melissa, Ryan and Monique, to school, and long walks with Janet in the sun. He adored his family and treasured the time he could now spend with them. There was never anything flash or extravagant. It was enough just to be together. His football career may have been winding down but his family life was in its prime. Indeed, many of those who met Rocastle during this time were surprised at just how down to earth he was.

'Considering what he'd achieved, we were expecting a bit of a prima donna,' the former Sabah FA president, Datuk Anifah Aman, told journalist Jason Dasey. 'But David was very humble and dedicated and would turn up early for training and be one of the last to leave. He made an effort to learn all the unfamiliar names of his team-mates and took a genuine interest in them.'

Shellito was also struck by Rocastle's kind spirit. 'I remember we were once on a plane,' he told me, 'and while we were sitting down a stewardess came across and asked if one of us would mind trading seats with someone else because a young family had been separated and wanted to sit together. "No problem," David said, and changed seats, not realising he would now have to sit in the smoking area. When he realised, he smiled at the stewardess and told her, "Just make sure there's plenty of wine coming this way."'

But Rocastle was primarily in Sabah to play football and sell tickets. Both aspects required him to be fit and to play well. Thankfully, the slower pace of the game facilitated this. He was able to play far more regularly than he had done in recent years, while he also found that he was able to dominate games, even at walking pace.

In a 4-1 home win against Perak, Rocastle even produced a moment of brilliance that is still remembered to this day. With Sabah on the attack, the Perak goalkeeper came racing from his box to head the ball towards the halfway line where Rocastle was waiting. Seeing the keeper was off his line, Rocastle cut across the ball on the volley, sending it soaring over the flailing keeper's head and into the net. It was such a cheeky effort that, after the match, the Perak manager renamed him 'David Rascal'.

Although the team was built around him, Rocastle hated being the centre of attention. 'He was more comfortable just being one of the boys,' Shellito said. 'He helped the team and helped the players. He didn't come here and say, "I'm David Rocastle, give me the ball." He was just so down to earth and all the players thought a lot of him.'

Memorably helping Sabah reach the 1998 Malaysian FA Cup final, as well as the final of the 1999 President's Cup, there was another game in which he experienced something that he had never encountered before in his career. As Rocastle was the fulcrum of the team, Shellito had always urged his players to give him the ball at every opportunity. But in one game he was stunned to find during the first half that his team-mates were ignoring him. 'He came in at half-time and he was furious,' Shellito told me. 'He said, "Coach, this game is fixed. They won't give me the ball." I said, "David, I don't think it's fixed." But he said that he had had enough. He was so disappointed.'

Friends and family can also recall Rocastle calling the league 'the most corrupt in the world'. With local players not being paid much, he felt they were open to bribery, which often left him taking all the free-kicks, corners and throw-ins so that they couldn't interfere with the game. One game his family recall him mentioning saw Sabah face a team which they had beaten earlier in the season by six goals. At this stage Sabah were already in the play-offs, while their opponents needed to win by seven goals to qualify themselves. To Rocastle's disgust, Sabah were four goals down after 20 minutes. While he tried to rise above it he felt it was all but impossible when others were letting him down.

Whether games were fixed or not Shellito doesn't know, but when Rocastle's contract came to an end, after 18 happy months, he had already decided to move on. Having received an offer to play for Clementi Khalsa, a small Singaporean club with crowds of just 4,000, he was ready for another adventure.

Subsequently, Rocastle travelled to Singapore for talks, with Clementi's owner, Balbeer Singh, putting him up in his downtown apartment for four days while he showed him around the city.

'There was a media frenzy when he was in Singapore,' Singh told me. 'Everyone was excited he was joining our league.'

Showing Rocastle around potential accommodation, and schools for his children, Singh also organised a family day at the Clementi Stadium. In an article for *FourFourTwo* magazine, journalist Neil Humphreys spoke of Rocastle's time there:

'The club had organised a family day for the community: face painting, five-a-sides and freebies, the usual Singaporean fare. The place was packed. It wasn't a Clementi family day. It was David Rocastle day. They had all come to meet Rocky. Frankly, the occasion was beneath an English Premier League footballer of his stature. But he signed every autograph and smiled at every asinine request. When I left him, he was showing a gaggle of eight-year-old stragglers how to jockey on the ball, how to drop a knee to slow down an opponent. His knee looked fine. He promised to meet again before the new season and went back to coaching the starstruck Singaporeans. No one had asked him to conduct an impromptu clinic. He could've left at any time. Other, lesser footballers, paid employees of the club, certainly did.'

Not only did he win over the hundreds of Clementi supporters who had turned out to see him, but he had also made a big impression on the Singh household. 'He would eat lunch with my family and I had little kids at that point in time,' Singh happily reminisced. 'He was so humble and brilliant with my son. I think it rubbed off on him as he grew to love soccer and is now training with the Barcelona youth team.'

Staying up until 4am drinking red wine, Rocastle was happy to regale Singh with stories about the old days. Feeling melancholy with wine, he reminisced about his time with Michael Thomas and Ian Wright, that momentous night at Anfield, and just how special Arsenal was as a club, from the unique tube station to the commissioner on the door. No matter where Rocastle was in the world, it seems that he always yearned for Highbury. They had been the happiest times of his life. The warmth and passion with which he spoke of Arsenal made a huge impression on Singh. 'I think he had really enjoyed his time in Malaysia,' Singh said. 'But it was clear his heart was always with Arsenal.'

Sadly, the move to Clementi didn't materialise. Singh recalls that there was an issue with a salary cap, combined with Rocastle's knee injury. There's no doubt he would have been the biggest star ever to have graced the game in Singapore, but it was not to be.

Returning to Sabah, the Rocastles stayed on for a further six months, such was their affection for Malaysia. While never officially announcing his retirement, it was clear that his time in the professional game had finally come to an end in paradise. The moment had arrived for him to turn his thoughts to what the future might hold. There was no doubt that he would have to carry on working, and there was thankfully no shortage of opportunities.

Jerome Anderson had already earmarked his client and good friend for a role at his agency. He believed that Rocastle's experience, intelligence and personality meant that he could be a great success in that industry. Coaching was also on the agenda. David Dein was always enthusiastic about the prospect of Rocastle taking his first steps at Arsenal, where he knew he would have a tremendous impact on the youth team. Another option was television. In recent years, the likes of Ian Wright, Paul Merson, Alan Smith and Lee Dixon have all become renowned pundits and there is no doubt that Rocastle could have made a name for himself in that arena. Well groomed and articulate, with an easy-going smile, he would have become a star.

Whatever he chose to do, Rocastle decided that his family would come first. He was determined to be there for his children, and watch them grow. But, with options being weighed up, he noticed two lumps in his armpit. Soon all his hopes and dreams were put on hold.

CHAPTER 34

FIRST HALF

Apart from the muffled singing of 'You'll Never Walk Alone' carrying through the walls, the dressing room was completely silent. The players sat shoulder to shoulder, slowly nodding their heads as their manager stood in the centre of the room.

'Remember, lads,' George Graham reminded them, determination in his steely eyes, 'keep it tight. We don't want to give away an early goal. We hunt in packs. We don't let them settle. Don't worry if we don't score before half-time. It will come. I'm telling you. Believe in yourselves. Believe in each other. Tony?'

Following on from Graham's relaxed and considered approach, it was now time for the captain to crank things up a notch. Standing to his feet, Adams let fly. 'We've come this far, lads, and we are not letting this fucking title slip now,' he bellowed, eyeballing his teammates. 'They've all written us off. Now is our chance to prove them fucking wrong. Let's go and fucking win it, for us, for our families, for the fans!' Rocastle patted Michael Thomas' on the thigh as the dressing room roared its approval. Everyone was together, as one.

This was not a team of individuals but a unit of compadres, willing to put themselves on the line for each other in the biggest battle of their professional lives.

As Adams led his team out, Graham stood by the door and shook each of his players by the hand, wishing them luck, as well as handing them a bouquet of flowers. This was Graham's final stroke of genius. Just over a month on from the dreadful events of Hillsborough, the disaster was still very much on everyone's minds. Indeed, not only had all the fences around Anfield been removed, but a police officer had reminded the fans, over a loudspeaker, that the whole country was watching on television and they should not invade the pitch, for fear of any trouble.

Emerging from the tunnel in their yellow away strip, the Arsenal players wore black armbands in memory of director Stuart McIntyre, who had died earlier that day. Running to all four corners of the ground, they presented the crowd with the flowers that Graham had given them. In an instant, the intimidating roar had turned to applause. This simple act had disarmed the Liverpool fans, who now had only respect for the Arsenal team.

Meeting on the halfway line, Adams and Liverpool captain Steve Nicol tossed the coin as Rocastle and John Barnes shook hands and embraced. Friends now, they prepared to be rivals for the next 90 minutes. The league title was up for grabs. It was do or die.

In the commentary box, Brian Moore and David Pleat oversaw proceedings, with the camera homing in on Rocastle clapping his hands together. 'And Rocastle is the man Liverpool will really fear,' Moore told the 8 million viewers at home, while Pleat added that for Arsenal to have any chance at all they had to be leading at half-time and would therefore be starting at a high tempo.

Then, to the deafening roar of the crowd, the referee blew the whistle for hostilities to commence. It was game on.

The early minutes were frantic and error-strewn, as both teams struggled to settle into the flow of the game, which descended into a midfield war of attrition. Standing out wide, Rocastle tracked his runner and kept it simple when the ball came to him. This was the time to play for the team. Not for any individual glory.

With Arsenal hunting in packs, never allowing Liverpool to settle, boos soon echoed around Anfield as Bould clattered into McMahon. A few choice words were muttered between the two as Bould retreated back into his position, satisfied that he had Liverpool's midfield linchpin rattled.

Content to sit back and keep their 5-4-1 shape, O'Leary swept up to deny Rush and Aldridge the space they craved in behind. Expertly marshalling the back five, Adams also kept a watchful eye on Dixon and Winterburn, ensuring they maintained their fullback positions, while Rocastle sat deep to nullify the threat of Barnes. Wave after wave of attack was subsequently broken down by good positional play or a flying tackle.

Clearly frustrated, Liverpool found themselves limited to long-range shots. Steve Staunton's effort might have stung Lukic's palms, but it was straight at him, while Rush's 25-yard pile-driver saw him pull his groin and need to be replaced by Peter Beardsley. Beardsley was, of course, a fine player in his own right, but he certainly didn't possess Rush's goal threat.

While it was Liverpool who enjoyed more of the possession, and seemed to be camped in Arsenal's half, it was the visitors who still crafted the best chance. Thomas' cross was met by the head of Bould, only to be cleared off the line by Steve Nicol. It was a reminder that Arsenal could strike at any moment, as the subdued Anfield crowd suddenly unleashed a roar to try to inspire their team.

Slowly but surely the away end filled up, as those who had been caught in traffic, or stuck on the train, made their way into the ground. Looking up at the scoreboard, they saw their team was still very much in the game and let rip a reverberating chant, 'Come on, you yellows! Come on, you yellows!'

The only time Arsenal appeared vulnerable was when an angled ball over Bould saw him lose John Aldridge. Dropping on the half-volley, just 10 yards from goal, Aldridge's wild swipe sent the ball sailing high and wide into the stands. Heading into the match, Aldridge had scored in six consecutive games, but this was a sign of just how tense the players were, as he snatched at a chance he would usually have taken.

Still, as the referee blew the whistle for half-time, Graham could be satisfied that the game had gone exactly as planned. But with his team still requiring two goals in the second half, he trotted down from the directors' box and prepared to let his flair players off the leash.

CHAPTER 35

THE END

The summer of 2000 saw David Rocastle make a surprise return to London. While he had enjoyed some fleeting visits since his move to Malaysia, he opted to stay in a hotel. However, on this occasion he wanted to stay with his mother.

'I was back at home for a bit with Mum, and so was my younger brother Sean,' Karen Rocastle told me. 'He came and he spent the whole week with family. He wanted to visit all of our cousins, and he wanted to go to the cemetery to visit my dad's grave, my grandad's grave, and my aunt's grave. He also went up to Norwich to visit my younger brother Steve and he was really keen to see all his old school friends, people he probably wouldn't be seeing if he was just up on a little fly-by.'

Ringing around all of his old school friends, he suggested that they have a reunion in the North Pole bar in Greenwich. As all the faces from the past met up, Rocastle laughed and joked about old times, appearing happy and relaxed. However, old school-friend Jenny Fraser recalls that he was also in a philosophical mood.

'David had always been very light-hearted,' Fraser told me. 'But on this night when we spoke he was a little more serious. I remember him telling me to follow my dreams. Do what you want to do. Don't wait. I put it down to all the knocks and twists and turns he had had in his own life.'

While everyone was thrilled to see him, no one knew that Rocastle was hiding a devastating secret. After months of putting it off, he had finally had the lumps in his armpit examined. Concerned doctors had subsequently sent his tissue and blood samples away for tests before delivering a shattering diagnosis. He had non-Hodgkin lymphoma, an aggressive form of blood cancer that attacks the immune system. Facing up to the fight ahead, Rocastle asked what could be done. In response, the doctor shook his head. Nothing. It was terminal. They could offer him chemotherapy to prolong his life, but other than that it was hopeless. At just 33 years of age, and less than a year since he had retired from football, he was now being told he had no future at all.

Hearing such distressing news would have led most to seek the support of friends and family. However, Rocastle was not like most people. He had grown up as the father figure in his household, always ready to take on other people's problems, but never burdening them with his own. Indeed, during his struggles at Leeds United and Chelsea, he might have appeared frustrated but away from the pitch he very rarely let such matters affect him. To his friends and family, he always had a smile on his face, no matter what he might have been dealing with.

Rocastle gently gave those closest to him the news, but he held back from telling them that it was terminal. 'I can remember getting the call in October, the year before he died,' Karen Rocastle revealed. 'He phoned Mum, who was always so close to him, and I saw her start to cry. "Mum, Mum, what is it?" I asked. In the end

I had to take the phone from her. I said, "All right, Dave, it's Karen. What's going on?" "All right, Karen," he said. "It's nothing, really, I'm just not well." "What's wrong?" I said, and he goes, "It's all right, I'm just gonna have some chemo and whatever, and everything will be fine." He never actually ever said the word "cancer" but when you hear the word "chemo", you know what it is straightaway. He told us they had caught it in time, that they were going to give him a blood transfusion, and look into his stem cells. He kept saying that it was treatable, so while we were all obviously concerned we never thought it was so bad. I think he was really trying to protect Mum as she had lost Dad at a similar age so didn't want her to worry.'

Sent to Wexham Park Hospital in Slough for life-prolonging treatment, he tried to ensure that no one saw just how fast he was deteriorating. Whenever his mother said she would come and visit, his stock answer was always, 'Don't worry. I'll come and see you.' Only his beloved Janet was allowed to see him in his condition, as he tried to hide the reality of the situation from the rest of the family. However, it was a secret that was becoming harder and harder to keep.

Junior Hamilton recalls taking him to the hospital and being shocked at his appearance. Having lost a large amount of weight, his once tree-trunk thighs were nothing but skin and bone. His cheeks had hollowed, with his glasses virtually being kept in place by his sharp cheekbones. His famous curly black hair had also fallen out. Most noticeable of all were the terrible burns across his chest, an after-effect of the chemotherapy. Not once did Rocastle ever state that he was dying, but all who saw him now began to suspect that the treatment was not working.

On one occasion, Rocastle had surprised his mother and sister with a visit, in an attempt to prove that he was well. 'That was the first time I had seen him properly,' Karen told me. 'He looked totally different. You wouldn't even think it was the same person. Honestly. You couldn't believe that just a year earlier he could have played professional football.'

Even though things were not looking good, his family recall his positivity; he never thought he wouldn't beat it. At one point he told his siblings that the doctors had told him there were three ways of treating his cancer, and he was already at the third level. While most would have panicked that the treatment clearly wasn't working, Rocastle remained positive that there would be another solution and made everyone feel that a cure would be found. Such was his positivity that he even turned away Marie Curie nurses as he was convinced he was going to beat it.

His condition was, however, going rapidly downhill. On 25 March 2001, Rocastle called his mum to wish her a happy Mother's Day. Breathless, he struggled to complete his sentences. 'I'm just tired,' he told his concerned mother. 'I'll be all right once I've had some sleep. Have a nice day. Love you.' It would prove to be the last time his mother ever heard his voice.

In intense pain, and falling in and out of consciousness, Rocastle was admitted to Wexham Park Hospital on Monday, 26 March. Even then, many of his close friends and family were unaware of his true state. Indeed, Paul Davis had been so taken by his positivity that he had told mutual friends he was on the mend.

However, by the Thursday it was clear that all was not well. That night Janet called Linda Rocastle from the hospital and told her that her son was asleep, and would receive more treatment in the morning when she would call again with an update. Yet before she hung up, Janet mentioned that the cancer had spread to his liver. Instantly, Linda knew this was not a good sign. After years of working as a nurse, she recognised that once the cancer had spread that far then the end was in sight.

As Linda broke down in tears, Karen decided to call the hospital.

Speaking to her son's doctor, Linda was told, 'Come straightaway. He might not last the night.'

Frantically arriving in the middle of the night, Karen and Linda were led to Rocastle's room. Frail and asleep, the former Arsenal star had an oxygen mask attached to his emaciated face, which slowly went up and down in accordance with his shallow breathing. With his mother and sister holding his hand and softly speaking to him, every so often he would open his eyes. To help him feel more comfortable, Linda rubbed lotion into his dry skin, while Karen called her brother Steve and told him to travel down from Norwich as quickly as he could.

As Steve raced to the hospital straight from work, Jerome Anderson also arrived to see his great friend. The memories were almost too painful for Anderson to discuss with me, even 14 years on. Unable to find the words, and welling up, Anderson had to cut our interview short.

Finally, in the early hours of 31 March, Steve Rocastle rushed through the corridors of Wexham Park to be at his brother's side. Kneeling down, he held his brother's hand when suddenly, after days of no movement, Rocastle jolted up, sensing his younger brother's presence. The two had shared their love of football together, from their days as children, kicking their mum's plastic fruit around the kitchen, to their adult years, when Rocastle had starred for Arsenal and Steve had gone to Norwich. It wasn't supposed to end like this. His big brother, who had once had the world, was indestructible, wasn't he? Yet moments later, with Steve holding his hand, the man with the never-say-die spirit slowly slipped away, heading towards the bright lights of a stadium in another world to project his talents. The man known to all as Rocky was dead at just 33 years of age. By his side, an Arsenal shirt with the name 'Rocastle' emblazoned across the back, a gift from David Dein. To the end he had been a Gunner.

When the news broke the following morning, it was greeted by total shock and despair. Ian Wright, who was on Radio 5 live, speaking in advance of that day's north London derby, referred to Rocastle as his 'best mate' and then broke down, unable to talk any longer.

In an East Anglia charity shop, Perry Groves was alone in a store-room, helping to sort books (a condition of a drink-driving charge), when he heard Wright break the news. He immediately dismissed it, thinking they must have been talking about someone else, until it became clear that it was indeed his old team-mate. 'I don't tend to cry,' Groves told me. 'But that news hurt. I was by myself and I couldn't stop myself. He was such a great guy. I couldn't believe he was gone.'

'I remember his wife Janet calling us at three in the morning,' Alan Smith told author Jason Cowley. 'It was terrible, just terrible. I'd never lost a close friend like that before.'

As the crowds flocked to Highbury, the news soon spread in a wave of disbelief. While fans tearfully shared their own memories with each other, former team-mates did the same. 'There were no airs and graces about him,' Paul Davis said. 'He would speak to everyone the same. He was a fantastic guy to have known. I just feel so sorry for his wife and kids.'

Graham Rix, who had spoken to Rocastle just two weeks previously, admitted that upon hearing the news, 'I cried my eyes out.'

Arsenal's current manager, Arsène Wenger, said, 'I cannot recall so many people wanting one person to win a battle. We wanted him better, we wanted him back at Arsenal to continue his coaching career. It was not to be and David will be terribly missed by all of us.'

His old scout Terry Murphy also shared his own memories of his former protégé: 'My lasting memory of David is of his feeling and compassion. I had recently lost my wife through cancer and, as ill as he was, he only thought of me. That was David.'

Even old adversaries were stunned at the news. Liverpool defender Alan Hansen stated that Rocastle was always modest and humorous, a player who was hard to upset on or off the field. On one occasion, when Hansen had tripped Rocastle in a game, Hansen recalled that he had merely smiled and said, 'Getting old?'

Kate Hoey, then Minister for Sport, said that 'his standards of decency and modesty made him stand out', while Chelsea chairman Ken Bates recalled his 'knockout smile' and how he 'always had a spring in his step and a sparkle in his eyes'.

The sportswriters each wrote loving obituaries. Rob Beasley in the *News of the World* summed up the common theme when he said that Rocastle was 'one of the gentlest and most genuine gentlemen in the game of association football'. Harry Harris in the *Daily Mirror* agreed, 'Everyone who came into contact with this fine player and lovely man is struggling to come to terms with his cruelly premature loss.' Michael Hart in the *Evening Standard* described Rocastle as 'a throwback to a bygone age; a young footballer who retained a charm and sense of perspective at a time when the egoists were about to take over the dressing rooms'.

Meanwhile, an Arsenal statement declared that the club had lost a 'legend' and Gordon Taylor, head of the PFA, stated, 'It's too tragic for words.'

With Highbury ready to pay tribute to its fallen hero during the north London derby, there was a real worry that the Spurs fans might disrupt the one-minute silence with catcalls and boos. As such, the referee was instructed to blow the whistle prematurely if this happened, to try to prevent trouble between the supporters. However, in a sign of just how much Rocastle was respected, the Spurs fans behaved immaculately as Highbury fell silent.

Up on the big screen, an iconic picture of Rocastle was projected, with his thumbs up, while the lettering underneath rammed home the tragic news: '1967–2001'.

In the centre circle, former team-mates who were still playing for Arsenal, such as Seaman, Keown, Dixon and Adams, tried to hold back the tears. There was a game to be won, and they wanted to win it for the man they knew as Rocky, but still the emotion got the better of them. Incredibly, as they thought of their former team-mate and friend, the ball moved in the centre circle, almost as if he had taken kick-off for them.

Fittingly, it was Robert Pires, wearing Rocastle's number 7 shirt, who opened the scoring in the 2-0 win. As the crowd burst into chants of 'Rocky! Rocky! Rocky!', Pires pointed to the heavens. Across London, another player was also dedicating a goal to Rocastle. Former team-mate Gianfranco Zola, who Rocastle had helped to settle in London, told the press after his goal against Middlesbrough, 'It's very sad news. He was a really good man, always positive and friendly. I really liked him.'

On 7 April 2001, David Carlyle Rocastle was laid to rest in Windsor's St John the Baptist church. Although it had been earmarked as a small, personal funeral, over 750 people crammed inside and out, while hundreds of onlookers gathered as if it were a royal burial. Adams, Wright, Thomas, Davis and Smith were among the pallbearers who helped carry their former team-mate's coffin on a highly emotional day. However, while the stars paid tribute to Rocastle at the wake, it was left to his old friends to bury him. In an ancient Caribbean tradition, close friends like Errol Johnson, Kevin Arnold and Gary Hill filled in the grave themselves, and didn't finish until their friend was at rest.

Since that tragic day, Arsenal and its fans have ensured that the memory of one of their favourite sons lives on. Around the outside of the new Emirates Stadium, giant images of former heroes stand proudly linking arms. Rocastle is depicted among the 32 given such an honour. He was also voted the club's 17th greatest player of all time. But perhaps the best tribute of all has been the sound of his name still being sung by the Arsenal faithful at most home and away games, some 14 years after his death.

Why is he so fondly remembered? Of course, one of the reasons is the impact he had at the club, bringing with him excitement and passion, as well as trophies. He was also clearly an Arsenal fan who lived and breathed the club. Yet other players could also be said to have these attributes, and are not immortalised as Rocastle has been.

In the process of writing this book, I realised why so many of us felt such an affinity with David Rocastle. Simply, he came across as a beautiful human being. Softly spoken, with a smile permanently etched across his face, he led many, myself included, to think of him as a friend. He was someone you knew you would get on well with. You knew he would be great company. You knew he would be loyal. You knew he would make you feel good about yourself. And isn't that what heroes are meant to do?

CHAPTER 36

CHAMPION

A strange atmosphere permeated the air at Anfield. Why aren't Arsenal being more adventurous? And why are Liverpool playing so poorly? It seemed neither set of fans was satisfied yet the managers of both teams certainly were.

Dalglish told his players to just keep doing more of the same. There was no reason to panic. It was Arsenal who needed to score twice. If they wanted to sit back, then let them. A draw, or even a 1-0 defeat, was more than enough to win the title. Graham, on the other hand, jogged down from his seat in the directors' box just as the players had entered the dressing room at half-time. As Gary Lewin massaged tired limbs, and coach Theo Foley patted the players on the back, giving words of encouragement, Graham stood in the middle of the room and waited for silence. Satisfied with his team's first-half efforts, he now urged his players on to the next phase of his master plan.

'We can be more positive and adventurous for the opening 20 minutes of the second half,' he said. 'Lee and Nigel, if the opportunity presents itself, push right forward and get your crosses in from the flanks.' Winterburn and Dixon nodded accordingly.

'David and Michael, come through on support runs whenever you feel it's right. I want us to bring Alan and Paul more into the game now because it's important we try to get an early goal.' Thomas and Rocastle looked at each other, a telepathic under-standing between two schoolboy friends on the verge of their greatest moment.

'If we get one, I know the second will follow. This could be the greatest 45 minutes of your lives. Good luck.'

With that, Adams clapped his hands and roared, 'Come on!' Leading his team back out on to the pitch, this time they were no longer daunted by the 'This is Anfield' sign. Instead, as they ignored it, Rocastle shouted a phrase from his childhood which would in time become synonymous with Arsenal: 'Remember who you are, what you are and who you represent!'

Now, rather than make his way to the directors' box, Graham took his place in the dugout, ready to dictate proceedings.

Once again carrying out Graham's instructions, Arsenal rocked Liverpool by immediately going on the attack. To their surprise, Merson and Rocastle now pushed in alongside Smith, while Win-terburn and Dixon virtually played as wingers. A Merson snapshot on the volley was an early warning signal that Arsenal were now going for the jugular.

In response, the Kop chanted, 'We're gonna win the league. We're gonna win the league. And now you're gonna believe us. And now you're gonna believe us. We're gonna win the league!' But as the ball broke in the Liverpool half, Rocastle prodded it past Whelan, only to be brought down 35 yards from goal. Eyes wide, he clenched his fists and roared, 'Come on!' at his team-mates, as Winterburn stepped up to take the free-kick.

Lining up on the edge of the penalty area, the Arsenal players suddenly swarmed into the box, as Winterburn lofted in a cross. Smith, darting in unmarked, headed the ball with the faintest of touches past Grobbelaar and into the far corner of the net. But as the Arsenal end erupted, the Liverpool players noticed that the linesman had raised his flag, only to lower it again. They surrounded him and the referee, claiming that Smith hadn't touched the ball (an indirect free-kick had been awarded), while the Arsenal fans held their breath, waiting for referee David Hutchinson's decision. The television replays clearly showed that Smith had got a touch, but in the cauldron of Anfield would the referee be strong enough to give it?

Turning away from the remonstrating McMahon and Whelan, Hutchinson pointed to the centre circle. GOAL! Just as Graham had predicted. But no one was getting carried away. The celebrations of the players was restrained, while the fans couldn't quite bring themselves to believe they might be on the cusp of something truly special. In the film version of Nick Hornby's *Fever Pitch*, Colin Firth perhaps summed up the general feeling when he said, 'Isn't that just like Arsenal? They need two goals so they score one just to get us all going.'

Liverpool were now rattled. Soon afterwards, Grobbelaar spilled a cross after colliding with Gary Ablett, which led to the two remonstrating with one another. Smelling blood, Graham stepped on to the touchline and gave Rocastle even more licence to get forward, his runs now having the Merseysiders on the back foot. In contrast, Dalglish seemed paralysed by indecision. Did he tell his players to sit back, soak up the pressure, and win the title by virtue of a 1-0 defeat? Or did he tell them to go forward, in search of an equaliser, ending Arsenal's title hopes once and for all?

Full of energy, Arsenal not only stopped Liverpool from playing, but also began to create chances of their own. Richardson was denied getting a shot off only by a last-ditch Gary Ablett tackle, while Rocastle threatened to beat the Liverpool defence single-handedly before a desperate challenge by Hansen. Frantically trying to regroup, Liverpool attempted to eat up time by launching the ball upfield, or passing back to Grobbelaar. With deliberate irony, the Arsenal fans chanted, 'Boring, boring Liverpool!'

But with just 15 minutes to go, the game exploded into life when Graham brought off Bould and sent Groves on in his place. The sweeper system was sacrificed for the sake of getting the vital second goal, which allowed Liverpool more space in behind. As both teams dropped any inhibitions, the season was primed to conclude with a spectacular finale.

End to end, Thomas looked to have spurned Arsenal's best chance when, with just Grobbelaar to beat, he lost his cool and prodded the ball straight at him. In response, Houghton proceeded to volley a good opportunity high and wide into the Kop.

The minutes were ebbing away. The Anfield crowd whistling. The away fans hoarse with desperation. Smacking his hand into his fist, Rocastle roared for one last effort. Eyes popping, shirt drenched, teeth gritted. He knew this chance may never come again.

As Kevin Richardson fell to the floor with cramp, Steve McMahon looked around at his team and held up one finger. 'Just one more minute,' he shouted. In the television gantry David Pleat stated, 'If Arsenal are to lose the championship, having had such a lead at one time, it's somewhat poetic justice they've got a result on the last day, even if they're not to win it.'

With time almost up, Barnes sought to carry the ball towards the corner flag. It seemed that all he had to do was keep it there and the title was Liverpool's. However, as Adams and Richardson desperately tried to get the ball from him, Barnes made a decision that would haunt him for the rest of his career. Rather than stay out of harm's way, he instead tried to beat the exhausted Richardson and head for goal, only for Richardson's outstretched leg to dispossess him. As he passed the ball back to Lukic, the whistles around the ground were now deafening. The referee glanced down at his watch. Only seconds remaining.

Holding the ball in his hands, as the Arsenal players ran forward, Graham leapt from the dugout and screamed at Lukic, 'Kick the fucking thing!'

But Lukic instead proceeded to throw the ball out to Lee Dixon on the right-hand side. This was it. Now or never. Up in the television gantry, Brian Moore watched on, enthralled, ready to deliver commentary that would become as recognisable as Kenneth Wolstenholme's 'They think it's all over. It is now!' from the 1966 World Cup final.

'And Arsenal come streaming forward now, in surely what will be their last attack.'

Dixon hit a long ball towards Smith on halfway, who had his back to goal.

'A good ball by Dixon, finding Smith ...'

In an instant Smith turned and clipped the ball to Michael Thomas, who was galloping forwards.

'... for Thomas, charging through the midfield!'

But as Thomas looked to shift the ball past Nicol, it hit his legs, which for a split second seemed to stop his momentum. Yet, with a slice of luck, the ball rebounded off Thomas' shin and suddenly saw him through on goal.

'Thomas! It's up for grabs now!'

For a second, everyone in Anfield and around the country froze. Behind the goal, Paul Davis, sitting with the fans, screamed 'SHOOT!', but for some reason his team-mate kept going. All the while, Grobbelaar was advancing and Houghton was catching him up. In the background, Rocastle, who had been charging up in support, suddenly slowed. Thomas was in the area. Grobbelaar was almost upon him, diving at his feet, when at the last possible moment the cool Thomas flicked the ball with the outside of his right foot over the keeper's outstretched arm, and . . .

'THOMAS! Right at the end!!'

'. . . GOAL!!!'

Racing away, Thomas writhed on the floor in sheer ecstasy, as his Arsenal team-mates rushed towards him. In the stands, the Arsenal supporters lost all control. The terraces became a seething mass of bodies tumbling forwards, scarves liberally thrown in the air, as the fans released a guttural roar of 18 years of hurt that had just been banished in the most sensational of endings.

But as Anfield didn't have a clock, not all of the players had yet realised the magnitude of Thomas' goal. 'When he scored, all I could think of was to try and keep calm,' Rocastle later confided. 'I never knew there was just a minute left. I don't think any of us did. When I asked the ref, "How long to go?" and he said, "Any minute now," I said, "Sorry?" and he said, "That's it." We were champions.'

As the final whistle blew, Rocastle sank to his knees and tried to take in the enormity of what the team had just achieved. Soon he was surrounded by team-mates, hugging, crying, screaming. George Graham emerged from the dugout and appealed for calm, wanting to be respectful, but to Liverpool's credit the fans stayed behind to applaud what they recognised as one of British sport's all-time heroic efforts.

'You could see the emotion in the players,' Rocastle said, 'how much hard work we'd put into it. Everyone hugged every player. It was like a brotherly hug, like you hadn't seen someone for a long time. And it was every player, even players on the bench and in the stands.'

Blood brothers to the end. This type of camaraderie and love between a group of players was rare, but the 1988/89 Arsenal squad had it in abundance. Rocastle had grown up with the likes of Michael Thomas and Paul Davis, while he had become great friends with Alan Smith. After such a hard start in life, when he had been forced to mature at a young age, Arsenal had become his home. It was more than just a football club to him. It was family. While the anthem may be symbolic of Liverpool, and Hillsborough, it was somehow fitting that, as Rocastle hugged his friends, the ground rocked to the sound of 'You'll Never Walk Alone'.

Leaving the warm embrace of Highbury had hurt him deeply. He always enjoyed close friendships at other clubs, as well as a good rapport with the fans, but deep down he knew Arsenal was where he belonged. And the fans knew it as well.

He never forgot who he was, what he was or who he represented. He was David Carlyle Rocastle, a proud black man from a London council estate, who represented club and country with the utmost respect and dignity. And on 26 May 1989 the man known to all as Rocky was a champion. But then he didn't need a medal to prove that – the boy from Lewisham had always been, and would remain, a champion, right until the bitter end.

ACKNOWLEDGEMENTS

Researching and writing a book is always a mammoth task. As such I am certain that without the support of the following people my hair, and life, would be a little greyer.

As always my patient and understanding fiancée, Charlotte Watkins, has been a tower of strength as have my wonderful parents, Jim and Jackie Leighton.

Alex Leighton, Anita and Roy Kenny, Alice, Rachel and Giles Watkins, Jonny Griffiths, James Gundy, Tom Jeanes, Ben Syder, Tariq and Edward Aris, Rhys Jones, Stefan Burnett, Neil Chakrabarti, Dick James, Ben Morris, Gareth Lloyd, Michael Warburton, and Degsy Williamson (lead singer of The Oasis Experience, the best tribute band on the planet) have all been on hand to boost my spirits whenever I required a laugh, a drink, or a kick up the backside.

There is no doubt that my job would have been all but impossible without the transcribing skills of Jessica Barfield while Arsenal fans, Jonny Wright, Chris Jones, Darren Bluman, and his sons, Jackson and Theo, reassured me in the early stages of my research that this was indeed a story that had to be told.

Thanks must also go to everyone at The FA, Arsenal, The Arsenal Supporters Club, Leeds United, Manchester City, Chelsea and

Hull City who helped put me in contact with many of David's team-mates and managers, as well as opened up their archives to me.

This book would not have been possible without the trust and support of the Rocastle family, namely Karen Rocastle, Sasha Edwards Rocastle, Junior Hamilton and Sean Medford, who I must thank from the bottom of my heart for sharing their memories of their beloved David with me. Thanks must also go to those who were happy to talk to me on condition of their identities remaining confidential.

Tracking down people to interview is always a daunting task but it was made much easier thanks to the generosity of the following individuals, who gave up their time to speak with me; Errol Johnson, Gary Hill, Jenny Fraser, Michelle Edwards, Jerome Anderson, David Dein, Ken Friar, Glenn Hoddle, Howard Wilkinson, Brian Horton, Ken Shellito, Terry Burton, Alan Sutton, Eamonn Salmon, David Moss, Terry Byrne, Mike Cheeseman, Nick Hornby, Paul Parker, Perry Groves, Brian Marwood, Kevin Campbell, Colin Pates, Viv Anderson, Gus Caesar, Jon Purdie, Kenny Veysey, Scott Sellars, Mark Tinkler, Gregor Rioch, Gavin Peacock, Michael Duberry, Fitzroy Simpson, Balbeer Singh.

Journalists, Neil Humphreys and Jason Dasey were also of immense help, particularly in regard to David's time in Malaysia and Singapore.

Mike Francis of The Gooner and Andy Kelly of www.thearsenalhistory.com were incredibly helpful in sifting through the Arsenal archives for me, while Darren Epstein was a great support and a constant source of fact checking and information. Their knowledge, and support, of Arsenal Football Club is second to none. All clubs would be lucky to have dedicated fans such as them.

Right from the start, my agents Gordon Wise and Richard Pike at Curtis Brown showed real enthusiasm for this project and without them I would not have had the opportunity to write a single word. From beginning to end they helped take the weight from my shoulders and made the whole process far easier than it might have been.

The same must be said for my publisher, Simon and Schuster, and my editor, Ian Marshall, with whom I have now had the pleasure of publishing three books. Ian's love of the game, incredible knowledge, and attention to detail never fails to amaze me and constantly elevates my work.

My little nephew, George Leighton, who will hopefully grow into a football fanatic like his uncle, may have tried to eat the book as I edited it but he provided me with many smiles along the way.

Last but not least, thank you David Rocastle. The phrase 'legends never die' was made for you.

INDEX